By the Skin of Our Teeth

Creating sustainable organisations
through people

By the Skin of Our Teeth

Creating sustainable organisations through people

CLIVE MORTON

MIDDLESEX UNIVERSITY PRESS

to Florence

Acknowledgements

My greatest debt is to the generosity of the interviewees who have given of their time and thoughts to make this study possible. For many this arose from their organisation's membership of and support for Tomorrow's Company, a charity established as a spin off from the Royal Society of Arts as a product of the Tomorrow's Company enquiry in the early 1990s. Other interviewees are part of my own network and again my grateful thanks go to them for their patience and support.

Next, I wish to acknowledge the support of those in the Morton Partnership who assisted with interviewing and analysis – Chris Bottomley, Karen Kircher and Jane Morton; and Lesley Sortwell who painstakingly transcribed the verbatim interviews and produced the manuscripts, translating my attempts into something readable! Thanks too go to Jill Swaby who assisted with the typing.

Then my colleagues at Board Performance Limited – Bob and Sally Garratt, Jesper Berggreen, Des Gould, Heather Matheson, Christopher Delacombe and advisers Sir Michael Bett, Jonathan Charkham, Chris Mellor and Mike Kinski who have all contributed to the thinking on board and director development outlined in chapter 9.

I also owe another debt of gratitude to Bob Garratt who facilitated the concept of the book with the original publishers, Harper Collins, where Lucinda McNeile was an enthusiastic supporter. Then followed an author's nightmare when Harper Collins made an inexplicable decision to put their whole book list up for sale affecting many authors like myself. Relief followed some twelve months later when Paul Jervis, John Sivak and Celia Cozens of Middlesex University Press seized the opportunity of publishing this volume. Their support and enthusiasm has been infectious and heart warming and I am grateful for their speedy publishing process, which has enabled us to retrieve some of the precious lost time.

I'd like to mention the origin of the term 'extrovert organisation' used frequently in the book. This was coined by Nicholas Timotheou, General Manager (CEO) of the Cyprus Telecoms Authority (CYTA) when Florence, Jane and I were helping with top team development in 2000, in CYTA's transition from 'public to private', in anticipation of Cypriot accession to the EU. Thank you Nicholas.

Lastly, to Florence, my wife, who yet again saw holidays and other quality time eaten up by the study, analysis, writing and endless corrections meeting this with her usual combination of stoicism, forbearance and love!

Without all this, it would not be possible. Thank you all.

Clive Morton
Cambridgeshire and Umbria
July 2003

Early praise for *By the Skin of Our Teeth* by Clive Morton

Every CEO, in every organisation should learn and then implement these ideas and I hope commercial companies will discover the real talent and enterprise of the voluntary sector. They are the extrovert and agile operators of the 21st century. This book should be on the desk of every CEO in the commercial sector.

Stephen Bubb, Chief Executive, Association of Chief Executives of Voluntary Organisations

Clive Morton's conclusion is inexorable - if sustainability isn't at the top of a CEO's or chairman's agenda then that company has a problem...

David Clutterbuck, Clutterbuck Associates

Anyone wrestling with the problems of management will find this book perceptively challenging and stimulating about the way ahead.

Sir Michael Bett, CBE, Chairman, Pace Micro Technology plc

In *By the Skin of Our Teeth*, Clive Morton correctly exposes the myth that ethical conduct is in inherent conflict with business success. ...His neatly expressed and convincing argument makes a rational case for more ethical stewardship of corporations and will be of interest to policy makers and trade unionists as well as executives themselves. ...I hope that, before too long, business agendas are guided by the ideas of Clive Morton and others who show that the obsessions with opportunistic mergers and treating people as disposable bits of machinery benefit neither shareholder nor society.

Philip Whiteley, co author of *Unshrink* and *Complete Leadership*

The pressure on businessmen and on business has never been greater, and change is occurring at an unprecedented rate and often unexpectedly. At such a time, the essential characteristics that Clive identifies are particularly relevant, namely not being world-class in everything that you do but having a high level of intuition and emotional intelligence so as to take advantage speedily in changing conditions.

Michael Rake, Chairman KPMG International

This thought-provoking and visionary book will be of value to business executives who aim to create a sustainable future for their organisations.

**Linda Holbeche, Director of Research and Strategic Development,
Roffey Park Institute**

I am sure that Clive Morton's *By the Skin of Our Teeth* will quickly become required reading for those who want to understand how to survive in this rapidly changing global environment we all operate in.

John Bridge, Chairman, One NorthEast

Clive Morton makes the all important point that there is no formulaic solution to the complex problem of running organisations successfully in the long term, especially in a world where the pace of change is forever accelerating. There are many different ways that organisations can be world-class, extrovert and agile, his well-argued principles for success.

Tim Melville-Ross, Current Chair, Investors in People UK

Clive Morton's tour de force on business sustainability provides a lively, real world account of how organisations are responding to the challenge of increasingly rapid change. Though wisely avoiding a simplistic blueprint for sustainability, *By the Skin of Our Teeth* offers an essential road map for any corporate boards and business leaders looking to succeed rather than just survive.

John Philpott, Chief Economist, CIPD

This book is for leaders hungry for learning to enable them to explore the new and exciting directions we will have to take in organisations over the coming decade. *By the Skin of Our Teeth* offers deep insight into the strategies and skills we will need in the coming decade to ensure organisational success and community development. Clive Morton argues for an approach to the world of work that honours and develops the human in us all and the need to build effective communities within and around organisations.... In contrast to the rather facile prescriptions of many business writers, Clive Morton offers a comprehensive, holistic and humane view of organisations' success that leaders from organisations in the public, private and voluntary sectors will find practically useful and personally inspiring.

Michael West, Professor of Organisational Psychology, Director of Research, Aston Business School, Aston University

Clive Morton guides us carefully across the ever-shifting sands of what constitutes best practice in managing for long-term success. This is a book that will reward those who wish they had more time to read and make sense of some of the leadership theory that pours out of today's business schools, consultancies and organisational change merchants.

Nigel Cassidy, BBC Business Reporter/Presenter

Clive Morton has assembled a cast of high repute and considerable diversity from whom consummate and poignant lessons have been drawn. His conclusion that this new era requires us to achieve balance in right and left brain activity is a point well noted. This book is mandatory reading for all leaders who are seeking a role that offers the opportunity for self-expression rather than a rigid script.

Jose Pottinger, Director HR, Cummins Engine Co Ltd – Europe, Middle East & Africa

Clive Morton has produced a new and inspirational book on leadership in the 21st century, which executives and students will find thought-provoking and of practical value. He has interviewed thirty-four chief executives and directors from some of the most admired organisations such as Toyota, Shell, BAA, Cisco Systems, KPMG, the Arts Council and technology start-ups.

Their leaders' comments remind us starkly of how much our organisations have changed in the last decade. What emerges is a coherent philosophy of leadership and best practices which executives can use to drive their organisations forward in today's challenging environment.

Professor Bernard Taylor, Executive Director, Centre for Board Effectiveness, Henley Management College

First published in 2003 by Middlesex University Press

Copyright © Clive Morton

ISBN 1 898253 56 0

A CIP catalogue record for this book is available from
The British Library

Design by Helen Taylor
Printed and bound in the UK by Hobbs the Printers, Hampshire.

Middlesex University Press, Bounds Green Road, London N11 2NQ
Tel: +44 (0)20 8411 5734: +44 (0)20 8880 4262 Fax: +44 (0)20 8411 5736

CONTENTS

Start-ups/Entrepreneurism/Phoenix/Networks

- AIT
- The Generics Group
- BioFocus
- Camelot
- Toyota
- Unipart Automotive
- Pertemps
- Lymphoma Association
- Ashton Penney
- The Strategic Partnership
- Telos Partners

M&A/Demerger

- Royal & Sun Alliance
- Cisco
- KPMG
- MCL

Public to Private

- AWG
- BAA
- BT
- GB Rail

Public sector and PFI – radical change within

- NHS – Peterborough Hospitals
- One NorthEast (RDAs)
- Arts Council
- LSC
- Patent Office
- Bovis Lend Lease

'built to last' and 'steady as she goes'

- Shell UK Exploration and Production
- Burall
- UNUM
- Gardiner & Theobald
- House of Hardy
- CBI
- Ashridge Trust

Foreword

Clive Morton is a remarkable man. He has for many years been at the cutting edge of business change. He was at the centre of things when UK business was learning its lessons about 'total quality' and 'world class' from the Japanese. He was there when a leading utility was being transformed from the bureaucratic to the adventurous. He is there now at the heart of the changes needed in the health service, chairing an NHS trust that leads the way in breaking down the old compartments that stand in the way of better and swifter patient care, and in corporate governance. He also provides a special brand of development training for board members and other future leaders.

At the same time he has since 1999 been a trustee of, and the valued chairman of, the Research Board for Tomorrow's Company. In this role he has overseen the development of a new agenda for the organisation. The agenda poses big questions about the future relationship between companies and their investors, between business and society, and about the nature of leadership and governance in the organisations of tomorrow.

It was therefore natural that many of the interviews conducted for *By the Skin of Our Teeth* should be with organisations that are members of, and close supporters of, Tomorrow's Company.

Clive makes the point that he believes that long-range retrospective studies – such as *Built to Last* – may be less helpful in the future because the pace of change has accelerated and people's expectations have changed as well. Readers can draw their own conclusions. I did a quick check of the current status of the thirty-four CEOs interviewed and to my personal knowledge there are at least 20 per cent who have moved or been moved on from the roles they were speaking about when interviewed.

There is, among some commentators, a knee-jerk reaction that somehow discounts the testimony of those no longer in their role. My view is the opposite: all of us in leadership roles need to be much more aware that in the midst of (corporate) life we are in (corporate) death, and perhaps we would show some welcome humility if we were more aware of this. In Clive's own case the publication of the book coincides with yet another new role, as Chair of the Postgraduate Medical Education & Training Board, to which he will bring his rich experience and from which he will distil wider insights.

Throughout this book the reader is made aware of the live and unending tension between what a business is and what it does. On one hand there is the underlying personality and character of a business. Without consistency in that, there is no trust and there are no relationships. On the other hand there is the need, well-described in the book's title, to move and change fast. That inevitably means hard decisions, with people losing their jobs and relationships being disrupted. Ultimately the disruption can only be explained, and the trust retained, if there is some purpose to the business in the first place and the changes in what it has to do. As Clive Morton concludes, the board cannot escape their responsibility for defining and holding to a clear purpose and set of values. While living each day as though it might be their last, leaders and organisations need also to take decisions and manage relationships on the assumption that their organisation just might last a very long time!

Mark Goyder
Director
Tomorrow's Company

Introduction

This is an inquiry into the sustainability of organisations in the 21st century. It covers the world of businesses, large and small, old and new, as well as the public and voluntary sectors. In writing this, the latest in a series of books in which I have sought to identify key factors that define the high-performing organisation, I have been driven by a concern that Sir Geoffrey Chandler identifies in his usual succinct and perceptive way:

> *'Financial failure affects companies and those who work with them. Moral failure affects capitalism'*

Business has been the dominant institution of the 20th century. It is business that provides national governments with their income, either directly through corporation taxes or indirectly through income tax. In addition, the social and environmental powers of business are immense and are being increased even further by globalisation.

Yet as we enter the 21st century, long-term business success is more uncertain than ever and business is very often seen as a cause of global problems when it should be part of the solution. So, it is important to explore the pressures on business and to identify the demands that will be placed in the 21st century on managers and directors if enterprises are to survive and prosper. Are there pointers to the sustainability of organisations? What are the lessons that we can draw from successful organisations in the private, public and voluntary sectors? What is the impact of this 21st-century global context? Exploring these issues is my purpose here.

Thirty-four Directors and Chief Executives from a variety of large corporations, SME companies, public sector bodies and voluntary organisations gave generously of their time to participate in lengthy interviews. In these, I explored with them a basic premise which I had formulated about business sustainability.

Based on my own experience and my previous writings, it seems to me that the fundamentals of business sustainability for an organisation in the 21st century are:

- to be world-class in all it does

- to be an extrovert organisation with keen antennae sensing trends and opportunities and involving its people in its future

- to 'catch the moment', exploit the window of opportunity

- and above all to be agile, proactively to anticipate and take advantage of trends, markets and the potential of resources – in particular, the human resource

The various answers I received add up to these participants' collective experience to date of sustainability. They help to identify what can be constant in a world which is in a state of flux.

Consider in more detail the issue of business success, described above. Accelerating business change means that business strategy has to be reassessed at increasingly frequent intervals. What therefore is, or can be, constant in today's organisation? Are there business principles or philosophies that continue to hold good? Can corporations evolve vision and values that can survive, unchanging, for the long term while engendering the ability to be fleet of foot, proactive, and adaptable?

By the Skin of Our Teeth draws a perspective on business success from the 'old economy' - the firms often described as 'built-to-last' - as well as from the public sector. It establishes parallels with the new entrepreneurial economy to define the foundations of corporate success. In both the 'built-to-last' world, besieged by external change, and the new economy, surfing and then diving, there are common threads. Neither can succeed without effective relationships, social glue, or networks. Neither can survive and grow without effective use and development of people.

However, the philosophy that people are the source of competitive advantage is neither universally believed nor acted upon. Many businesses may pay lip service to the concept, but then behave in a cavalier fashion towards people, whether those they employ or those in a stakeholder relationship to them. As a result, such organisations tend to survive only by the skin of their teeth. As a consequence individuals experience high levels of insecurity, and communities experience instability and uncertainty, in a globalised world.

This book helps organisations to chart their course from the past, in which people were a resource to be managed (or exploited), to one for the present and future in which people are a key source of sustainability. The basis for the transformation is effective relationships. I use examples from both my own experience and the interviews, of recent, successful change to illustrate effective systems of corporate transformation to world-class competitiveness.

The fundamentals that I explore here deal with the crucial 'pinch points' of managing in the 21st century. I commence with the value proposition. Is it possible to establish values that unify diverse resources and that convey meaning to the enterprise? Do these values have a place in achieving sustainability? With so much faith now being placed in entrepreneurship across the world, what role is there for personal belief and spirituality?

Business often lacks an overarching philosophy that is sustainable and that can give meaning for the enterprise and those that work within it. It is very clear to me that, without meaning and philosophy, emotional commitment cannot and does not follow.

The issue of leadership naturally comes next. I believe that leadership is about dealing with dilemmas, making choices, and striking a balance when outcomes are far from certain. Today, we know so much more than we used to about human nature, psychology, motivation and methods of achieving commitment. Yet in the individualistic, Western hemisphere fundamental lessons are still ignored. Our leadership role models still owe much more to macho, distancing approaches based on speed of decision making or transactional cost, than to those based on transformational change, relationship unifying, team-working philosophy, and the gathering of contributions valued for their diversity and creativity.

The global context is powerful. Competing models of leadership and management can inform and teach, rather than just being seen as manifestations of cultural differences. The crucible for much of this is the boardroom. Is team-working at this level attainable, and is it compatible with the focus on individual, hothouse development?

Mergers and Acquisitions have been the constant topic of debate in all financial centres worldwide. In terms of relationships, M&A activity represents an oxymoron. The pressure for mergers and acquisitions has been inexorable, despite the accumulating evidence that 70 – 80 per cent of such developments fail to deliver shareholder value, let alone wider 'stakeholder' benefit. Analysis shows that M&A failures are consistently due to incompatibility of cultures, values, relationships, and personalities. All these are people factors, yet these are the issues least likely to be discussed, measured, or considered at the M&A table. Further, the lessons of post M&A integration appear to be disregarded totally in the headlong, herd-like rush to demonstrate early cost savings to a City seemingly focused on the fee-earning potential of M&A activity without a thought for the long term. I will describe the experiences of several organisations that have merged or de-merged.

I make a distinction here between the needs of new talent streams of entrepreneurship (beacons of business growth) and knowledge workers (latter day journeymen, commanding their market value and at the same time eminently disposable). For organisations and communities as a whole, the issue is one of knowledge creation, management and sharing, not the 'knowledge is power' of yesteryear.

The agile organisation is totally networked, having decided what are its core businesses and what is better performed by others. This is not a simple subcontracting of services, but the building of value-adding partnerships, the sharing of thinking on strategy, and the contributing of intellectual capital as well as working capital.

The agile organisation is deeply involved in the solutions of its outsourced providers, is keen to see contribution and development within their ranks, and takes a long-term view of business-to-business relationships, which are characterised by 'voice' not 'exit' as a priority.

The characteristics of the network today are also different. Yesterday's network had the reciprocal bargain as its raison d'être. Today's has the sharing of knowledge at its core, and involves the sharing of the trials and tribulations of the entrepreneurial experience, gleaning advice from those who have already travelled successfully down that road.

How do we achieve relationships in a world without certainties? The characteristics of world-class relationships here are trust, openness, belief in reciprocity and win-wins, and a willingness to help and be helped.

The traditional sectarian divides between public and private sectors continue, even though they both now do learn much more from each other and share many of the same choices about policy and forms of working. We will explore what lessons there have been here, and what is in prospect for the future.

I believe the sector of most significance, in terms of both change and influence, is the voluntary sphere. Recent studies have shown that, in the United Kingdom, upwards of a million people are employed in the voluntary sector, broadly defined, and that over eighteen-million volunteers contributed their time to charities, which is the equivalent of a further two-million workers. This pattern is repeated throughout the developed world.

The voluntary sector is no longer the dumping ground of organisational downsizing, or the realm of largesse from the good and great and those with time on their hands. The sector aims for efficiency, effectiveness and influence just as much as any other sector and, as the State retreats from universal provision and benefits, it will have a larger, more central role. The voluntary sector contributions reported here add realism and richness to the debate. Many of those contributors pursue their voluntary sector involvement in parallel to their 'proper jobs', and the transfer of learning and experience between the two stands out in their remarks.

The organisation that succeeds through the 21st century will need to be super-sensitive to the external environment, whether this is the environment of competition, of customers with global choice, or of social, economic or ecological influences. These organisations will have gone beyond the mentalities of 'what we ought to do' or the demands of the 'licence to operate'. They will recognise fully the need to contribute to, and gain from working in, the communities within which they exist. Their antennae will be attuned for the dialogues that build and sustain relationships.

These communities need redefining. They are no longer marked by a physical radius around the place of work. They are defined and bounded by their existing and potential stakeholders (customers, suppliers, partners, collaborators, et al). Their policies and practices of corporate social responsibility will benefit from business case reciprocity and sustainability, not be a manifestation of their defence mechanisms. Such proactivity will lead to new business development, and give them the potential of strategic choice based on the degree of consumer trust they enjoy. Involvement in the future, internal change, and employee development will all find their catalyst here – particularly from those contributing to other organisations part-time alongside their 'day job'.

These beliefs thus form my 'manifesto' for organisational sustainability. In the chapters that follow, I describe the evidence base that my interviewees have helped me to assemble. My sincere thanks go to all of them for their patience and their insights. Any errors of reporting or interpretation are, of course, mine alone.

Chapter one

THE CONTEXT

THIS BOOK IS ABOUT the survival and sustainability of organisations in the face of overwhelming and endless change and uncertainty that takes on a totally different character after 9/11. Much has been written about the impact of this uncertainty at both the macro and micro levels. At the macro, geopolitical level it affects governments' international strategies. At the other extreme, the impacts are on individuals, their migration and travel, the amount of racial tension and other influences on individual choice.

For organisations, the traumatic events of 9/11 have had impact on security issues, the mobility of key people, and international strategies. But they have often had a much deeper effect. Just as world leaders reacted to the events of 11 September 2001 in moral and value terms, for organisations and those who work in them, the deeper reactions have been to question meanings and value sets to which previously we often have given little attention.

The challenges that these events represent to an assumed way of life at a geopolitical level have their reflections both within and between organisations. This book is about the successful ability to cope with change. Part of that success comes from understanding the impact of events on choice. Individuals and organisations will make informed choices on their work and futures based on context, scope and what they are comfortable with.

Just as liberal societies have embraced the freedom of the individual as an article of faith, arguing that what is good for the individual is good for society, so opposing forces have espoused that firstly, checks and balances are needed to rein in selfishness, greed and discrimination and secondly, that liberal societies cannot do without an active moral defence in order to sustain them. (Tom Bentley and Ian Hargreaves, Demos 2002).[1]

The research that underpins this book shows that the element of today's liberal society, both within and between organisations, struggles with the same reflected dilemmas as society as a whole. It indicates that individualism, with its powerful positive virtues, counterbalanced by unbridled competition which negates teamwork, produces issues which organisational leaders have to manage actively. It also finds that the

1

successful organisations studied have arrived at a prominent conclusion about the linkage between moral, ethical and values issues and sustainability. Just as at geopolitical level a moral defence is needed.

The two diagrams which follow demonstrate the height of the hill to be climbed, where gaining trust and confidence is concerned.

The Future Foundation has managed to trace declining trust in companies in the last two decades, representing a fall from 60 per cent in 1980 to 40 per cent in 2000. This is put in even more stark contrast by MORI in February 2003 from their longitudinal study on *Who do we trust to tell the truth?* showing business leaders convincing only a quarter of the population. No doubt business can take comfort from scoring higher than politicians and journalists.

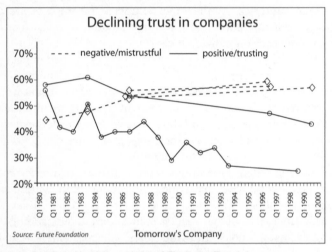

Source: Future Foundation   Tomorrow's Company

Reproduced with the kind permission of The Future Foundation

A Question of Trust – Who do we trust to tell the truth?

Top Five Occupation	2003 (%)	2002 (%)	Bottom Five	2003 (%)	2002 (%)
Doctors	91	91	Trade Union Officials	33	37
Teachers	87	85	Business Leaders	28	25
Professors	74	77	Government Ministers	20	20
Judges	72	77	Politicians Generally	18	19
Clergy	71	80	Journalists	18	13

Base: 2,141 British Adults aged 16+ (Feb 2003)   Source: BMA/MORI

The link between the individual and the organisation reflects the dilemmas and the challenges of sustainability. Both organisations and their employees seek a moral base, a meaning and purpose behind their existence and work. The sustainable, successful organisation has sought to bridge this gap. The events of recent times, including the global issues over sustainability, have sharpened the focus in these organisations.

Typically, there has been a focus on vision and values, or mission and purpose, depending on the language used. There are very few of these prominent organisations, large or small, that have not tried to bridge two gaps. First, is the understanding gap over vision and values. What are they? What do they mean? Do they have day-to-day relevance and applicability? Second, is the ownership gap. What do these words mean to me? Do they give me a vision I can relate to? Can I identify with the values espoused? Do they express values that give my work a meaning and purpose? And, most telling, do the behaviours in the organisation reflect the espoused values? (This, for individuals post 9/11, became a defining question.)

For many organisations this searching after perceived truth is off limits. For them, the focus should be on specified performance measures, no more, no less. A proportion of the organisations studied are just this, single minded, purposeful but not embracing the wider issues; accepting the context and climate as it is, behaving in a 'commercial' way, conforming to the constraints of the market.

A more fundamental issue surrounds the word 'sustainability'. This is very often allied to the environment, the way we carry on, will there be a world worth living in for our children? However 'sustainability' can be used in a wider context, which includes economic and social pressures as well as those of the environment.

The PWC Global Survey 2003 of 1,000 CEOs entitled *Leadership Responsibility and Growth in Uncertain Times* defines sustainability in the following terms:

> *'We prefer the single world 'sustainability' – borrowed from the world of sustainable development and used in this context to mean adding economic, environmental, and social value through a company's core business functions. Another way of saying it is 'doing business with your grandchildren's interests at heart'.'*

Martin Wolfe, economics commentator for the FT, has given a challenging global metaphor to this context.

> *'Think of a stretch limousine driving through an urban ghetto. Inside is the post-industrial world of Western Europe, North America, Australasia, Japan and the emerging Pacific Rim. Outside are all the rest.'*

Yet the proportion of the human population that belongs to this elite – 32 per cent in 1950 – is falling: today it is 19 per cent and is predicted to be 13 per cent by 2050.

So we can conclude with the environmentalists that the whole system as we know it is not sustainable in economic and social terms, as well as ecologically. *'We live in a globalising world. That means that all of us, consciously or not, depend on each other.'* (Zygmunt Bauman, Emeritus Professor of Sociology at the University of Leeds).

In modern day institutions, the issue of making choices between conflicting and compelling dilemmas has become the hallmark of leadership. Cultures and organisations have become plural and dialogue is vital. The structures and frameworks that have served us well in the past are not now able to help resolve today's moral dilemmas. Both Al Qaeda and Western nations have used (very different) moral stances to justify their positions. Further, it is remarkable that the management ethos apparently adopted by Al Qaeda seems to mimic the thinking of Western networked organisations. This dichotomy over moral stances exists at the micro level in organisations as well as at the geopolitical level. *'The challenge in any multicultural society is to gain a shared framework in order to flourish.'* (Amitai Etzioni – *Sustaining the Community of Communities*).

Etzioni argues that *'the most profound problems that plague modern societies will be fully addressed only when those whose basic needs have been met shift their priorities up Maslow's scale of human needs. That is, only after they accord a higher priority to gaining and giving affection, cultivating culture, becoming involved in community service and seeking spiritual fulfilment'.*[2] Etzioni was aiming this at individuals in society. I will be arguing that the same applies to organisations that make up the institutions in our society (see Chapter 9). We have for too long segmented our society, institutions and communities into definable parts and lost the synergy which comes from exploring how we can leverage one for the benefit of the others. For instance, in *Beyond World Class* (Macmillan 1998), I demonstrated that the individual, the organisation and the community needed each other for growth (*Beyond World Class*, pp ix and 276). My thesis was that *'no organisation or company is an island and cannot hope to maintain or go beyond being world-class unless it operates in partnership with the world outside the factory gates'* (p vi). Further I argued that *'a company can, by operational excellence, become 'world class' but its products are likely to be commoditized and unless it reinvents itself through innovation and a wider perspective, it will cease to be world-class and probably will cease to exist'* (p vi).

The world has moved on since 1998 when *Beyond World Class* was published. The issue of the ever-increasing pace of change has become dominant, the dot.com phenomenon has come and gone, and the world order has been turned on its head by 9/11. The seemingly unassailable, ever-ascending stars like Enron and Worldcom have suddenly crashed to earth.

Just as Etzioni argues that, for fulfilment, individuals need to progress up Maslow's hierarchy so I will be arguing that for organisations to avoid surviving by the skin of their teeth they have to do something similar – progress beyond efficiency through effectiveness to being completely nimble in today's turbulent world.

Notes

1   Bentley, T & Hargreaves, Demos 2002
2   Etzioni, A *'Sustaining the Community of Communities'*, Demos Collection 16/2001

Chapter two

THE BASIS OF THE RESEARCH

MY RESEARCH FOR THIS BOOK goes back nearly twenty years and I see it as a progression of my understanding and knowledge – against a moving target. Our collective understanding of people and organisations has advanced just as industry and the nature of companies has changed.

The 'Holy Grail' in the mid-1980s was the implementation of the quality movement, espoused from the 1950s onwards. The unique experience I had with Komatsu in setting up their first European plant fired my imagination and gave me the opportunity to write *Becoming World Class*. Out of this period grew the 'lean production' philosophy espoused by Jones, Womack and Roos in *The Machine that Changed the World*. Suddenly, everybody was benchmarking against the automotive industries and this highlighted the stark contrasts of production man-hours per vehicle between Japan and the West. This was not new. In May 1980, for example, Ford compared the labour needed to produce its Transit van in the UK with that needed to build a Toyota Hiace van. The total man-days needed were 12.5 for the British van compared with 2.4 for the Japanese van.[1] The authors of *Supporting Workplace Learning for High-Performance Working* have found that, despite the twenty-plus years of lessons learnt on the topic, precious few organisations in the developed West have consistently adopted the 'hurdles of high performance' working. Those who have learnt the 'tricks' have been either in automotive manufacture or close to it. The service and public sectors seemingly are still unconquered.

The attention of management moved on. The quality movement was acceptable for the 'dangerous enthusiasts', provided their application was confined to the shop floor where they could practise continuous improvement to their hearts' content.

The holistic lesson practised in Japan was missed and continues to be missed. This is that the quality philosophy was a philosophy affecting how a whole system should operate, from shop floor manufacturing to supplier integration, to customer involvement, to service function support, to top management embracing the philosophy and changing behaviour as a result.

Over the past twenty years, this class system of separating

leadership from the means of production has bedevilled efforts by western organisations to become 'world-class'. Today, many business leaders have given up on earlier aspirations of achieving overall world-class performance. The vast majority of those interviewed in this study have said it is necessary to be selective when you define 'world-class'. Their view is that in the round it is too ambitious to attempt. I propose to return to this issue, to see whether this is sensible pragmatism or whether, as Professor David Ashton and Johnny Sung suggest, we are lowering our sights.

My personal education progressed in the 1990s as I deliberately tried to implement the lessons from my experience of working with the Japanese in western companies. Much of this is covered in *Beyond World Class*[2] and *Leading HR*[3]. One conclusion I came to was that many of the techniques of 'high performance working' could be easily applied at shop floor level but organisations found that improvement was transitory due to lack of behaviour change in middle management and, more importantly, at top management level. This was compounded by continuous tinkering with change methods. Almost as dangerous as no change at all were too many confusing, conflicting and overlapping initiatives destroying continuity.

Evidence of the fundamental importance of consistency came from what, in my view, is the book of the decade, *Built to Last* by Jim Collins and Jerry Porras.[4] Their work demonstrated the powerful effect of continuity, particularly in terms of the constancy of values, affecting long-term performance in the companies they studied.

The undermining effect of negative behaviours in top and middle management has been increasingly recognised, with more and more organisations revisiting the half-century of work by psychologists and sociologists from Jung to Lewin. The context, in my perception, is now different. Whereas the socio-technical movement of the 1970s focused on work groups at shop floor level, and psychologists were employed to aid effective individual recruitment, in the last decade the focus has shifted towards the self-development industry and the means of understanding behaviour and its effects at the top of organisations. In rare cases this has even extended to examining and developing top teams.

In western, developed countries, due to the overwhelming cult of the individual, the jury is still out as to whether the top is a place for team working. Few have made the connection between divisive behaviour at the top and failures in corporate governance, preferring to rely on conformance to 'tick box' rules, eg conflict of interests, numbers and role of non-executive directors, separating roles of

Chairman and Chief Executive et al.

The growth of the corporate governance ethos has been propelled by demands of stakeholders over spectacular failures and implosions such as Maxwell, Marconi and Enron, not by perceived internal needs for productivity, harmony or avoidance of disruption. So, from the sense of cohesion and support for high-performance working, we have started at the wrong end. For the improvements at shop floor to gain pertinence and spread through the organisation, corporate governance could have been designed around behaviours that would have supported change and given consistency and continuity. Two internal attributes or values would have been openness and transparency, to build trust within to support change. Instead, openness and transparency have been forced by the corporate governance movement, often on unwilling boards by scarred and suspicious stakeholders who have suffered from past dramatic failures, fuelled by mistrust over obsessive secrecy and misuse of power. Hence the corporate governance parameters are a series of checks and balances designed to protect the interests of stakeholders, not essentially to improve the sustainability of organisations or the economic and social interests of the communities which the organisations serve.

The 1990s saw a radical re-examination of the purpose and function of organisations in relation to their wider stakeholders. Charles Handy posed a question in a lecture to the Royal Society of Arts and Manufactures in the early 1990s, *'What is a company for?'* which triggered an in-depth inquiry by the RSA which led to the concept of the 'inclusive company' in relation to stakeholders. Much of the work of Tomorrow's Company, set up as a direct result of the RSA inquiry, feeds into the research in this book since the core of the question of *By the Skin of Our Teeth* is about the issue of sustainability and survival in an ever-changing world.

Similarly, I believe the issue of stakeholder relations has often been prompted by looking through the wrong end of the telescope. The quality movement argued that stakeholder relations could greatly contribute to productivity, profit and internally driven sustainability. However, later developments in corporate social responsibility lean heavily on the licence to operate, on the moral case, on the threat of 'society bites back' rather than the internally driven business case. This research will look at what motivates the board in terms of external stakeholder relations and corporate social responsibility.

Here it is important to be clear what is meant in this context by sustainability (or 'durability', the term favoured by Tomorrow's

Company)[5]. Essentially, it is the view as seen from the bridge (to use the merchant shipping analogy) – the view being that of individual organisations (or that of their leaders) on what they see as important for survival and growth in their particular context. I deliberately do not look at this from the viewpoint of particular global stakeholder interests such as:

- the environmental dimension, global warming et al

- the economic dimensions, the 'real' economy (trading goods and services) and 'shadow' economy, (global capital and foreign exchange markets) defined by Philip Sadler in his book *Building Tomorrow's Company*[6] or the social dimension (social cohesion, social capital and social institutions) other than providing the wider context for the examination of sustainability (or durability) for the 'view from the bridge'.

Why be so restrictive? This book is designed to help practitioners running organisations in their quest for sustainability and growth. It is about tapping into the experience of a wide range of successful entrepreneurs, leaders and managers who have navigated the increasingly stormy seas provided by the external environment, economic and social context. This book is not a polemic aimed at governments and lawmakers in order to regulate the effects of ever-increasing change – that is for others. I take the perspective of the practitioner who has to choose how to make the best of the opportunities offered, who sees that most organisations eventually fail and that increasing uncertainties provide now an even greater challenge to survival than past track records would indicate. This is about what business leaders can achieve in an increasingly uncertain climate.

Hence in terms of the economic dimension I take Philip Sadler's definition, *'At the level of the enterprise, economic sustainability is simply defined as the continuing ability of a business to be competitive and to create sufficient added value to meet the expectations of investors while making adequate investment in its future'*[7] – not the sustainability of the whole global economy. I do, however, extend this definition to cover organisations that are 'not-for-profit' or in the public sector since, as we shall see, the pressures and much of the context are the same.

Of course, having deliberately restricted the definition of sustainability to the organisation and its stakeholders, we will find, I predict, that part of the quest for survival and growth requires the leaders of these organisations to work with wider stakeholders to affect and moderate the external context.

This external context has become increasingly important over the last three decades as diagram 2.1 illustrates.

By the Skin of Our Teeth
Creating sustainable organisations through people

1970s Static Organisations	1980s Creative Destruction

Industrial relations
   Issue of organising large workforces
   Protected markets
   Nil labour flexibility
Unitary or pluralistic frameworks?
   Socio-technical theory and practice
Sustainability not an issue
	Start of privatisation
	   Labour/Union showdowns
	   Labour flexibility low
	   Inward investment
	Learning from the Japanese
	   Total quality
	   - QCD
	   Teamwork
	   Continuous development
	   Communication
	Becoming world-class

1990s Lean Production	**2000s Agile Production**
Business process re-engineering De-layering: outsourcing Self-employment mindset Supply chain change But Bottom-up OK Need top-down and 'middle-up-down' Beyond world-class but riding high on creative accounting	Networked organisations Intensive use of IT/Knowledge management Focus on core competence Labour flexibility high/global v local issues But Sustainability low Therefore *By The Skin of Our Teeth* premise - World-class in all we do - Extrovert organisation - Agile, proactive: seize the moment

Diagram 2.1

The nub of this enquiry is how do successful organisations cope and sustain in this increasingly turbulent context? I asked the leaders interviewed whether they subscribed to the basic premise:

1 Basic premise

That the fundamentals for business sustainability in the 21st century are to be:

- world-class in all we do
- an extrovert organisation with keen antennae sensing trends and opportunities
- agile, proactive, responsive, taking advantage of trends, involving and developing the human resource, 'to catch the moment'

I then sought their views on the following:

1 Vision and values proposition

- What can be constant in a world in a state of flux?
- Is it necessary to focus on something constant such as vision and values?
- How does this relate to a compelling work ethic? Is work/life balance an issue?
- Have the vision and values stood the test of time?

3 On leadership and entrepreneurial ability

What place have the following in developing leaders?

- Knowing yourself and others – is this deliberately encouraged?
- The role of emotions and emotional intelligence – is this explored?
- The individual and the team – what understanding, what adjustment?
- If leadership is all about effectively dealing with and resolving dilemmas (ie short-term v long-term), can you recount how your organisation dealt with a crucial dilemma? Did it demonstrate leadership?

4 Are you an extrovert organisation?

In other words, do you get involved outside your day-to-day business with other stakeholders, community, etc?

- Does this help the business – or is it a diversion?
- Do you find you are influential outside the business?
- Does it help anticipate external change?
- Who does it?
- Who contributes to the antennae?
- Does it help in other ways, eg with resolving dilemmas and/or business development?

5 How important are internal and external relationships to you as an organisation?

Where are you on the scale starting with risk assessment to ensure there are no bad relationships that may undermine objectives and at the other extreme, deep co-dependency, which may restrict independent action?

- Do you have any policy on the subject? Is partnership an issue for you?
- How important are your relationships to business success and durability?

- Has the importance changed with the advent of distance-type relationships in virtual organisations?

6 **On durability in an economic, social as well as environmental sense, do you regard the talk as rhetoric and aspiration or do you think it is achievable? Is 'creative destruction' more realistic?**

- What are your goals in this sense?
- What motivates the Board: society biting back, the moral case or the business case?

7 **On agility and innovation**

- How do you 'catch the moment' in your organisation?
- How do you encourage creativity and innovation?
- Is it about being in the right place at the right time or can we engineer it?
- From which end of the telescope should we and do we look?
  - leaders perceiving the opportunity and then investigating the resource?
  - or building the resource to create the opportunity?
- Does the former lead you to conclude that agility can result from concentrating on the core resource and outsourcing the rest?

This chapter has put the current research into context – both the historical context of our increasing knowledge about organisations and the external environment that affects their performance and longevity. It has also put forward a definition of sustainability to which we will return.

It is clear by inspection, even before we look at the research data, that the old formulaic solutions to longevity and sustainability are not appropriate in today's complex environment. It is also clear that regulatory approaches towards governance of organisations are reactive, prescriptive and do not provide answers for 'high performance working' and business continuity. In effect they treat mostly symptoms, not causes. Similarly issues concerning stakeholders are often treated as defence mechanisms, not as tools for improving the effectiveness of organisations or improving the environment in which business works.

Lastly, the structure of the interviews is now reflected in the following chapters. The results to the enquiry over the basic premise follow in chapter 4; the vision and values search in chapter 5; leadership and entrepreneurial ability in chapter 6; the extrovert organisation, relationships, durability in chapter 7; and agility and innovation in chapter 8. Chapter 3, which follows, introduces the organisations studied with supplementary material in Appendix I.

Notes

1   Ashton, D and Sung, J *Supporting Workplace Learning for High-Performance Working* ILO 2002

2   Morton, C *Beyond World Class* Palgrave 1998

3   Morton, C Newall, A Sparkes, J *Leading HR* CIPD 2001

4   Collins, J and Porras, J *Built to Last Century* 1994

5   'Durability' is favoured by Tomorrow's Company for the business sense of 'ensuring that a business will be there in the future', reserving 'sustainability' for impacts on the planet and society.

6   Sadler, P *Building Tomorrow's Company* Kogan Page 2002

7   P46 *Building Tomorrow's Company*

Chapter three

INTRODUCING THE ORGANISATIONS

AUTHORS HAVE CHOICES on where they source material for research. A rigorous academic approach for a study such as this could have started with an in-depth analysis of companies and organisations based on their published results (which are usually aimed at shareholders). It could then have related the organisations' actions and policies to evidence of an end result in terms of their performance. That was the methodology used in *Built to Last*, and in that context it worked.

Here, I was looking for evidence that paralleled my own experience of change, survival and growth over the past decades. So I believed this needed to be an experiential study, not heavily reliant on statistical results, which can be both myopic, by focusing on shareholders, and very transitory. There are two reasons for this.

The first, which builds on the process I outlined in *Becoming World Class* and *Beyond World Class*, is that I believe that by bringing together the asymptotic curves of theory and practice it is possible to establish workable solutions for replicable success in organisations. Yet, as chapters 1 and 2 recognised, the old rules may now no longer apply. Globally, change is happening at an increasing rate. This leads to the second reason for the approach used here. When we find organisations that have been striving for success we need to ask how does the process feel? How do they deal with 'the world in a state of flux'? What is their philosophy?

Success in business used to be seen as the ability to run a well-oiled machine. Crisis management needed to be eliminated, otherwise the prevailing ethos would always be fire fighting. With the world in a state of flux, do these successful organisations see the need to create 'breakwaters' and 'harbour walls' to give a sense of constancy and continuity, so that goals of sustainability can be achieved? How do they deal with the wider stakeholders?

Other studies have documented the increasing desire for understanding of the meaning and purpose of work. This may possibly be the gravitation towards 'inner-directed' values that was predicted by Francis Kinsman in *Millennium* (1990)[1] and reinforced by Richard Donkin's *Blood, Sweat and Tears*[2]. Is the growth of the use

14

of values a response to satisfying individual and collective needs? Are we seeing the turning of the full circle, from the paternalistic unitary framework of the 1960s through the pluralistic phase of the 1970s to an alignment by values in the 21st century?

To answer this, the research needed to look at the process and experience of change, and to test out the basic premise at which I had arrived. This premise is reflected by my choice of *By the Skin of Our Teeth* as the title. It was chosen because, for me, it encapsulates how many organisations – in private, public and voluntary sectors – seem to perceive survival and sustainability today. We have to do so many things right to stay in business. It used to be that there was conventional wisdom about success. A formula was defined and refined, based on past successful experience and was then to be rolled out and applied by competent managers in other organisations. But today so many of the external environmental conditions are subject to such rapid and radical change that simple aspirations to efficiency, quality and best practice are not enough to guarantee survival, let alone growth and durability. Long-term business success remains as uncertain as ever, but accelerating business change means that business strategy has to be reassessed at increasingly frequent intervals.

Consequently, it seems to me that the fundamentals of business sustainability for an organisation in the 21st century are:

- to be world-class in all it does
- to be an extrovert organisation with keen antennae sensing trends and opportunities and involving its people in the future

and, above all,

- to be agile, proactively to anticipate and take advantage of trends, markets and the potential of resources, in particular, the human resource – to catch the moment- the window of opportunity.

Yet the perspective that people are the key the source of competitive advantage is not universally recognised or acted upon. Many businesses may pay lip service to the concept, but then often act in a cavalier fashion towards people, whether employed by them or in a stakeholder relationship with them. As a result, in a globalised world, individuals experience high levels of insecurity, and communities experience instability and uncertainty.

So who was I to include within the study, to supplement and contrast with my own experience of leading change in private, public and voluntary sectors? Mark Goyder, the Director of Tomorrow's Company, kindly wrote to many of his members to ask for their co-operation with this study. I supplemented those selected and willing with my own network of organisations of which I had been a director, and those for which latterly I had worked in a consulting and coaching capacity. The choice of Tomorrow's Company members was deliberate. Members not only, by definition, align themselves with the 'inclusive leadership' philosophy of Tomorrow's Company, but invariably they will have striven towards the typical characteristics of the inclusive approach. These are defined by Philip Sadler in *Building Tomorrow's Company*[3] in the following terms:

'Such companies remain competitive in the face of a changing environment for the following reasons:

- *They have clear purposes which are stated in other than purely financial terms; purposes that are on the one hand inspirational for employees and on the other provide a social as well as economic reason for the company's existence.*
- *These purposes are supported by a set of shared values which are deeply embedded in the company's culture and which have stood the test of time.*
- *They have developed sound corporate governance practices, with effective Boards of Directors and well-regarded reporting practices that are inclusive in the sense that they cover the whole range of a company's activities, including its impact on society and the environment.*
- *They have developed deep knowledge of what it takes to be successful in their particular industries and markets... The critical success factors have been identified and are systematically tracked by measurements.*
- *They set challenging performance targets and carefully monitor progress towards their achievement... If necessary, short-term profits will be treated as of lesser importance than continuing progress towards the longer-term goal.*
- *They deliver excellent value for money to their customers in terms of both quality of product and service, and create strong customer loyalty.*
- *They have committed loyal employees who feel the company is loyal to them in return.*
- *They have developed relationships of mutual trust with carefully selected suppliers.*
- *They are well respected in the communities in which they operate, and act as corporate citizens, taking a full part in the affairs of the local communities in which their operations are based.*
- *They have built a reputation for quality and integrity with the public at large. This reputation is often associated with a brand that is, in some cases, the company's most valuable asset.*

- *They are innovative and strive for continuous improvement.*
- *Their organisation structures and processes are well aligned with their strategies... They put decision-making powers as close to the customer interface as possible.*
- *These companies are characterised by a corporate culture in which people and relationships are highly valued and in which integrity and ethical behaviour are important values.*

As a consequence of possessing these characteristics (above) they have proved to be sound long-term investments for institutional funds and individual savers alike.

They also set an example for other companies to follow. Being highly admired and among the leading companies in their industries, their practices and policies provide models which other companies are following.'

By inspection, this definition of Sadler's, which is sourced from the research evidence of Kotter and Heskett (1992), Collins and Porras (1995), Pfeffer (2000), Collins (2001) and also related to the RSA Inquiry on Tomorrow's Company, aligns closely with the results of my findings in *Beyond World Class* (chapter 7 pp 194-224). These were drawn from some of the same studies, and supplemented by others.

Hence I would suggest that there is overwhelming evidence for the 'basic premise'. Therefore a sound methodology is to examine the experience of like-minded leaders of organisations in striving for sustainability in today's world of turbulent change. It could be argued that with such a selection I am preaching to the converted. However, the reader will find many interesting dissenters! Also, few of my interviewees would claim to meet in full Philip Sadler's exacting standards.

A parallel work to *By the Skin of Our Teeth* is *Hidden Value – How great companies achieve extraordinary results with ordinary people*[5] by Charles O'Reilly III and Jeffrey Pfeffer. The authors wrestled with the same dilemma of research methodology, and chose to focus on eight 'great' companies selected from their database as exemplars whose practices illustrate how companies can realise the full potential of their people. The authors' methodology was driven by their analysis of how managers learn (in contrast to how most management books are written).

'What we observed was that managers seem to learn best when they are provided with rich descriptions of how other managers and organisations operate, rather than the simplified, pre-digested 'lessons' that are conveyed in most management books. Research shows we

learn best by watching and listening to others facing diverse situations and then trying to apply the insights to our own experience.'

I share their logic, and also believe it is more helpful to practitioners to tap into such case study approaches than be presented with prescriptive recipes.

Thirty-four leaders of organisations were generous enough to collaborate with the research in this book, and they represent a spread of organisations across private, public and not-for-profit sectors. The full listing is shown in Appendix I together with the distribution amongst the sector categories of:

• large companies employing over 250 employees

• SME companies employing up to 250 employees

• public organisations

• not-for-profit organisations.

Although this method of classification fits most purposes, for this analysis I have re-classified the organisations in terms of the ways they have outwardly demonstrated their reaction to the challenge of survival and growth. Typically this is through new forms of organisation. Implementing a new structure in an organisation is a natural way of signalling change, both inside and out.

The leaders of these organisations gave me their personal perspectives, sometimes separate from their organisational roles. It is appropriate here to name this 'cast of characters' as well as the organisations they represent. For further details on the individuals and their organisations please refer to Appendix I.

THE CAST OF CHARACTERS

I Start-ups

The first category is the start-up. The start-up can be all about entrepreneurship, or it can involve a re-start – a phoenix arising from the ashes. It can also involve that really new form of organisation, the network. Of our list those that fit here are:

a New start-ups in the fields of technology

AIT – Richard Hicks, Non-Executive Chairman, entrepreneur in software development

BioFocus – Keith Moscrop, former Business Development Director, serial entrepreneur in electronics and biotech

The Generics Group – Duncan Hine, former Chief Executive

Camelot – Dianne Thompson, Chief Executive

b Not-for-profit organisations

Lymphoma Association – Alan Bartle, former Chief Executive

c Phoenix

Toyota – Dr Bryan Jackson OBE, Deputy Managing Director

Unipart Automotive – Paul Forman, former Managing Director

d Consultancy/Outsourcing

Pertemps – Tim Watts, Chairman (son of founder)

Ashton Penney – Bill Penney, co-founder

The Strategic Partnership – Peter Smith, Chief Executive

Telos Partners – Peter Ward, Principal

II   Mergers and Acquisitions

The second major category is mergers and acquisitions – a movement which reached a crescendo in the early 21st century where fashion overtook necessity. Some of our list of organisations are products of M & A activity in the past decade and have demonstrated sustainability, although showing shareholder value has sometimes been a struggle. They include:

- Royal and Sun Alliance – Syd Pennington, Group Director Executive Office and Change Management
- KPMG – Mike Rake, Chairman, KPMG International
- Cisco Systems – Todd Abbott, former Group Vice President, EMEA
- MCL/The Performance Solution Ltd – Sally Vanson, former Head of Human Resources at MCL and Director of The Performance Solution Ltd

III   Public to Private

Precisely because governments decided over the last two decades that many public sector bodies were not sustainable, and were better off in the private sector, a vital category of demonstrated change is the move from public to private ownership. Our sample here includes:

- AWG (formerly Anglian Water) – Chris Mellor, former Chief Executive
- GB Rail – Jeremy Long, Chief Executive and co-founder
- BT – Bob Mason, former Human Resources Director

- BAA – Tony Ward OBE, Group Services Director
  Sir John Egan, former Chief Executive, now Chairman of Inchcape

IV PUBLIC SECTOR AND PFI – RADICAL CHANGE WITHIN

Privatisation and the continuing struggle government has with the size, cost and effectiveness of the public sector has driven radical change hence I sought the views of:

- Department of Health/National Health Service (macro) – Professor Sir Liam Donaldson, Chief Medical Officer, Department of Health
- Peterborough Hospitals NHS Trust (micro) – Malcolm Lowe-Lauri, former Chief Executive
- One NorthEast (a Regional Development Agency) – Dr John Bridge, Chairman
- The Arts Council England – Peter Hewitt, Chief Executive
- Learning and Skills Councils – Jenny Clarke – Head of Workforce Development
- Patent Office – Philip Johnson, Head of Marketing
- Bovis Lend Lease – Mike Walters, Executive, Lend Lease Europe

V 'BUILT TO LAST'/'STEADY AS SHE GOES'

This final category may appear somewhat of a catch-all. However, the internal movements in such organisations may take the form of continuous change but they can be radical. Name changes, re-branding and demerger can make tremendous impact and complement cultural change. On the other hand for some organisations it can be 'steady as she goes' without radical change:

a Private sector

Shell UK Exploration and Production – Mark Hope, Director of External Affairs

UNUM – Lawrence Churchill, Former Chairman and Chief Executive

Burall Ltd – David Burall, Non-Executive Chairman and grandson of founder

House of Hardy – Richard Maudslay, Managing Director

Gardiner & Theobald – Marion Weatherhead, Partner

b Not-for-profit

CBI – John Cridland, Deputy Director General

Ashridge Trust – Professor Leslie Hannah, formerly Chief Executive

Now, having explained the reasons behind the choice of methodology and introduced the cast – both the organisations and their leaders – we turn to the discussion of their stories. First, in chapter 4, we see how they reacted to my basic premise, and to the three suggested fundamentals of business sustainability, being world-class in all it does, being an extrovert organisation, and being agile and proactive.

Notes

1   Kinsman, F *Millennium: Towards Tomorrow's Society* W.H. Allen / Virgin Books 1990

2   Donkin, R *Blood, Sweat and Tears: The Evolution of Work* Texere 2001

3   Sadler, P *Building Tomorrow's Company* Kogan Page 2002 pp248-250

4   Morton C *Beyond World Class* Macmillan 1998

5   O'Reilly C & Pfeffer J *Hidden Value and How Great Companies Achieve Extraordinary Results with Ordinary People* HBSP 2000

Chapter four

BASIC PREMISE
POLICY AND STRATEGY TO MEET THE CHALLENGE

HOW DO SUCCESSFUL ORGANISATIONS cope and sustain themselves in this increasingly turbulent context? In the interviews reported below, I asked the leaders whether they subscribed to the basic premise that there were three fundamentals for business sustainability in the 21st century, namely that the organisation needed to be:

* world-class in all that it does
* extrovert, with keen antennae, sensing trends and opportunities
* agile, proactive, responsive, taking advantage of trends, involving and developing the human resource to 'catch the moment'.

I sought responses from the leaders of a number of different types of organisation. The respondents fell into five categories, as shown below. I asked interviewees to consider each of the three different elements of this basic premise.

I   Start-ups/Entrepreneurship/Phoenix
II   M&A/Demerger Organisations
III Public to Private
IV Public Sector and PFI
V   'Built to Last' Organisations/'Steady as she goes'

I   START-UPS/ENTREPRENEURSHIP/PHOENIX

The organisations in this category represented four different types of enterprise. First, there were the new start-ups, operating in various fields of technology. They were:

AIT Group plc (software design and application)
BioFocus plc (combinatorial chemistry)
Scientific Generics (incubator technology)
Camelot (application of technology).

The not-for-profit sector was represented by the Lymphoma Association. The 'phoenix' companies were:

Toyota Manufacturing UK Ltd
Unipart Group Ltd

Finally there were a number of consultancy and outsourcing ventures.

These were:

Pertemps Ltd
Ashton Penney Ltd
The Strategic Partnership
Telos Partners

A   NEW START-UPS IN THE FIELD OF TECHNOLOGY

Element 1: World-class in all we do?

Did these start-up ventures accept it was necessary to be world-class in all that they did?

The AIT Group plc went through the most amazing roller-coaster ride in 2002. When I had interviewed Richard Hicks in 2001 it seemed that the pattern for success and sustainability was set. The ideas and values with which Richard and Clive Hicks had started in the 1980s had led them to build a highly successful software application enterprise. It was leading edge in its field in financial services and eventually made it to Number Five in the 2002 *Sunday Times 'Survey of Top 100 Employers to Work For'*.

Yet within the next year, due to stock market sensitivity over technology shares exacerbated by two profit warnings in close succession, AIT shares slumped from over £5 per share to 32 pence, closely followed by suspensions from the listings. Richard and his partners spent six months attempting to re-finance the company, in the process moving AIT from start-up technology to Phoenix! Richard Hicks says:

> '*I find it pretty depressing to realise how quickly a company's good reputation can be so quickly, but hopefully temporarily, damaged.*'

In the current re-assessment and recovery phase, AIT is still using to good effect the philosophies that helped to build it to its 2001 levels. In sustainability terms, 'today' this is reality. In a funny sort of way, the AIT experience is totally faithful to the start point of this book – that change can come from a totally unlikely quarter and completely knock your company sideways. The extreme sensitivities in the unforgiving stock market mean that there is no room for error, miscalculation or over optimism about forthcoming contracts – you can be 'darling' one minute and 'dead in the water' the next.

In 2001, in an open and honest interview, Richard Hicks acknowledged that, essentially, the future was in the hands of others. This was no entrepreneur who believed in control from the centre. Richard was determined to hand on the day-to-day running of the business to others. One year later, and non-executive Richard was in the driving seat again. But he still held to the view that you have to give people a reason to work for you.

> 'Increasingly, in the Western world, all employees are volunteers, where the most precious resources are those which are ever more mobile. The first battle for business sustainability in the 21st century is going to be giving people a reason to work for you. So it's the connection that can actually be made with people, and the whole set of relationships that you have with people, that makes them turn up for work at your office and not somebody else's.'

In Richard's view this leads on to the idea that the first port of call in aiming to be 'world-class in all we do' is to be an employer of choice.

> 'I think that with the huge increase in mobility, you are going to have to be the employer of choice if you want to be sustainable. In software, a huge throughput of staff is impossible – you just can't carry things through. It's partly being the employer of choice; but I suppose it is also a commentary on the nature of the organisation. There has been a lot of talk about outsourcing, about virtual organisations; and they're intriguing conceptually, but real organisations have a lot more solidity than that.'

Skills give different passports to mobility. Twenty years ago this was a major factor of difference. Richard reflected:

> 'Why was it different? I suppose it was geographic stability, stability of staff, and just social custom and expectations of not changing your job. There was undoubtedly an idea in people's heads that you didn't change jobs often. And there was a more practical issue, which was that people probably had fewer skills which, maybe, were not so generally transportable. If you're a twenty-five to thirty year old now, the way you get to travel is by being a Microsoft Certified Engineer. Skills give different passports to mobility.'

This is a major reason why companies have to be sensitive to the need to be employers of choice.

As he examined the proposition about being 'world-class in all we do', Richard made some very interesting points that give a perspective on issues also raised by others. But why does a business that does not operate globally have to worry about issues of world-class performance?

> 'Nobody would argue that you're likely to be successful if you're not world-class in anything you do. The interesting thing is why, now, is it more necessary to compare yourself with somebody other than the guys down the road? Is it because so many more of us are operating in a globally competitive market place? Even the sweet shop on the corner has been assaulted by change. Even small retail outlets

compete with global businesses – so I think there's no such thing as a cosy local business any more.'

For Richard, the issues were not so much about whether the basic premise held good in all situations. Rather, he saw the benefit of asking the question and examining whether things were different to the previous model. Whether, for success, you needed to do things differently.

'One can't argue that 'world-class' is a good thing to be; and you can't argue that 'being extrovert' is good; and 'being agile'; and so on. But I suppose what all that requires you to do is to prove (or at least demonstrate in some way) that the context has changed. Software is the archetypal intellectual capital. It is pure intellectual capital. There is nothing physical about software and its potential for replication is vast. When we're talking about software it's difficult to create barriers to entry.'

In the past stable conditions and barriers to entry enabled simple businesses to grow organically, as Richard illustrated. For him, running a business is always a mixture of art and science. He related a conversation with a very successful Canadian entrepreneur who had commented that the two richest people he knew were one who made coat hangers and one who made paint. Both were astonishingly rich. Anyone could make money with a simple product in a stable environment. The problem today, as Richard argued, is:

'There are just very few of those opportunities around any more, opportunities that could create real growth.'

For Richard, this discourse reinforces the imperative that he started with, the need to be an 'employer of choice'.

BioFocus is a more recent start-up than AIT and operates in a totally different industry. But again the focus is on people. Keith Moscrop, former Business Development Director, talks about the energy of release for the scientists in moving from 'Big Pharma' – the multinational pharmaceutical corporations – to a minuscule company which they owned and could do so much with.

'They had a very clear view of how they wanted to be seen, as good quality scientists delivering good quality service and products. For them, the release from the constraints of their previous employment was probably the single biggest motivator. They now can do things that, previously, committees or individuals in the big organisations had, for one reason or another, stopped them from doing. It doesn't mean that they have a free hand, because obviously we have a very small amount of money. But it still, nevertheless, gives a sense of freedom, and people really exploit that.'

To Keith, as for Richard Hicks, if the motivation is there the results will follow.

> *'People are essential to this. It is essential that they should be fired up, but people are the cause for the things not happening as well. I think it is how you face those issues that is important.'*

The Generics Group is less than twenty miles from BioFocus yet a world apart in terms of technology and its business model. However, similarities quickly emerge. Duncan Hine, who was the Chief Executive when I interviewed him, confirmed that being world-class is essential to being part of the marketplace. He immediately linked that to the quality of recruitment:

> *'The first thing is that we have to be very good at all we do. I wouldn't presume to say world-class in everything; but the reason we only recruit the top 2-3 per cent of graduates from good universities is that it is a start to being world-class. It gives you that potential.'*

Duncan explained that Generics were often chosen in competition either to somebody else giving a similar service or to a client company doing something themselves. He commented:

> *'I think one reason behind being competitive is that we challenge the option to do nothing. We often have to suggest something to somebody – even knowing it wasn't in their budget. .... The only way to do that is to be compelling and highly competitive, which I suppose in a sense translates into being world-class.'*

The intellectual base of the Generics organisation is clear. It is a classic definition of the 21st century company. Seventy per cent, or probably more, of its assets are represented by the brains of its employees.

Perception of the company from the outside is everything, whether from the potential postgraduate recruit or the potential client willing to sub-contract a large portion of their technology business to someone like Scientific Generics. The theme is 'world-class assets equal world-class businesses'.

With Camelot, use of the term world-class also rings true. Most countries around the world run lotteries and they are all country-specific. Camelot has no direct competitors in the UK. The competition is in the ways that customers spend their 'gaming' money. Camelot is a monopoly operator – so why is world-class important?

Dianne Thompson, the feisty Chief Executive who turned the tables on Richard Branson in 2000, is clearly a force to be reckoned with. She illustrates how much of it was 'a close run thing' (to emulate Wellington.)

'I think ...people who weren't involved remember the fight, remember the scene of me going into court, coming out of court and eventually winning. We lost on August 23rd. On 24th August we decided to fight on, and by Friday 25th we were in court. But at the same time we were out there fighting, we were actually closing the business down because we didn't think we could win.

The odds did look stacked against us because as directors we had a fiduciary duty to our shareholders that meant we had to close the business and to exit with as much return on their assets as possible. So we went on fighting, but at the same time we went through this business and we axed absolutely anything and everything that we could. We stopped all market research, all new product development. , We disbanded our interactive team because all of that [was due to] come through in 2002/03. All of that just got scrapped.'

This necessity to face both ways (i.e. being prepared to shut everything down whilst fighting to retain the licence) caused a hiatus in the business. Momentum for future sales and products inevitably was lost. Dianne disclosed her impatience over media expectations in this recovery phase.

'I get slightly cross that people are saying already that we're failing because sales are falling. In fact we won in December and Richard Branson conceded that he wasn't going to challenge in January 2001. I think it was as early as March or April 2001 that the front page of Sunday Business was 'The Camelot Queen loses the sparkle'. You think, 'For God's sake, give me a break here!' We eventually lost seven months because of the contest. But actually we lost about eighteen months because of losing people [because of disbanding teams].'

The negative effects on ongoing business of bidding for a re-franchise will often be unappreciated from the outside. The tension between a focus on the bidding team and keeping 'the ship of state' going is a classic dilemma (to which we will return in chapter 6 on Leadership). However the issue of one stream of activity affecting the other is often overlooked.

'In the bid process itself, there were two types of people here. There were people working on the bid and then the rest of us. What I was saying to everybody else was, 'They're doing a great job on the bid. Don't worry about it. We've got to concentrate on keeping the fundamentals right'.'

With hindsight, Diane now recognises that this inadvertently disempowered everybody. People were scared of taking any decision in case theirs was the one thing that backfired and caused a big problem.

> *'When I took over in January I inherited a company that was totally risk-averse. People were battered and weary and bruised and there was a real sense of lethargy here in the building. People just wanted to know, 'Am I out of a job or not, just tell me'.'*

Not surprisingly, Dianne is unimpressed with the franchise bidding system, which she believes is an incredibly wasteful process.

> *'I look back on the process and it's incredibly wasteful. It took us two years. I don't know how much the Branson team spent on it. I could well believe he spent £12m. We spent £4m here, and that didn't include any of the costs that he would have had to pay like salaries or buildings. Our bid was 15,000 pages long and God knows how many rainforests that took. The whole thing was totally wasteful. Also the Commission couldn't do day-to-day running of the Lottery because they were too busy evaluating the bid.'*

Despite this history behind her, it is now business as usual. Dianne is aiming to be world-class.

> *'I would absolutely agree with the world-class bit. One of the projects that we're working on here is called 'Model Company'. We are trying to establish benchmarks of what world-class behaviour is in a whole variety of fields and for that behaviour to be our goal. I think that, in certain things, we really are state of the art. I believe our social and ethical reporting is very world-class. We're trying very hard on our people policies to become real state of the art and leading edge. We've got a project running to benchmark every area of our business to find what its world-class level should be.'*

All these start-ups have been through turmoil in one way or other. They could be forgiven for giving up on high-flown ambitions of being world-class; yet each came back to fundamental agreement with the basic premise. I believe this is a reaction that balances short and long term. Crises come and go and our entrepreneurial leaders react to them. However, they recognise that, for sustainability, they need to be continually checking that they are up with the competition.

Element 2: Extrovert organisation?

Richard Hicks at AIT has practised the 'extrovert organisation' in many and different ways. Typically, individual entrepreneurs rely on their own involvements in the community, or on other boards, to provide the 'extroversion'. Richard and his colleagues have spread this much wider, and integrated it with the inputs into the organisation.

> *'It's absolutely what we do. A good question with other stakeholders. Definitely with our staff – there's a structured, demonstrable history of that. Definitely with the local community. Bear in mind there are less than five hundred people in the whole organisation. We've got*

two full time staff concerned with community affairs. One of them is a local headmaster and another an artist – solely concerned with the internal/external community.'

This approach is based on some deeply held beliefs about the role of 'trust' in transactions. Richard has been influenced by *Bowling Alone* by Robert Putnam.

'It's about social capital in America, plotting the decline in what [Putnam] calls social capital over the years and suggesting the things that recreate social capital.... He says that, broadly in society, trusting societies are much more efficient. In every transaction, leading our lives is much more efficient if we can do it in an environment of trust.[1] It's self-evident really. Trust is something you can bring into a relationship with every one of your stakeholders.'

For Keith Moscrop at BioFocus the issue of being an 'extrovert organisation' is about being a customer-orientated business.

'As far as customers feeding back to the business, listening to the customer has been a key feature of our services and product development. It's a quasi service, really, because we actually bring our own technology platforms to bear – but again the research needed for these developments is heavily influenced by the customers' feedback. Each of our big contracts, of which we now have half a dozen, is structured around the way the customer wants us to deliver.'

The same theme is reflected by Duncan Hine, former Chief Executive of The Generics Group, but in a more systematic way:

'Extrovert is quite an important word to us in terms of the nature of people in the organisation. One thing we insist on is that everybody is engaged to some degree in the selling process. The reason the selling process is important is that it's an extrovert thing by nature. They must go out and find people who want work done, persuade the people to give us the work, do the work and extend it.'

At Camelot the effort to be an extrovert organisation is not focused on direct sales but on the value of employees and customers in general rather than physical assets.

'I agree entirely with the extrovert view, particularly for an organisation like us where we manufacture nothing apart from dreams! So people and our own consumers are our only resource.'

Dianne sees the need to be extrovert in terms of the competition.

'Yes we're a monopoly. There is only one UK National Lottery but we operate in the gaming market and that's a very vibrant, very dynamic market place. You have to be extrovert or the competition will take the market share.'

Element 3: Agile, proactive, 'catching the moment'?

Oddly, the start-up companies did not have too much to say on this topic. I think this is because, to them, it is a non-question. It is something they take for granted. They do not come from the same place as larger organisations that have felt the need to be more entrepreneurial. It is already in the ethos.

Richard Hicks of AIT makes the distinction between large and small organisations and links agility to diversity:

> *'Large organisations inherently tend to create standards and standardise processes and so on. I think if you want responsiveness you do have to build diversity.'*

For Keith Moscrop at BioFocus, the small enterprise has created space for people coming from large organisations to be agile and satisfy customer demands.

> *'We were told by one customer that we were approximately three times more efficient than his own staff. If you just take that premise, that we actually serve the customer in as dynamic a way as we can, the interesting thing is that, by good fortune, that attitude has actually created space for those middle managers to do things for their customers that they wouldn't do in a rigid organisation. There's a degree of freedom down the organisation that has grown up which has been encouraged by that culture.'*

In Generics, agility is central to the ethos. However it is evolutionary, bottom-up, but not unbridled. It is very business-focused but the development paths are not led from the top. As Duncan Hine explained, there are at least two audiences that need to understand the constraints:

> *'Agility is very important to us here. What we do is the summation of what all the bright young technical people think we should do and what we can find customers to pay us to do. So, in fact, agility is a Darwinian thing here. It's by natural selection. Even though you might have a brilliant idea and be convinced that this will make lots of money over the next three years, unless you can persuade somebody to buy some work in that area or invest in it, you won't be doing it.'*

This onus on the instigator of the idea to embrace stakeholder groups beautifully links the 'extrovert organisation' philosophy with agility. Duncan Hine explained

> *'It's almost a proof test in the sense that it's not enough to have an informed opinion. You've actually got to find somebody externally who will commit their resources to it, either in terms of investment in cash or a purchase order. And if you're not getting interest from*

people we're not going to do it in the lab just because it looks very interesting.'

For Dianne Thompson at Camelot, agility has a lot to do with positioning the product in the market place. Dianne's background is in retailing and she regards Camelot as being as near to retailing as you can get. She illustrates the need to lead from the top in a commercial organisation in a heavily regulated environment:

> *'We're in a very odd position. We're a private company, and a commercial organisation that's very heavily regulated. To give you a specific example, we've recently launched an instant millionaire ticket – a scratch card with five £1m prizes. We applied for a licence to do that in 1999 and we were turned down by the Commission because they thought it would cause excessive play. We applied again the following March and they turned it down again. The only reason we got it the last time was that news was being leaked out from the Branson camp as to what was in his bid. And in his bid was a £1m scratch card game. So I rang my people downstairs and said, 'Get the licence out, change the name.' We had been going to do a type of 'Who wants to be a Millionaire' – the 'Instant Millionaire' – and we submitted it like that. We didn't do any work on it, just changed the name, changed the dates and put it back in. They had two choices. Either they turned me down – in which case I went out publicly and said, 'How can he (Branson) be saying he's going to do it, because we've been turned down three times now?' or they had to give it to me. They gave it to me and it was one of the most successful games we've had.'*

What is striking here is that, apart from assuming agility is 'in the blood' and not needing to be fostered, the contrasts are made with constraints of both larger, more institutionalised organisations and differing industries. Hence agility and the ability to innovate are seen to be cultural issues, not a function of technology or inherent intelligence (although clearly these factors add their own value).

B   NEW START-UP/ NOT-FOR-PROFIT

The Lymphoma Association is a relatively new charity, which started in Tim and Felicity Hilder's dining room in the 1980s. Tim had non-Hodgkin's Lymphoma and survived for over twenty years after the initial diagnosis – which was quite exceptional. Tim and Felicity realised from experience that there was little co-ordinated non-medical help for sufferers, relatives and carers. Hence the Lymphoma Association was born out of voluntary help to meet the need.

Alan Bartle became Chief Executive in 2001 and was able to describe the growth from early beginnings to the situation today:

*'We have an annual budget of going on for £0.5m, which in the
charities sector means that we are in the lower-medium size range.
The organisation aims to provide information and emotional support
to people who are affected by lymphomas, that is cancer of the
lymphatic system. We are the only organisation that works exclusively
in the lymphoma field. The organisation has undergone quite a
considerable growth in the last five or six years. It has grown in that
time from being an operation of volunteers in the dining room of the
founder's house to an organisation that has its own office.'*

I was rather hesitant in asking Alan the questions that I had posed to
the private and public sector organisations – did world-class have any
relevance? Alan didn't shy away from the issue:

*'I don't think the fact that we are a charitable organisation detracts
in any sense from whether or not one is world-class. World-class may,
however, be a difficult concept to quantify or define. I would actually
express it as saying that we want to meet the needs of everyone that
approaches us. We want to meet the needs of the patients and their
families but we need also to be satisfying the funders. I also believe
that although we are a UK-based organisation we have a
responsibility to see what's happening globally, and we are doing just
that. We can find out the best of what is happening elsewhere, make
sure that we are setting ourselves targets as high as everybody else
and learn from what they're doing and attempting to achieve.'*

This answer of Alan's linked very easily with the next element of the
basic premise, 'the extrovert organisation'.

*'In terms of being extrovert, I think we're fortunate in that we're a
national organisation. We certainly have to be aware of the UK scene
– and increasingly I believe we have to go beyond that. That's both
in terms of how we meet the immediate needs of our clients and in
terms of what's happening in the charitable sector generally.'*

Similarly Alan saw the relevance of the link between having good
antennae and reacting in a timely way.

*'In terms of being agile and proactive, being responsive is part of it;
but also being reactive, because in the particular disease setting,
things do happen and we have to be ready to react or be responsive.'*

So, the basic premise was relevant to the Lymphoma Association,
despite its very different history and activities.

C 'Phoenix' Organisations

Two of the organisations studied fit well into this category, Toyota
Manufacturing UK and Unipart Automotive.

Toyota was established in the UK in 1992 at Burnaston, near

Derby, on a greenfield site in much the same way as Nissan MUK had been established in the north east. It also had many things in common with Komatsu UK, a firm which forms part of my own experience.[2] In many ways Toyota Manufacturing UK is a start-up, but in other respects its development is part of a well-trodden path. The manufacturing systems are imported from Japan and the ethos is very much the parent company's way of doing things.

The second company, Unipart Automotive, was originally the parts side of British Leyland (BL) which was government owned in the 1980s. Unipart started as a buy-out when BL (which by then had been re-named Rover) was sold to BAe. Its business is the provision and distribution of parts to original equipment manufacturers (OEMs) and the supply of replacement parts to distributors. It has grown organically, at 5 per cent, year on year, to £650m turnover and employment of 6,000 people by 2001. So it is a start-up but with people, equipment and other inheritance from BL.

There is another link of interest between them. Unipart quickly saw itself as a learning organisation and, under its first managing director John Neill, adopted many Japanese manufacturing techniques. It disseminated these amongst its suppliers and employees through Unipart U, its corporate university.

I interviewed Dr Bryan Jackson OBE, deputy managing director of Toyota Manufacturing UK Ltd, who provided me with his views in a personal capacity, not necessarily on behalf of Toyota. I also interviewed Paul Forman, former managing director of Unipart Automotive. Again, I have grouped their responses according to the three elements of the main premise.

Element 1: World-class in all we do?

For a manufacturer that is seen as the most successful in the highly competitive large volume producer segment, Bryan Jackson was of the view that you cannot be world-class in everything! He pointed out that first it is necessary to define:

- What is 'world-class'?
- How do we judge 'world-class'?

Yes, he acknowledged that Toyota had world-class manufacturing systems but essentially the judgement was down to customers; they, after all, buy the product. Hence the key question is, 'What is the need in the market place' and 'What will provide for this need and sustain the organisation?'

Paul Forman voiced a similar reservation. He did not believe that, in an increasingly fast-changing and global business, organisations could be 'world-class in all they do'.

> *'If you take our example we hope to be world-class as a branch distribution function and as a sourcer and brander of products. To try and be world-class in, say, our warehousing – or a number of other areas – would just stretch us too thin.'*

Not to do this would mean that you would end up doing everything badly, rather than a few things well. As Paul commented:

> *'There's only so much psychic energy you have as an individual and as a management team.'*

He believes in focusing on the greater demands that they are seeing in their market. These are changing quicker and quicker, and:

> *'Unless you are on top of your game in a few key areas, you won't have the capability to follow major trends in absolutely every part of the value chain.'*

Yet Paul Forman differentiated between being world-class, and having access to world-class capability.

> *'I think you should have access to world-class capability in everything you do. That's a very different proposition.'*

Element 2: Extrovert organisation?

The responses from these two participants in world-class manufacturing businesses were similarly consistent when we talked about the extrovert organisation. Bryan Jackson accepted the concept without question because, he said, otherwise you operate in a vacuum – remote from customers, competitors, society and the environment. Paul Forman felt that the need to be in touch was always there historically, but the pace of change today made it even more necessary:

> *'I don't think it has ever been different. I just think that your antennae need to be keener now because the trends are more fleeting than they were – probably because customers are more demanding. The customer-driven company, which is the consequence of having an extrovert organisation, is not a new concept but I do think now your antennae need to be keener.'*

Element 3: Agile, proactive, 'catching the moment'?

On agility and 'catching the moment' both these respondents embraced the concept, but rightly stressed the contextual difficulties. Bryan Jackson said that aspiration to agility was fine, but what was needed internally, day to day, was a flexible response in the management process. Product development inevitably took a long time. A new car takes five years or more to design and develop. It is important not to dramatically change direction in the market place.

Obsolescence is not good. It causes confusion, and you need a longer-term view. The key, he believes, is taking people with you after having established a product/plan.

Paul Forman also put the question of agility into context and emphasised the contribution of people in teams:

> *'Having an organisation that can catch the moment is running before you can walk....My experience of the real world is that the start point is just getting people to do their best to work as a team.*
>
> *Pro-activeness and responsiveness are organisational traits. The increased commercial and mental agility implied in the phrase 'catching the moment' to me is a second tier of development. If you can get it, undoubtedly it can give you competitive advantage; but getting the basics right is very important. I think agility would be a good end-game or organisational goal.'*

Overall, both these companies provided realistic but optimistic responses which, yet again, put the customer and the employee at the heart of the basic premise.

D   CONSULTANCY/OUTSOURCING

In this section I have grouped together four companies that are all relatively recent in terms of business and all in the service sector. They all provide solutions to a range of businesses. They are:

- **Pertemps** – which provides temporary and permanent people to business. I talked with Tim Watts, the chairman.
- **Ashton Penney** – which provides interim management to organisations, where I interviewed Bill Penney, the co-founder.
- **The Strategic Partnership** – a management consultancy where I spoke with Peter Smith, the chief executive.
- **Telos Partners** –another management consultancy, where I interviewed Peter Ward, a partner.

The unifying feature for these companies is that, having relatively few core staff and being 'extensions' of their client's business, they tend to comment on the way other organisations do business rather than their own. Because of this, they tended to agree without much question with the basic premise, in the round, without distinguishing much between the elements. They would then go on to comment on how culture within organisations potentially undermines aspirations.

Hence Tim Watts, who runs the oldest and largest of these providers (turnover £600m, employees 2,000), said that the basic premise was a good summary, but went on to an analysis of what held companies back. His emphasis was on what his injection of new employees can bring.

> 'What I would add is the importance of removing all static from the company. They are what kill companies. If companies have a hierarchy like, for example, the army, then those that will survive the 21st century need the 'privates' to be at the top. I see that the new people in (companies) are the ones who bring the new energy. Using the analogy of a tree, the oldest employees are the trunks that support the life of the tree. But the new leaves absorb the external environment and carry out the photosynthesis to send the messages through the branches back to the trunk.'

Bill Penney saw the basic premise as a dilemma between being 'reactive' and 'proactive'.

> 'I would totally endorse the basic premise. The difficulty, in my view, is the distinction between being reactive to the things that are happening around you and being proactive and actually making things happen. I think there's a subtle tension between the two. So you have one or two people who catch the vision that you've got and that validates the vision. Then you go on to convince the other people.'

Bill shared his frustration at getting across the message about his business offering and stressed the importance of targeting the right people:

> 'We are a growing company in a market that I've seen from its inception to becoming newly mature. I've spent twelve years banging my head against a brick wall trying to persuade companies that interim management is relevant. Originally, companies reacted to it by seeing it as a distress purchase, putting a finger in the dyke. The ideal client at that stage was the chairman, the chief executive, the plant director, the person that was feeling the pain. We're now at the point where we're saying the people we really ought to be talking to are the personnel directors (now that the others are convinced).'

Peter Smith was worried that 'world-class in all we do' could be limiting if it led companies simply to benchmark against the average. He used terminology from Collins and Porras[3] in making his point:

> 'It (the premise) is fine I but it is also important for an organisation to have 'big hairy ambitious goals' with targets greater than what it appears to achieve at any one moment.'

Commenting on the 'Extrovert Organisation', Peter felt that people were less aware of the environment around them today:

> 'Networking is not a cultural habit in the UK. There is a need continually to monitor internal and external factors of what is going on. Every meeting and conversation presents a potential opportunity

for this and, if this is not recognised, then the organisation could be missing out.'

If the basic premise is sound, why then is it not working in organisations? Peter Smith explained:

'(There is) lack of empowerment. Giving people responsibility and allowing mistakes is not as commonplace as it should be. Big global organisations are beginning to break down into smaller units without full responsibility, innovation and accountability.'

Peter Smith felt that companies do not pay enough attention to corporate governance or to the relationships between different parts within the organisation. They 'muddle through' with structures that inhibit managing success.

'Boards are too far apart from the rest of the organisation and not effectively monitored. Directors need to be out and walking the talk. Look at Marks & Spencer: how come customers stopped buying but it took three years for the board to hear this? It is odd that senior general managers behave like normal people, yet as soon as they get on the board they change and become distant.'

This conclusion rang very true to me. It is consistent with other findings, which are brought together and discussed in chapter 9.

Peter Ward of Telos Partners took a philosophical view of the three elements of the basic premise. He maintains that the challenge is largely about having the 'will to do it'.

'If you want a business to last, the first and absolutely foremost thing is the will to make it last. There's a core ideology which people buy into that will sustain the business through thick and thin.

We all know that unifying purpose is absolutely vital. You can be world-class in a process, you can be world-class in thinking and that buys you the right to start off. Then, if you're world-class, you're probably thinking about regeneration. It's a will to continue, to be self-determining.

If somebody walks in and says, 'You could grow twice as fast if you work with me and here's a couple of million' and you accept the offer, you will have lost it because your self-determination is gone. You've cashed in.'

In a similar way to Peter Smith, Peter Ward focuses on a dysfunction that destroys the intention of sustainability. For him, this is the fickle nature of the short-term shareholder. Looking at what was a then recent experience in the City of London, he casts doubt on the contribution of shareholders to sustainability.

'It is complete nonsense to suggest that Goldman Sachs needed to

float because they were limited in their ability to raise capital.
Another interpretation of their action might be the cynical
exploitation by one generation of former generations for their personal
gain.'

Because of this, Peter Ward felt that the prospect of owners sustaining
their business can be damaged by bringing in external shareholders.
He gave an example:

'We have a new client, trading at £2.80. Their shareholders are
saying 'When you get to £3.00 we're going to sell you'. What sort of
shareholder is that?'

The question for Peter was whether people wanted a 'transactional
shareholder' or whether they wanted somebody who was going to stay
with them over the long term. He advised:

'If you want somebody to stay with you over the long term, then you
look for a different type of shareholder. You actively seek them and
court them and keep them on side.'

II M&A/DEMERGER ORGANISATIONS

In the organisations I surveyed there are four significant companies
that have experienced merger or demerger. Some of these have
policies of 'acquire for growth'. The four are:

Royal and Sun Alliance Group Ltd
KPMG Ltd
Cisco Systems EMEA (subsidiary of Cisco Systems Inc)
MCL Group-Performance First Ltd

Royal and Sun Alliance (RSA) is one of the world's largest insurance
groups. In recent years it has been through enormous upheaval in
terms of products, position in the market place and financial viability.
I interviewed Syd Pennington, then Director of Customers and
People. He described how Royal and Sun Alliance has had to go back
to its fundamental roots to establish what it was, and where it needed
to go in the marketplace and in motivating its workforce. With an
enormous range of insurance (from pet insurance to nuclear power
stations), diverse origins pre-merger, a presence in fifty-two countries
and 52,000 employees around the world, this has been a massive
challenge. A major review was carried out to establish how RSA
added value, what the goal was, and what was the differential. The
objective was to make external and internal brands with a focus on
providing insurance solutions not pushing the traditional products.

With the background of this close examination of where RSA

found itself, both internally and externally, the basic premise of this book came as no surprise to Syd Pennington. The only difference was one of terminology – he would have called the extrovert organisation 'innovative'. There is no doubt that the insurance industry has had to look to the customer situation much more and, in RSA's case, be more 'extrovert' in listening and tuning its antennae.

In terms of agility, Syd felt that the modus operandi had moved from 'product producer and processor' to 'solutions provider'. However he was not sure whether they had yet made much progress in shifting from the 'day job' to thinking outside the box'.

Overall, as with others in this category, the concern was more with issues of size and diversity, and how to manage internally, than with being 'world-class' as such.

Mike Rake, now Chairman of KPMG International was similarly getting to grips with size, with total revenues exceeding $14 billion and 50,000 people in Europe alone. He sees size as a problem for accountancy firms. 'The bigger they are the more trouble they seem to get into.' His quest was 'to find a different method to self organise'. The interview with Mike predated the demise of Andersons and his words, in retrospect, look prophetic.

Mike's issue with the basic premise was that it was a real challenge to keep agility in a large people business that tends to work in silos.

> 'We're talking about a large people business. To keep the business agile and flexible and able to move fast and to understand and react and deal and anticipate external events is a real challenge in a professional service firm.'

I was able to interview Todd Abbott, then Group VP Cisco Systems EMEA, about their phenomenal growth through acquisitions. Cisco have not diversified into other industries but have used acquisitions to build capability through people in their chosen sector. They are now the largest manufacturer of networking solutions worldwide.

Todd defined Cisco's business as having a focus on helping enterprises and small and medium businesses to enable them to deliver, or to achieve the productivity gains from Internet business solutions.

> 'The true benefit has been around productivity increases for businesses through connecting their various constituents, their employees, their customers, their suppliers and their investors. So it's truly about providing the information each constituent needs in a self-sufficient manner so as to enable more enriching interfaces amongst its constituents. That's really what the Internet's all about. Our focus is around enabling those kind of systems, those kind of

*applications, and those kind of interactions, to happen at a much
more rapid rate.'*

The whole sector has taken an enormous hit in the wake of the burst
of the dotcom bubble but Cisco maintains it is the only profitable
company in their market of internet business solutions. Why? Todd
explained:

> 'We've always been very focused on the use of the Internet to run
> our business, so we are a much more productive company than any
> of our competitors. If you measure that by revenue per employee, we
> are always at the top of the list. Only one firm has exceeded us in
> the last several years but it has now started to slip back.
>
> So, firstly, it's been a very relentless focus on productivity and
> realising the benefits of using the technology that we sell. Secondly,
> we've had some luck. Our focus has always been on the new
> technologies around networking and specifically IP. So the internet
> protocol foundation has been an enabler for a lot of converged
> applications and converged systems and these happen to be our
> strength.'

Cisco demonstrates the concept of an 'extrovert organisation with
agility' in its strategy. As Todd expressed it:

> 'A cornerstone of our strategy has always been to look for market or
> economic disruption. Those are the times to take shares and move
> into new markets. Five years ago, when the EEC markets were
> collapsing, we actually started to invest while everybody else was
> contracting, figuring that it was going to be a long downturn in
> Asia. We took a lot of share from our competitors at that point.'

In common with others interviewed, Todd wished to be selective in
the definition of 'world-class in all we do'.

> 'When you talk about world-class, I think you have to identify what
> it is that you need to be world-class in. What really adds value to the
> business model? You can focus resources on what is truly value
> added, the value proposition to the market.
>
> The vertical business model is too hard now. The market's moving
> too fast. It's still difficult to be number one and number two with
> every component of the Internet so you've got to pick what your
> strengths are, focus a resource there, and partner with the rest. The
> need to partner now is much greater than it's ever been.'

Sally Vanson was Director of The Performance Solution and at the
same time Head of HR at MCL (previously Mazda Cars UK). The
Performance Solution demerged from MCL after Itoshu, MCL's
major shareholder, decided to diversify out of automobiles. Following
this, Ford took over Mazda factories in Japan and the raison d'être of

the original businesses, supporting Mazda, disappeared.

The Performance Solution grew out of the expertise in HR and focused on 'personal and organisational development, particularly in the areas of leadership, team development and coaching'. Sally Vanson describes the complete reversal of cultures during this transition period.

> *'Through a five-year transition the whole of the culture in MCL has changed. One of the major changes has been a move from a very patriarchal, autocratic motor industry structure. In this, the original MD reckoned that we made five business decisions a year and he made them. So he recruited managers around him who were compliant, who didn't raise their heads above the parapet, were task orientated, were definitely not strategic thinkers and were very processed. In the last two years we've been recruiting exactly the opposite - mavericks, free spirits, entrepreneurs, people who will challenge.'*

Sally described how The Performance Solution is now selling business services to other business. This has again has caused a change in culture.

> *'The value of our people has become much more significant because our knowledge, our asset base, now resides in them as opposed to lumps of metal.'*

In examining the basic premise Sally takes an interesting post-TQM view, having been thoroughly exposed to it in the MCL days. She says she no longer believes in the total quality route:

> *'I think, actually, people will give up part of the quality in order to get the fast response so it's very much the 80/20 rule now. If people get 80 per cent of it right, that's okay. The days of zero defects have gone. The reason is speed. We have a saying that an Internet year is three months.'*

Sally described how, in the old Mazda days, the annual business plan would be broken down into quarterly reviews. But there is no time for that any more.

> *'What we used to do in a year we now do in three months. I think it is because of the Internet, the information available and the speed at which people want things.'*

There can be tensions between quality, quantity and generating the right response. An anecdote from Sally provided a very good example of this. In one call centre staff selling cars were tasked to make twelve customer-related outbound calls an hour. One day somebody made a call to Nat West and was on the phone for forty-five minutes. The member of staff got reprimanded for spending so long on a call with a customer and didn't get his bonus. However the potential sale was 15,000 cars! The company eventually got the contract for the cars. However the member of staff concerned, who had actually done a superb job, was not perceived to have done so because he hadn't met his short-term target. As Sally reflected:

> 'There's something about the issue of quality there. It doesn't need to be perfectionism. I think that's the big change. In the nineties it was very much total quality. If you could have perfection in two weeks, why take something less than perfect in a week? I think that's completely reversed.'

Sally regards the issue of being an 'extrovert organisation' as one that concerns especially the area of staff development. She sees agility and innovation in people terms and in particular as a gender issue. She cites Charles Handy's prediction that women will become the general managers and MDs of the future, with men becoming technical specialists because, biologically, there are such trends.

> 'I'm not saying men can't be intuitive but, because women seem to be more intuitive, they seem to be able to catch the moment more easily. I think men can do it but they haven't been allowed to. It is that peripheral vision, being aware of what's going on behind you as well as in front.

> [From] caveman days men have much better focal vision which means they can see much farther forward. Women have much wider peripheral vision which means they can see further behind their heads than men can. It comes back to when we lived in caves, the job of the man was to hunt the lion and to focus on it and kill it. The woman had to look after the children, the fire and the cave, but she also had to keep an eye out in case the lions crept up and ate the children. So actually we developed physically like that. For me that's catching the moment in business – the men need to be able to look round.'

This suggests a fascinating additional dimension on why 'men don't ask for directions' and women (reputedly) can't 'reverse park'!

This group has a diverse mix of companies, which thus have differing rationales for mergers and/or demergers. The premise appears to hold good but the management preoccupations are different. R&SA were looking to make sense of the merger of equals within a rapidly changing insurance world; KPMG were grappling with the problems of size and co-ordination; Cisco looked for growth and opportunity that markets offered with the impression of an express train; and Mazda/Performance Solution were into creative destruction in the demerger process. But, despite the different drivers, the premise holds good.

III PUBLIC TO PRIVATE

I also carried out interviews at a group of companies that are the children of the Thatcher era of privatisation. They have matured from the first flush of commercial freedoms in being released (or ejected?) from the public sector. The firms are:

AWG

G B Rail

BT

BAA

Their public sector backgrounds mean that there rightly remains a public sector ethos of universal service. Consistently, they lost some monopoly and focused on cost reduction in their journey from public to private as competition, transparency and challenge increased.

Typically, such large ex-public sector enterprises spent much time examining alternative business models and income streams. The balance between regulated and non-regulated business would have been regularly debated in their boardrooms. Industry comparisons loom large. Benchmarking would be de rigueur and 'world-class' systems purchased from ever-willing consultants and business schools. So, how did they react to the three elements of our basic premise for business sustainability in the 21st century?

Element 1: World-class in all we do?

The interesting conclusion from the interviews in this sector is that, following the benefits and scars of this experience, our leaders are very selective about issues of world-class performance.

Chris Mellor, then Chief Executive of AWG plc, said:

> 'World-class in all we do, yes, that's an aspiration, but is it an unrealistic aspiration? Isn't that really why many companies have gone down the outsourcing route, recognising that you can't be world-class at everything?'

Jeremy Long, Chief Executive of GB Rail plc, commented in a very similar vein:

> 'World-class in all that we do? Actually, I think there are very few organisations that, in all truth, will try and do that. I think what you find is that successful organisations are clearer about what it is they're trying to be world-class in.
>
> I'm being controversial, but I think it's very easy just to say an organisation should look to spell out quality in everything. Budgets, in reality, don't run to it.'

Bob Mason, formerly of BT, saw the aim of being world-class as the entry ticket. It was what got you into the game.

'It's a bit like getting to the Olympics because you've met the Olympic qualifying standard. Because of globalisation, companies (who don't understand) will get a very rude awakening.'

Drawing on the experience of BT, he says:

'What every company is striving to do is, for a moment or a period in time, to be unique but these temporary monopolies that they might enjoy are a matter of months.'

Sir John Egan, former Chief Executive of BAA felt that being 'world-class in all we do' was only part of the answer. His concise view, which reflects his extensive experience with both Jaguar and BAA, was of a 'central concept':

'I would add a central concept. Business is about satisfying customers, it's about engaging your employees in bringing their brains and enthusiasm to work, it's about all of the various stakeholders that you have. You must make sure that you're giving a good return to your shareholders. You have to make sure that you are co-ordinating your supply chain in a way that is competitive. You must make sure that you have a relationship with the environment and your surrounding communities which is wholesome and you run your business with their support. When I say 'be world-class in all we do' that's what I mean.'

Element 2: An extrovert organisation?

This second tenet of the basic premise found much resonance with these privatised organisations. There was no difference of view on the importance of understanding trends and having effective antennae, particularly where the competition was concerned. Jeremy Long of GB Rail said:

'I totally agree with your [concept of the] extrovert organisation. I've felt for a long while [that people] in business [have a] degree of short sightedness, of not seeing trends even though they really are staring them in the face. You have to get the management to have the confidence to go out and look at their competitors. The confident management team is the one that's actually out there, always looking to see who else is doing it better, as opposed to the arrogant team that just never believes they're going to find it. It's a form of creativity for me.'

In common with some other comments, the term 'extrovert' didn't meet with totally universal approval. Tony Ward of BAA expressed it like this:

'I wouldn't choose the word 'extrovert'. I know exactly what you

mean and I can demonstrate that it's part of our characteristic. A
crude analogy might be in the way that market research is introvert in
terms of its approach. Also, I think, there are many extroverts, if you
use the word in personality terms, who can't empathise. So I think
extrovert is just the wrong word. I would talk about future focus and
external awareness but I think the basic premise is exactly right.'

The end effect, however, is the same. For Chris Mellor, formerly of
AWG, the extrovert organisation was about being able to reconcile the
irreconcilable:

'The way we get out and involved is through what we call
'sustainable development' which is really about the reconciling of
irreconcilable things. It is about creating the economic growth of the
organisation whilst protecting the environment and whilst becoming
a good corporate citizen and playing a role in the community you
serve, wherever you happen to be.'

Chris argued that being 'extrovert' also provides an opportunity for
employees to develop through working on community projects and to
be proud of being in a company that actively contributes to local
communities.

'Being seen to do good things for the environment and the
community makes people proud to be associated with, and work for,
the company. It improves our image and the payback for us – apart
from enhanced reputation – is that, in my view, people who
participate in these programmes come back better managers or better
workers than had they not done so.'

Bob Mason also believed that activity of this sort contributed heavily
to external reputation and brand, and also has internal benefits:

'Yes, (being an extrovert organisation) does help the business. There's
quite a lot of evidence for it. I think the strategic example is that,
ultimately, it positively impacts the company's reputation. By doing
that, it positively impacts the brand. It says this company does
actually care about the community in which it does its business. The
more tactical example is when you get into employee involvement
activity in the community. There can be a real pay off internally.'

John Egan made a telling point when he pointed out that people are
more engaged with the outside than their employers realise:

'For us, it was very obvious that BAA would be known as a benign
and quality neighbour. Our contract with the community, and
inspiring our people to give to the community around them, was
absolutely non-controversial. Don't think that only 10 per cent are
fully engaged. Everybody, to some extent, is more engaged.'

These organisations, with roots in public service and a newly found life in the private sector, are interesting hybrids. They have found their own level in terms of being world-class, are very sensitive about wider stakeholders and hanker after agility – as we shall see.

Element 3: Agile, proactive – catching the moment?

All respondents in this group agreed that agility was a function of creating the right atmosphere and environment within the enterprise. Chris Mellor of AWG saw this as the opportunity for commercial advantage, by creating the opportunities for innovation through emotional intelligence, by having the aim of the whole organisation as being able to spot opportunities:

> *'It's about trying to create an environment, culture, call it what you will, where people can see the opportunity and are motivated or empowered to do something about it.'*

He pointed out that it was vital to engage the whole organisation and not see this as a role for only the senior people:

> *'We do have power to do something about it but we can sit here for days on end and not have the ideas, whereas somebody down below does spark but feels powerless to do anything about it.'*

Similarly, John Egan put the priority on an alert workforce who used their brains and 'wore the badge' for the company:

> *'You have to make sure that you've got an alert workforce who engage their brains and, so it's not just your brains you use, you've got a lot of people wearing a badge'*

For him, agility was about giving the licence to experiment, encouraging diversity and creativity, and valuing incremental improvement. It was not necessarily about looking for the great leap forward:

> *'You've got to teach your employees to experiment and try and do things. Everybody is experimenting with process improvements of one kind or another.'*

Jeremy Long of GB Rail made the strong point that it was one thing to get these ideas but that this was easier than implementation:

> *'Most innovation is coming from people who are otherwise flat out doing the day job. You've got to persuade those people that it's worthwhile, because for them it's taking on extra responsibility. Otherwise they come up with a good idea, are told 'Okay, do something about it' and they think 'Oh hell, I wish I hadn't raised that'.'*

This discussion on the basic premise gave the interviewees the opportunity to expand on their philosophy. Much of this was about achieving employee motivation or 'energy' to propel the organisation. All these examples of 'public to private' have had to change the environment away from the previous, public sector influenced, 'entitlement culture'. Some of the talk was about the ethical and spiritual dimensions, opening out to cover social capital or the 'glue' between individuals, teams and organisations.

Chris Mellor described:

> '*A genuine sense of wanting more vision, but clear accountability and a high degree of devolved responsibility for delivery, within the framework and the strategy that you've outlined. Culture is the key, particularly among the top one hundred or so managers. Getting their behaviours right and appropriate, the one team approach, the sense of co-operation rather than being in boxes, that's the glue that helps you get on with your own thing.*'

He went on:

> '*What do we stand for, what sort of a company are we? What are we doing, where are we doing it? There's almost a spiritual dimension to that, to the behaviours that the senior management exhibit as they try to do what they are trying to do.*'

The theme of spirituality was also taken up by Tony Ward of BAA:

> '*I feel there is another dimension. In order to have sustainability there has to be an ethical element. I think you could have all the best things going for you and you'll get rejected if you behave unethically. It is a spiritual dimension, the way you run the business internally, and it can be a spiritual dimension in the way you relate to your customers.*'

Bob Mason also referred to the link between ethics and stakeholders:

> '*I think it's this concept of attraction. If customers and consumers in the future see companies as anything less than 100 per cent ethical, they won't shop there, they won't want to buy.*'

With the 'public to private' organisations, the links between the three elements of the basic premise are easy to see. These organisations have had to 'crank the handle' over creativity – their heritage meant that they had been risk averse. They too have delved into 'meaning and purpose' with its ethical and spiritual dimension, something to which we will return in chapter 9.

IV PUBLIC SECTOR AND PFI

Hardly a day passes without the Public Sector being in the headlines. The issues of efficiency and effectiveness loom large. Government's tenure today seems to hang on the thread of demonstrable improvement in public services in much the same way as political parties need to depend for election on the basis of their management of the economy.

Perhaps, oddly enough, the issue of sustainability looms large just as much in the public as in the private sectors, but for different reasons. Over the last three decades governments of differing hues in the UK have applied a variety of organisational, ownership and partnership forms to the public sector – firstly to decrease its dominance on the public purse and, secondly, to radically improve performance. As a result we have seen compulsory competitive tendering in local government, outsourcing, public-private partnerships (PPP), public funding initiatives (PFI), agencies to achieve devolution and more focus and, privatisation, the last of which has been considered above.

Insecurity in the public sector has increased as a result, both for individual employees – who fear they may be outsourced to the private sector with its perceived lower security of tenure – and also for organisations as a whole who collectively fear that their political masters may conclude that the whole operation is best off outside the public sector. Hence sustainability is an issue that is alive and well, even though the transfer of an undertaking can be good news rather than the worst, as feared.

The organisations in this grouping, although not privatised, have been through enormous and radical change and their raison d'être and modus operandi have been the subject of examination and re-examination over several decades.

Department of Health/NHS
Peterborough Hospitals NHS Trust
One NorthEast
Arts Council England
Learning Skills Council
Patent Office
Bovis Lend Lease

So how do they view the three posited elements of organisational sustainability?

Element 1: World-class in all we do?

The private sector comparison looms large. The success of applying tools such as total quality, 'lean production' and process re-engineering in manufacturing industry worldwide has been enthusiastically promoted by management consultants into the service, public and not-for-profit sectors. The language has travelled even if the results have not.

The answer that we find in the public sector to the first element of the premise, 'world-class in all we do? is not surprising – 'Yes, but...' Professor Sir Liam Donaldson, Chief Medical Officer of the National Health Service (NHS), which employs over one million people, occupies one of the two most senior executive posts in the Department of Health. He saw the issue as largely a technological one, and about tailoring to patient needs.

> *'I think world-class resonates more at the technological end of things so that you get the best innovations in as early as possible and so let people benefit from the technological side of healthcare. The other aspects of quality are much more about being perfect at tailoring things to each individual patient's needs in a way that is world-class.'*

This sounds very much the way that manufacturing would talk – see the responses from Bryan Jackson of Toyota, above, or Richard Maudslay of House of Hardy, below, about being at the leading edge and perfectly answering customer needs.

Again in the NHS but managing a discrete operating unit – Peterborough Hospitals NHS Trust – former Chief Executive Malcolm Lowe-Lauri felt that being 'world-class' on its own was not an aspiration since, as Liam Donaldson recognised, health care differs according to the national and regional context world-wide.

> *'The culture or ethos of healthcare around the world depends a little bit upon the society that it's delivered in. So, to that extent, some things can't be benchmarked worldwide, but many can.'*

Malcolm felt that, although benchmarking was not inherent in the NHS culture, it needed to be so in order to monitor the progress of the Trust, both in the interest of the public and employees. Malcolm's view was:

> *'The challenge is how you use that benchmarking to push the standards towards 'leading-edge'. As a generalisation, in many parts of the NHS, the attitude would be to accept 'mediocrity'.'*

One of the biggest problems hospitals and other health trusts face is the inhibition on learning from each other, and being able to compare performance. The Department of Health has introduced many standards of performance but few that really reflect the patient experience or the efficacy of treatment. So Malcolm Lowe-Lauri, rightly in my view, takes a local health system view. His agenda was about a 'can do' culture at Peterborough.

> *'What matters is how you go about achieving your goals and motivating employees to achieve them. To change people's view of the*

*Health Service it is necessary to deliver. It is essential to become
more accessible, to open up communication and services to patients
and families'*

I obtained a fascinating overview of 'world-class in all we do' in both
public and private sectors from Dr John Bridge, Chairman of One
NorthEast, the regional development agency for the north east of
England. He wished to stress the importance of the public sector in
performance terms:

> *'Something like 40 per cent of our GDP in the UK is generated
> through the public sector. We miss a trick; we don't understand that
> the public sector has got to be world-class as well.'*

That certainly doesn't let the public sector off the hook!
And now for something completely different, Arts Council England
(ACE). Here, Peter Hewitt the Chief Executive sees the issue as:

> *'Judged against international standards, the ACE is seen as a leader
> in the Arts themselves and in Arts and Education, regeneration,
> regional development, research, social inclusion, criminal justice and
> so on. The prime Government agenda is value for money for the
> people of the UK.'*

This highlights the issue. For the public sector there is rarely value in
international comparisons. It might help prestige but rarely does it
help the issue of sustainability at home. Probably the only exception
is sport where international comparisons are everything and resources
are provided to enable global competition.

An organisation that has similar interface with the private sector is
The Learning and Skills Council (LSC) where Jenny Clarke is head
of Workforce Development. Although public sector, like John Bridge,
she is focused on the enabling role of the LSC to enhance private
sector performance.

> *'The 'best' companies always look outside their own immediate
> environment, never stand still and are never satisfied with the status
> quo. To achieve that, the environment must be created in which
> individuals flourish and have the scope to take charge of their own
> destiny.'*

The thought of successful organisations never accepting the status
quo is a resounding theme. It has its echoes in the discussion of
leadership later in this volume.

Another public sector body that has a perspective on both the
internal workings of the public sector and the degree of competition
in the private sector is the Patent Office, an Executive Agency of the
DTI. Philip Johnson, Head of Marketing, who was interviewed by

Chris Bottomley, fully supported the premise for world-class organisations. He took his views from interacting and observing the Patent Office's many business customers that are showing high levels of innovation and entrepreneurship. .

> 'Businesses increasingly are, or must be of, world-class standard to survive.'

This interaction with leading edge development in UK business often causes tensions in terms of internal administration – an experience the Patent Office shared with the LSC and RDA:

> 'The issue is the culture within the Patent Office itself which contrasts with the business cultures that they touch daily.'

Philip's feeling was that the world-class attributes of their customers should be transferred to the internal workings of the Patent Office.

I have included a private sector organisation, a PFI deliverer, in this section because of the impact they are having on the public sector. Mike Walters, Managing Director of Bovis Lend Lease, runs a project-based organisation famous for its partnership approach with clients, community and suppliers.

Bovis Lend Lease naturally takes a pragmatic contractor's view. Not surprisingly, transferring knowledge and quality approaches are high on the list of priorities.

> 'We make extensive use of circles of quality to look at lessons learnt. We use our intranet to open up channels about who to contact to get information rather than putting everything on the system and then trying to keep it all up to date. We also encourage team and peer reviews as another way of transferring knowledge, i.e. getting people to speak to others on the other side of the world. When we were looking at how to create effective knowledge transfer we used BP/Bovis Alliance as a benchmark and listened to many of the lessons they had learnt.'

Mike Walters felt that doing business today was operating in the sort of atmosphere encapsulated by Tom Peters in 'Thriving on Chaos'[4]. Mike felt that, in his business, a matrix organisation fitted best as an encouragement for learning and joint working. He said that, in our basic premise, we should focus on looking after the core business. Because of 'Thriving on Chaos' he was against following prescriptive systems and fads since they could eclipse what the business was about. The example he gave was Rover, which historically adopted TQ wholeheartedly but, in his view, neglected new model development. The quality may improve but the product becomes outdated. (Aficionados of TQ would, I am sure, wish to point out that

TQM should apply to design and design strategy as well!)

Element 2: An extrovert organisation?

Public sector organisations find the concept of the extrovert organisation more difficult. After all, their experience has been that you generally don't want to attract 'customers' to what is often an under-resourced and overloaded service.

As Professor Sir Liam Donaldson pointed out, the NHS is strong in engaging with stakeholders to progress specific areas of healthcare, e.g. partnerships with local authorities, non-governmental organisations (NGOs) and patient representative groups. Also, individual professionals have strong links with peers nationally and internationally. Where Liam Donaldson saw a gap was in the NHS not doing something for the local community because it felt it was already providing services.

Malcolm Lowe-Lauri from the Peterborough Hospitals' perspective saw this as an opportunity to move a Health Service provider from being essentially introvert to extrovert.

> 'Partnership is key and critical with suppliers, other service providers, and the wider community. The Trust cannot achieve its objectives without achieving integration amongst key parties.'

The theme of partnership was taken up by Peter Hewitt of the Arts Council. He saw partnerships as the key for artists being connected into opportunities for networking. The key partnerships were with broadcasting, commerce and industry, and education.

Jenny Clarke of the LSC saw businesses increasingly using the benefits of the 'extrovert organisation' and also felt that the LSC should develop this characteristic as well for its own benefit.

The Patent Office, as we have seen, is essentially reactive by the nature of its business: organisations or individuals approach it for the necessary approvals. However, like most of the public sector studied, there is a dawning realisation that looking outward for inward benefit is the way forward.

I can recall that, only a few years ago, the NHS was always on the 'back foot' from a public relations viewpoint. In Peterborough, a deliberate move was made to go from reactive to proactive – moving onto the 'front foot'. This significantly improved knowledge and reputation as managers were able to help focus on the good news stories to balance the inevitable 'NHS in Crisis' headlines so loved by sub-editors.

Mike Walters of Bovis Lend Lease needs no convincing of the benefits of being an 'extrovert organisation'.

'This is a given and we do it all the time. For example, we belong to ten to fifteen organisations so we are involved out there all the time. We also have an annual Community Day for everyone run by the Lend Lease Foundation. Everyone in the organisation spends one day out in the community doing something every year.'

He is very clear that, this way, Bovis meets clients through being out there.

Generally, the public sector finds this element of the basic premise the most difficult. It is not at all clear to those in the sector that to be involved outside is relevant, helpful or even a good use of public resource. If our premise holds good then this will force them to address a particular problem in terms of creativity.

Element 3: Agile, proactive, catching the moment?

Again this is a difficult fit for the public sector. Unlike product development in the private sector, it has not been seen as the key for greater future business. Innovation can tend to be confined to technological contributions – particularly in the NHS. However, as Liam Donaldson explains, even that is necessarily highly regulated and is still ahead of managerial and organisational change:

'Even innovation of technique has now come under the microscope in that no longer can a heart surgeon try out something different, manipulating a piece of surgery that he thinks might help. I think it's managerial and organisational innovation which is more constrained.'

Liam recognised that for innovation to happen successfully in the NHS, boldness and risk taking are necessary in organisational terms. He was a supporter of the changes at Peterborough, particularly in ophthalmology, but saw such moves as a calculated risk because of the likelihood of challenge from vested interests.

'A good example is with your initiative in Peterborough on cataract surgery. You innovated, but you took a risk there because if the Royal College had got up in arms you might have got into hot water.'

In his interview, Malcolm Lowe-Lauri, who had been in the thick of all the changes at Peterborough, reinforced this view:

'NHS employees have a high level of professionalism but this can lead to an insular state of mind reinforced by their own professional bodies. Overcoming that in order to 'catch the moment' is quite a challenge.'

John Bridge, in taking a macro-economic perspective, posits that constancy in macro economic stability oddly encourages change.

'I think what can be constant is macro-economic stability. I was an

economics teacher in the 1960s and 70s when the belief was, erroneously, that somehow or other you could fine tune the British economy like a radio by adjusting a whole series of parameters. It was just a very false world that we drove ourselves into. What you've got today, almost as a pre-condition for change, is stability. It's almost a paradox but it's not; because if you've got that sort of stability, then it actually encourages change.'

John again recognises the crucial need for agility in the public sector in order for the private sector to 'seize the moment'.

'If we had a really agile, very alert, entrepreneurial public sector you could do a lot.'

We all know it can work. It depends on the individuals concerned and their perception. I remember in the late eighties finding an entrepreneurial civil servant in the NorthEast, Peter Carr, then Director of Employment for the Government Office. He put together all sorts of inner cities funding to help set up the Pinetree Centre[5] which still runs today, providing a one-stop-shop for those with disabilities seeking training and work. He saw the opportunity of working with the private sector and his 'activism' enabled private sector monies and enthusiasm to flow on a matched basis with public sector contribution.

Another example of the public sector enabling agility comes from Peter Hewitt.

'Artists have a very special role to play in society. They are able to articulate the inexpressible. Policy makers like myself advocate the Arts as a means of creating a more tolerant and receptive society – with more emphasis on the intrinsic spiritual and cultural impact.'

Perhaps the annual controversy over the Turner Prize and the quality of its submissions should be seen in Peter's terms of articulating the inexpressible!

Jenny Clarke of the LSC saw the education system as a negative influence, the trend of which is often continued in employment:

'Employees can by nature be passive, particularly having gone through our education system. Clearly some organisations then introduce yet another form of 'schooling' which inhibits creativity and freethinking.'

The responses from public sector bodies reinforce the anticipated concerns over performance and longer-term viability of services and employment. It is small wonder that politicians are continually concerned over public sector performance and, equally, those working in the public sector are very focused on today, on 'best value' and aren't always encouraged to look forward or outside. Hence the struggle with 'extrovert' and 'agile'. As John Bridge pointed out:

> *'Something like 40 per cent of our GDP in the UK is generated*
> *through the public sector. We miss a trick; we don't understand that*
> *the public sector has got to be world-class as well.*
>
> *If we had a really agile, very alert, entrepreneurial public sector, you*
> *could do a lot.'*

Not surprisingly the private sector companies performing public sector work act like private sector companies but with a public sector set of priorities.

V 'BUILT TO LAST' ORGANISATIONS/'STEADY AS SHE GOES'

In this final section, I have included a number of for-profit companies and not-for-profit organisations that have stood the test of time. The private sector firms are:

Shell UK Exploration and Production
UNUM
Burall Ltd
House of Hardy
Gardiner & Theobald

In the not-for-profit sector, the organisations I talked to were:

CBI
Ashridge Trust

A PRIVATE SECTOR

The largest and most prominent of the organisations in this section has to be Shell. Mark Hope, Director of External Affairs with Shell UK Exploration and Production (Expro), was immediately in agreement with the basic premise, although with qualification:

> *'If you're not world-class, you don't do it. You get someone who is to*
> *do that bit.'*

However, due to poor communication, Mark argued that some businesses can get away with less than world-class, at least for a time.

> *'In the short run you can be less than world-class, because*
> *communication is still quite poor between countries and between*
> *businesses within the same country. But in the long run I'm sure*
> *you're right.'*

So you need to recognise the dynamic.

> *'Building capability in yourself and your team is something you*
> *have to work at continuously. It goes back to: what can be constant*

in a world of flux, where everything is changing? One key thing
that's necessary, however narrow the niche you're in, is building your
capability to work that niche. You can be sure if you're world-class
today and you're just doing the same thing next week, you're
unlikely to be world-class next year.'

For the second and third elements of our basic premise on
sustainability, Mark took a similar view to Richard Hicks of AIT – the
'employer of choice' view, which he extended to those supplying to or
contracting with the organisation.

'The best people want to work here. I don't think it matters whether
people are staff, consultants, advisers or whatever. If you are running
a business of any sort or size you want there to be a hum around the
place. It must feel like a place where bright, motivated people are
achieving good things – and that will attract other bright, motivated
people (be they staff, consultants or contractors).'

Lawrence Churchill, former Chairman and Chief Executive of
UNUM, a niche player in disability insurance and part of UNUM
Provident Corp USA, which has been established since the 19th
century, had a slightly different view. For the first element, Lawrence
felt that you had to be selective – it was necessary to be world-class at
your core skill – not in all that you do. The differential for UNUM is
to be:

'...skilled at disability insurance and the management of the
associated risk. We have an effective methodology for the rapid
transference of ideas. Knowledge sharing is a core competence of
UNUM.'

Whilst supporting the concept of the extrovert organisation (the
second element of our premise), Lawrence felt it should be balanced
by 'introversion' – looking within, not neglecting those relationships,
giving stability. This, to me, is unspoken – taken for granted.

David Burall of Burall Limited has a well-defined philosophy,
which is cemented into the history and growth of the company over
the last one hundred and ten years (see Appendix II). David agreed
with the basic premise. His preoccupation is with his restlessness:

'Never being satisfied with the status quo. Being curious and
innovative, not wanting to tread the conventional route. I don't
believe much business is done on the golf course, it's more hard work
and contact. Being outward looking also, ...whilst I've been very
committed to the business, it's never been all my life.'

His connections, and having good antennae, expanded the Burall
business.

'I worked with the consortium to bid for the franchise for Peterborough and was a founder investment director of Hereward Radio. I had four reasons: one, I wanted a printing company to look more broadly at communication; secondly, Buralls was very much a Wisbech business and I wanted to extend its reach – we were serving the national population but I wanted to extend to the wider business community of Peterborough; thirdly, I thought I might make money out of it; and, fourthly, radio companies need quite a lot of print so it helped me get into the radio industry.'

Richard Maudslay, Managing Director of House of Hardy, fishing tackle manufacturers, takes a very straight up and down view of the basic premise on sustainability:

'You've only got to be better than the other chap. It's a bit like being chased by the bear. It doesn't matter how fast you can run as long as you can run faster than your pals. That's it in its crudest way. It's not so much being an extrovert organisation but you've got to understand what your customers want.'

He thought that the term 'extrovert' was

'...a terribly upmarket way of saying 'work out what your customers want by asking them'. Nothing fancier than that.'

Richard related a telling story about listening to his Japanese customers.

'I said, 'I've dealt with the Japanese before and I know that you always want something that's different. We're going to sit here and you tell us what you want.' There was a deathly silence, a lot of muttering in Japanese and then huge smiles spread across their faces. They said, 'This is very good – we've been coming here for six years and this is the first time anyone has asked us what we want.' They said, 'What we want is very simple. We are little people fishing for little fish on little rivers and we want little fishing tackle, please'.'

Of the third element, agility, he said that for him the challenge was learning how to deal with customers once or twice removed, and who all have very different needs:

'Presently, I'm in a situation where we sell to retailers or are even three-removed. In the UK we sell to retailers who sell to the customer. In overseas markets we sell to the distributor who sells to the retailer who sells to the end customer.'

Marion Weatherhead, partner of Gardiner and Theobald, the international project managers and construction cost managers, was supportive of the basic premise but felt the emphasis depended on what the client wanted.

'We will provide a traditional service if that's what you want but we are at the vanguard of change so we serve a whole range of clients. An extrovert organisation? Yes, we seem to be everywhere and, because we're involved in many industries, we're sensing what's happening, we're talking to people involved in different organisations, different groupings, trying to stay close to clients and potential clients.'

Again, the firm comes across as highly customer focused.

B   NOT-FOR-PROFIT

I spoke with John Cridland, Deputy Director General of the Confederation of British Industry (CBI). He was thoughtful about the three elements of the basic premise.

'I think that does sound right. I think the second and the third elements have the advantage of being crunchy and measurable. I think the challenge for the first, certainly in my experience in the CBI but more helpfully in many other companies that are members of the CBI, is that it really is very difficult to judge whether one is genuinely world-class or anywhere close. So, of the three elements, being world-class is aspirational and often lacks tangible benchmarks.'

John thought the potential relationship between the three elements was interesting in benchmarking terms.

'What I think is interesting is where the first of the three relates to the other two, because that makes it far more lateral. Often what you really need to do is look at yourself against an organisation which is totally different in shape. That's quite hard to do, and because it's hard to do, it doesn't get done often enough.'

Leslie Hannah, formerly Chief Executive of Ashridge Trust, a leading UK Business School, found the basic premise resonated with him. His caveat was over defining 'world-class'. He felt 'European class' was more appropriate to Ashridge.

'In our case, we're not competing in America or Asia, we're competing in Europe. Our competition is IMD, LBS, Cranfield and NCIAD It is not really Harvard, Duke.'

Even American clients display 'European' reasons for coming to Ashridge:

'They say, 'We come to Ashridge because we want to demonstrate we're a global company. We're an American company: 60 per cent of our employees are American, 40 per cent are European. The fact that we bring our Americans to Ashridge for management training convinces the Europeans we're a global company'.'

The second element, extroversion, is encouraged at Ashridge by giving staff one day a week to consult outside the organisation – product ideas and good customer feedback flow from this.

The third element, agility and creativity, is encouraged at Ashridge to the marked extent of devoting time to it

'We have a week in January when no member of staff works (in the normal way) and everybody comes in and works in everything from the Alexander technique to creativity workshops and there's quite a lot of brainstorming and special events and focus groups. It's a week where the organisation is devoted to navel-gazing and market analysis and a freewheeling discussion of anything anyone wants to bring up.'

This has been a wide- ranging chapter, which has covered the full span of reaction from our interviewees over all the elements of the basic premise. It has shown the great variety of contexts in which organisations find themselves and by which they are challenged. What emerges is a surprising consistency of agreement with the basic premise, together with an underlying theme from these leaders, that organisations have to be 'employers of choice' and that sustainability is pursued through the people themselves. There is no doubt about the pace and impact of change or about the need to be 'out there' anticipating change before it gets too late. This is equally well appreciated in the not for profit examples and the private sector. As we have seen, the public sector struggles with this as a priority – leaving it to the politicians and policy makers.

The issue of 'meaning and purpose' is a recurring theme in these conversations, and it forms the link into our next area of examination – Vision and Values.

Notes

1   Fukuyama, F *Trust* Penguin 1995 proposed similar arguments
2   Morton, C N *Becoming world-class* Macmillan 1994
3   Collins, J & Porras, J *Built to Last* Random House 1994
4   Peters, T *Thriving on Chaos* 1987 Macmillan
5   Morton, C N et al *Leading HR – delivering competitive advantage* CIPD 2001

Chapter five

THE VISION AND VALUES PROPOSITION

WHAT CAN BE CONSTANT IN A WORLD in a state of flux? Is it necessary to focus on something constant such as vision and values? How does this relate to a compelling work ethic? Is work/life balance an issue?

'It's the way you keep everybody within the organisation thinking alike and pursuing the goal in a co-operative way. For me that's one of the things that Vision and Values are about.'

Richard Hicks, AIT

'What I think our life is about is a) fulfilling my life and equally importantly, b) helping individuals of organisations realise more of their potential.'

'What I'm aiming for is an integrated, meaningful, rewarding existence. Some of it will earn cash and some of it won't.'

Bill Penney, Ashton Penney

'I don't think there is a work/life balance and soon as you start thinking in terms of work/life balance you've probably missed the point. It's work/life integration. You shouldn't need to make choices if you're working with an organisation that believes in your beliefs.'

Peter Ward, Telos Partners

I   START-UPS/ENTREPRENEURSHIP/PHOENIX

A   NEW START-UPS IN THE FIELD OF TECHNOLOGY

Richard Hicks of AIT provides this thoughtful answer which shows that, for him, focus and quality provide the rationale behind Vision and Values. AIT has to be the best at what it does, which is to provide CRM solutions in financial services not in a specific locality. The other imperative is the commitment to quality. So, he argues:

'The short answer is that you can't contrive constancy in the outside world ...it's the way you keep everybody within the organisation thinking alike and pursuing the goal in a co-operative way. For me, that's one of the things that Vision and Values are about.'

Richard also comments that, in a command and control structure, there is limited scope for people's imagination and inventiveness. But in organisations which are building intellectual capital you do need to use people's brains so vision and values become just one of the ways in which you communicate. When I pressed him about the difference this made in practice, Richard provided this great example of customer focus and quality of service:

> '*A few years ago we were building the software for a new type of banking machine which then was called non-cash till services. There were only two of these machines in existence, one of which we had in our building and the other that was in the manufacturer's showroom. A situation arose where they needed to launch this machine in Scotland and the manufacturer of the machine couldn't find anybody who had the authority to ship it to Glasgow. One of our staff hired a van, put our machine into that van and drove it to Glasgow and the launch went out on time. Without that initiative it would not have happened – a function of empowerment.*'

I asked Richard how the individual in the anecdotal example understood what he needed to do and what he could do. Richard's response was couched in terms of both behaviour and size:

> '*The simple answer is that, when you're smaller, it's just what you do. People are just seeing the principles of the organisation in the way you behave but that's not news to anybody because that's how it is. People who are successful in small organisations often are successful because of the right mix of skills. What sustains that beyond the twelve people to one hundred people and beyond? It's story telling within organisations.*'

To me this is the essence of how vision and values should be created – not invented by a 'Board Away Weekend' unrelated to the business, but in the way Richard describes. It is about observed behaviours and the struggle always is over issues of size – how do you translate this type of instinctive behaviour and readiness to take initiatives into larger organisations?

We had time to dwell on the related topic of the work ethic and how this has changed over time. Richard reflected on how, in general, the work ethic has changed and, specifically, for the younger generation and – in the AIT context – 'knowledge workers'. He felt that, twenty or thirty years ago, there was probably a convention of some sort about a work ethic that it would be difficult to identify in a lot of people today. The work ethic was, in part, determined by the social context.

> '*Work ethic is a psychological transaction that you have with your employer. Intuitively, I feel that for a lot of people it is probably very*

*different now than it was some while ago. Young people expect more
from work. They want to go to work and be fulfilled, find some
purpose, find some meaningful work.'*

Here I believe Richard has hit the nail on the head. His ideas confirm
other research, to which I will refer in chapter 7, that shows that, as
generations work their way up Maslow's hierarchy of needs, they
desire purpose, meaning and – in Maslow's terms – self actualisation.
I will return to this and develop this argument further in chapter 9.

Keith Moscrop of BioFocus saw the answer to 'what's constant in
a state of flux?' in terms of 'creative destruction'.

*'What's constant in our sector is that the pharmaceutical industries
appear to be steadily going backwards. I mean they are merging and
converging. You know they've got these huge organisations that
haven't solved the people problems. So the people that are made
redundant and start up businesses like ours can certainly start
moving fast and deliver some interesting results.'*

However, Keith is realistic about the impact and limitations of the
biotech sector, particularly in view of the costs of taking drugs
through clinical trials into the market place.

*'I think large pharmas are going to end up concentrating on
manufacturing and selling and they'll leave a lot of the early stage
discovery to companies like ours. Having said that, if you took all
the biotechs and the service platform companies that are around in
the world today, together they still only add up to the research effort
that the largest companies put in.'*

Returning to the subject of vision and values, Keith maintains that
this has not been seen as a corporate issue but rather as a collection
of individual aspirations fuelled by release from the sphere of
corporate rules and regulations. For BioFocus, which was about two
hundred strong when we talked, he said: -

*'I think that probably there would be only about ten people in the
company that have got an overall view of where we want to go and
we discuss that from time to time. The others are thinking, 'I want to
be in drug discovery'. I think, from time to time, people like the
glamour of being associated with a fast growing small company. I
think it is a collection of personal ambitions, quite honestly.'*

This picture is one of pragmatic growth based on those business
opportunities created by the willingness of the big 'pharmas' to
outsource drug discovery. The expansion of BioFocus from its
original Sittingbourne laboratory included the acquisition of two
more sites near Cambridge. There had deliberately been no attempt
to merge the cultures and Keith saw distinct variations in work ethic

between the sites. Also, driven by the need to recruit high quality people from wherever they came, there was an increase in diversity.

'The different culture has happened by accident, by being there and working on it. The first site where we started in Kent at Sittingbourne has got lots of young people there. They are collectively less mature, but very flexible with energy and commitment.'

The second and third sites in Cambridge, which came by acquisition, were more comfortable with the 'hands on' management style of BioFocus.

'On this site the staff are on average a little older, and many have families. They are settled, and they have really appreciated the efforts that the new management team put in to make their life better, even though you can't meet all of their aspirations. Because we delivered the plan to bring in a wider range of work and to diversify the whole atmosphere here is very positive.'

The Generics Group has had to cope with the issues of growth and the definition of vision and values. However, in this case the stimulus was somewhat more external. Duncan Hine immediately recognised the words, consideration of which had been triggered by the effort of floating the company.

'One of the key tests is: 'Can you explain your business model to a third party sufficiently lucidly that they will put their money into it?' So you have to put a lot of effort into understanding what it is you actually do and what you're going to do. It produces a model that you can use for internal communication too.'

Asked 'what's the glue that's held you together?' Duncan answered in terms similar to Keith Moscrop.

'I think the part of the glue that holds us together is that essentially it is a peer group company. The goal of most people here is to do something for a company that then makes a huge amount of money out of that technology. The glue, if you like, comes from that dimension.'

Again, issues of recruitment loom large and, interestingly, a comparison with Toyota emerges. Duncan Hine explained:

'There's a great debate to be had in Generics that mirrors the debates about Toyota and Nissan in the UK. Are they what they are because their model works brilliantly, or are they actually what they are because they reject twenty out of twenty-one of the people they interview for every job and select the one person who naturally is a Toyota production systems thinker? We are very conscious when we're recruiting that we pick good communicators. One of the key tests is 'Will this person work in front of a client?'

To Generics, it is clear that employability is defined much more widely than just intelligence and qualifications.

> 'There is at least 50 per cent of the recruiting process which runs along the personality dimension as well as the dimension of intellectual qualification, technical knowledge, and experience.'

The next issue common to all employers is, once having recruited excellent quality employees, how is alignment achieved and where are the pressures of work/life balance? Duncan Hine sees little problem in motivation – the Generics employee is typically highly self-motivated. But he explains that this can cause problems for work/life balance.

> 'I think that the real issue for us is about sustainability and efficiency in terms of this work/life balance. Lots of these people have got PhDs, and you can't get a PhD without being driven. The problem is that, for many of us, that tips over to be a kind of behaviour that says: 'I'm not going in until I know whether this works or not. Oh my goodness, it's four o'clock in the morning!' So we will watch out for people who are getting too driven, too obsessed and so on, spending too many hours on a long term basis.'

His second concern is over individuals and teams. Although, clearly, the individual motivation is not in doubt a lot of the people are very itinerant, doing lots of work in other parts of the UK or overseas in Europe or elsewhere. So time must be given to integrate individual effort into teams.

> 'There's lots of work done in hotel rooms, departure lounges, etc. Is there enough overlap with the rest of the team to get sufficient interaction going?'

The third issue Generics faces is yoking this individual effort to commercial priorities.

> 'The other thing that helps with that part of the discipline, of course, is the climate. You do have hard deliverables and a proposal and a timescale. All the jobs are accounted in hours and you've got a timesheet to fill in every Friday.'

All of which is about balancing commercial interests of the employer with the 'what's in it for me?' for the employee.

For Dianne Thompson at Camelot the vision is situational and a function of the company's development. We saw in the last chapter that Camelot and its staff had been through a roller coaster ride during the period of the renewal of its licence. As a result, in Dianne Thompson's words, people were disempowered, demotivated and risk averse. Dianne, in common with others, describes the situation of needing to change the vision: she explained that the first vision meant

the lottery operator was efficient but not as effective as she would wish
– it missed opportunities for creativity.

> 'Our vision was to be the best lottery operator in the world. You could
> argue that's a good vision and, in fact, we certainly became that. It
> was a vision that was designed to help us to win the bid. As a result
> of having that as our vision and our strategy, we went for and got
> ISO 9001, Investors in People, and BS7799 security award. It also
> caused us to do our first social and ethical report. You could say it
> achieved its objective. However, what it also did was to force us to be
> process-led. It was, I think, part of the reason we lost our creativity
> and innovation.'

Dianne explained how a new vision was developed that would change
the organisation's focus:

> 'After we won we went through a process that decided that what we
> were all about was serving the nation's dreams through the National
> Lottery. We already had values in place and they are **'FITTER'** –
> **fair play, integrity, teamwork, trusted to deliver,
> excellence** in all we do and **responsible** to all our stakeholders.
> We'd got the vision, we'd got the values, but not the behaviours. In
> fact we are just putting in this programme called 'Winning Ways'
> which is about the five behaviours that we want people to have. They
> are passionate, creativity, empowering, partnering and ownership.'

With a comprehensive vision, set of values and defined behaviours the
issues of work ethic and the balance between work and life cannot be
far behind. Dianne comments:

> 'I always say life at Camelot is not a job, it's a way of life. When we
> start selling on the net, it will be a twenty-four hour business. It is
> difficult. Camelot has always prided itself that it's a very family
> focused company. What we've been very good at, I think, is the small
> number of instances where there's been something very personal for
> one individual.'

The personal touch is not without its rewards. Dianne kindly showed
me a letter of appreciation which is self-explanatory.

> 'Dear Madam
> I hope you will allow this intrusion into your busy life as I would
> like to thank you. On April 1st of this year I completed five years as
> a member of staff at the warehouse and received a congratulatory
> letter via HR. This in itself was more than I expected since, in my
> previous job, I had worked for thirty years without any recognition.
> This was not all. I understood that champagne was also to be
> presented but, since my wife and I are both teetotal, I told John Kay,
> my boss, I would forego that pleasure. Later I learned that the
> procedure was being reviewed so I was quite delighted to receive a

Red Letter Day package containing details of various events or goodies I could apply for. As neither my wife nor I drive, I opted for the Green Range Hamper from Fortnum and Mason's. This has arrived and we are really delighted with the contents. So, thanks very much. If this isn't the wow factor, I don't know what is.'

This clearly greatly pleased Dianne, especially because:

'Somebody in the warehouse who doesn't know me from Adam has taken time out to actually write it. It's easier for you and me because we can just dictate it to a secretary. I was really chuffed with that when it came in yesterday.'

Camelot's vision and values programme was implemented in 2001 and 2002 and clearly had good effect in boosting morale. However, due to external factors (including poor publicity over distribution of lottery monies) Camelot's revenues continued to decline despite high-profile advertising which in 2002 prompted a re-think of the product range and its marketing approach, together with cost-cutting which saw the departure of some directors and about eighty staff. As I write, the issue of the Camelot and Lotto image is being revisited to re-energise and boost sales. All of which shows that companies can do the right things, but still be severely affected by the external environment.

B   New start-up – not-for-profit

Like most small organisations, the Lymphoma Association has little resource to devote to such sophistication as 'vision and values'. However, Alan Bartle does know what is common between his seventeen staff – commitment. Commitment to the purpose is what Alan describes as the 'constant'.

'If there is a constant in our organisation I think it would probably be summed up as commitment to the purpose. Treatments are constantly changing so, therefore, information is constantly changing. I think the constant in what we are doing is the commitment to the patients, the commitment to ensuring that the patients have the information and the support they need. It is to do with empowering the patients so that the patients are better able to interpret what is happening to them.'

The vocational dedication shone through when we talked about work/life balance.

'People in the charitable sector often have that work ethic in the sense that they're not actually interested in what time they started or what time they finish their particular task. The important thing for them is completing the task. Increasingly today there is less job

*security in all sectors. I do think the work and life balance thing can
become an issue.'*

C 'PHOENIX' ORGANISATIONS

For Bryan Jackson, the vision for Toyota MUK is to be the best
volume automobile manufacturer in Europe. This must be not just
expressed in writing but reflected in the culture and operations. For
Bryan, the expression for vision and mission must be simple,
understood and, as he put it, the 'music and words must match'.

In similar vein to Collins and Porras' work in *Built to Last*, this line
of thinking goes back to Toyota's credo which is eminently simple and
embracing:

'Making better cars for more people at less cost.'

This credo goes back to the time, in 1936, when the founder Toyoda-
san decided to sell the patent rights of an automatic loom to Platts
and used the proceeds to manufacture cars. The now famous Toyota
Production System was in embryo then and embraced stakeholder
principles in stressing avoiding damage to the environment – 'land is
expensive'!

Bryan Jackson told me that all new employees at Burnaston are
informed of the vision and values. Issues of focus and leadership are
illustrated by an appropriate analogy. 'On any road there are lots of
turn-offs with some dead ends, but it is the leadership challenge to get
back on the road and safely drive along.'

In terms of the work ethic, Bryan acknowledged the pressures
between family expectations and the demands of the job. In his view,
the simple issue of too many hours at work is the start point. The way
people are treated is the catalyst for achieving balance and leadership
is crucial.

At Unipart Automotive, Paul Forman took a bottom line
approach when answering 'what can be constant in a world in a state
of flux?' but saw 'value laden aspects' as translating across
international activities.

> *'(There are) some very hard-nosed things like the need to generate
> returns whatever the debt/equity structure. That the more value-
> laden aspects, like respect for the individual, the value of teamwork
> and the organisation being more than the sum of its parts, can be
> constant is equally valid in our Chinese and North American
> activities. If you get the people side right, treated right and involved
> right, the customer service side will follow as a result.'*

Paul agreed that vision and values did provide a constant around which employees could gain confidence.

> *'We've demonstrated leadership not only on commercial issues but also value-laden issues. That is, how we acted rather than simply what we've said which is important and certainly constant in a world in a state of flux.'*

Clearly, the vision and values are applied with a hard commercial expectation.

> *'In our organisation, we have a five-year mission, three year themes and one year strategic imperatives and these are cascaded through policy deployment to all of our 6,000 people with the ethical side. But we are in a capitalist environment and it's all about generating wins, at the expense of our competitors, to our customers' benefit.'*

In terms of the results, Paul can point to a dramatically lower staff turnover rate.

> *'We managed to halve our staff turnover rate in nine months which, on a 6,000 employee base, is significant. We did it by actively listening and then acting on the results. Listening is massively important and giving consistent messages is very important.'*

In terms of the constancy of Unipart's vision and values, Paul believes there is a distinction on the renewal of the vision as opposed to the values:

> *'From a commercial point of view, the principles of integrity, team work, respect for the individual and killing the competition will be consistent all the way through our five- year mission and will not necessarily change. I don't believe people can have strategies, as such, beyond about two or three years. Further than this is beyond a credible timescale for planning since there is so much change going on in the automotive sector, quite apart from in the business environment generally.'*

All of this gives a picture in Unipart of a pragmatic leadership from the top which has embraced the stakeholder concept but kept careful control.

D   CONSULTANCY/OUTSOURCING

As Chairman of Pertemps, Tim Watts represents the largest of this group of organisations. With a workforce of some 2,000 and with the placing of 30,000 temporary workers per week, he is dealing with a very large and diverse population. Much of the organisation's vision and values comes from the force of his own personality and his deeply held beliefs about the potential within employees.

His answer to what can be constant in a world in a state of flux is brief and to the point:

> *'Belief in what we are doing and a philosophy of teamwork and that everyone is equal. Pertemps is different, because it is part of our lives, but it is hard to encapsulate.'*

As to the role of vision and values, Tim starts with his role and quickly embraces the self-determination of employees (the company is employee-owned to a great extent).

> *'My role as chairman is to inspire, create loyalty, and to talk to people from the heart. We continually transform ourselves but everyone at Pertemps does this. We create an 'own your future' concept to the employees. Employees hold 50 per cent of our shares so the company owns itself.*
>
> *The employees wrote our vision and values as they did our strategic plan. Everyone built up the ten values so they do not need explanation. They are simply how we go about our business.*
>
> *I believe that imagination plus vividness equals reality. Why do people plan for their holiday more than their life? We encourage everyone here to use his or her imagination and make it reality.'*

Tim tried to introduce work/life balance into the work itself on a self-determination basis with a little help from the company, essentially to elevate from the grind:

> *'This is vital to Pertemps' way of life. People work hard but we also put a lot of emphasis on well-being, and also to supporting each other when someone has a problem – at home, for example. I like people to have fun at work, and also have the chance to unwind.'*

Bill Penney of Ashton Penney expresses values more in terms of customer service since there are few direct employees and they are widely scattered.

> *'One is that we're about customer service and sensitive to the needs of our customers. The second is that the essential value of the organisation is that we will adapt, change and react as the needs of environment and opportunity develop. Third, we've always used technology as a means of freeing us up from the constraints of a structured organisation.'*

Bill's personal values shone through when we talked about the work ethic and philosophy. He is an ordained clergyman who also runs a business and has clearly thought through the implications of being in seemingly different camps:

> *'I'm very reluctant to put anybody in a job they don't enjoy doing and don't find rewarding. That's the bottom line. From a personal point of view I have long ago ceased to make a distinction between*

*work and leisure. How does being an ordained clergyman square
with running a company and being involved in the company and
the nitty gritty of profit making? I think our life is about a)
fulfilling my life and, equally importantly, b) helping individuals in
organisations realise more of their potential. That's what I'm doing
in the pulpit on a Sunday, that's what I'm doing when I'm talking
to a friend in a pub and that's what I'm doing when I'm working in
the company employing people and working with clients. What I'm
aiming for is an integrated, meaningful, rewarding existence. Some of
it will earn cash and some of it won't.'*

I could identify with that. The conversation continued to the 'bottom
line' for individuals as Bill saw it.

*'If people are not enjoying what they're doing, being challenged by
what they're doing and getting no personal satisfaction from what
they're doing, either they're in the wrong job or the job is wrong for
them.'*

We debated the decline of mainstream Christianity in the UK
workforce with, perhaps oddly, the increased expression of values,
beliefs and 'spirituality' unrelated to religion. Bill cited one of Chris
Mellor's favourite examples (see the AWG experience cited in the
Public to Private category).

*'I like the example of the sweeper-upper at NASA who was asked
(by an idle TV crew) what he was doing …he said, 'Putting a man
on the moon'. It's a question of the ethic of buying into what this
organisation is about. Our organisation is very lucky because we're
in a field which does not have too much repetitious stuff.'*

However, no doubt we have lived in Panglossian times and, however
good the values and philosophy are, events come along to disrupt
things. (This reminds me of Harold Macmillan when asked about
what had had the greatest impact on his premiership, responding,
'Events dear boy, events!')

Peter Smith, CEO of The Strategic Partnership puts the
responsibility for the formulation of vision firmly with the Board, but
involving stakeholders.

*'The way in which boards articulate their vision is still too top down.
Vision must encompass the values and relationships with stakeholders.
Boards cannot do this on their own. At the end of the day, employees
want to work for someone whose values link to their own.'*

Peter has strong views about executive remuneration and how this
issue is perceived by employees:

*'Remuneration – if employees see a board with their fingers in the till
all the time then the reaction is, why should they put effort in when*

they are not fairly compensated. Vision must have core values that
must be lived day by day and which people understand through
seeing them lived.'

Changes in society, such as the increase in transparency and the
breakdown of social values, have made the formulation of
organisational vision and values even more essential.

'The changes in communications have played a big part. Boards
cannot hide behind a smoke screen. Employees and stakeholders can
see what is going on.

Communication is a difficult thing to keep going. It takes up an
enormous amount of time. It takes time to walk the talk and this is
against the pressure of deadlines.'

Peter believes the work/life balance is directly related to issues of
meaning and purpose.

'The biggest influence on work/ leisure and lifestyle balance is, 'Am I
happy in my job, do I like the people, have I job satisfaction'?
Companies have to understand they are made up of people and rely
totally on them. The way you behave to them is the most important
thing you do'

Peter Ward of Telos Partners is finding greater fascination in
businesses that 'see there's more purpose to the enterprise than just
transactions'. This starting point gets to the heart of this book. As
we've seen, there are differing formulae which can be used to pursue
business. As Peter puts it, there are businesses that cynically exploit an
opportunity then stop.

'For those businesses that want to continue to survive and thrive
there are investments that need to be made. There are other
companies that only have the ambition to exploit an opportunity and
stop. There is nothing intrinsically wrong with being one of the latter.
Transactions make the world go round. But what fascinate us are
those businesses that see there's more purpose to the enterprise than
just transactions. Once you get in and you start to work and talk
and deal with the people, relationship-based businesses seem to have
much more grit.'

As he says, for a long-term sustainable business, the business model is
completely different. Peter went on to recount an experience with a
client which, like many of the examples from Collins and Porras *Built*
to Last, had been in business for over one hundred years but had never
articulated its values even though they were solidly there all the time.

'Interestingly, we're working with a big engineering company at
present – it's been around for 130 years and we asked, 'Has anyone

ever written a book on your history?'We found a 'first hundred years account'. Guess what you find? Financial conservatism, engineering excellence applied to customer problems, and an interest in the people. Now try and move that business, try and change its culture from that. Not a chance! What you can do is to get people to apply these principles to today's situations.'

As a professional in his field Peter rightly wanted to differentiate between the common parlance terms used, not unlike Richard Hicks at AIT who we cited at the beginning of this chapter.

'Purpose is about something that doesn't change. It's what we always stand for. Vision describes what it's going to look like at some time in the future. But values are also timeless. They are a belief system that just doesn't change.'

All of this forms a very compelling argument to convince those with a focus on the 'bottom line' that concentration on vision and values pays off. Peter also starts from an interesting point with the issue of the work ethic and work life balance:

'It's interesting to hear you talk about the compelling work ethic and the work/life balance issue. I don't think there is a work/life balance and as soon as you start thinking in terms of work/life balance you've probably missed the point. It's work/life integration. You shouldn't need to make choices if you're working with an organisation that believes in the same things that you do.'

This belief is not dissimilar to Bill Penney's view about not being able to separate work and leisure, a view which has attracted other free spirits to Telos.

'Your purpose actually helps you with recruitment. People start to self-select. Our happy band is all ex-corporate. They've all had line roles. Some have been consultants but have had line roles in consultancy so they know what works and only advise clients on the basis of actual experience. They have joined Telos because their beliefs are aligned with the organisation's.'

I feel we have come full circle on this issue – from Richard Hicks to Peter Ward – and with many valuable thoughts and differing points of view in between.

II   M&A/DEMERGER ORGANISATIONS

Syd Pennington of Royal & Sun Alliance (R&SA) was fascinated with the concept of consistency in the face of change. His thought was that perhaps the only constant is change itself, but the thing with which it was extremely difficult to come to terms was the incredible pace of that change.

> *'The only consistency might be constant change. We business people have lived with the consistent need to change but not with the pressure and the speed with which it's happening now.'*

It was interesting to examine the results of the worldwide 'root and branch' survey of staff views carried out by R&SA. Syd and I discussed how all the results came down to defining values that were already present in the organisation.

> *'The one thing that keeps cropping up is that, if you're in the insurance business, you need integrity above everything else to be seen to be fair.'*

However, unsurprisingly, some of the values varied in different parts of the world. As Syd put it, a UK-based business is much simpler. Integration across the world has to come back to customer confidence.

> *'You've got to have some constants and some consistency. If you're in the business of risk and reward, I think you've got to be consistent as far as the customer sees you.'*

As Syd acknowledged, getting all segments of the organisation up to speed behind the core concepts of truth, trust, teamwork, openness and honesty is a long-term project.

> *'We go as fast as the slowest ship in the convoy, and some parts of the organisation haven't moved as fast as others.'*

With all the investment across the globe in such intangibles I asked Syd whether any hard results were coming through. An important issue for him was the ability of the organisation to access and share knowledge effectively.

> *'We started off on the basis that, if we only know what we knew, how do you find that if you've got 52,000 people around the world? On many occasions the people have met the same issues somewhere in the world at some stage, and what we're seeking to do now with technology and with culture is to share best practice.'*

Clearly, from this, Syd acknowledges that both technology, and particularly culture change, are necessary to make sharing of knowledge effective.

> *'It's all about culture. You've got to get away from the situation where managers believe that knowledge is power to one where it's mature to borrow an idea from somewhere else before you go and buy it externally.'*

My interview with Syd took place before 9/11, the stockmarket declines and the other disastrous events which affected the insurance industry in 2001/02 and R&SA was overtaken by the sort of change that causes business to live 'by the skin of their teeth'.

In addition, the leader of much of this change, the ebullient CEO Bob Mendleshon, was forced out of office in the autumn of 2002 by shareholder concerns. All of this, of course, tends to show that there can be no set formula for business sustainability, although another possibility is that perhaps four to five years is too long a period for such a change programme. Even at the time of the interview in August 2001 there were clear signs of shareholder discontent as the following excerpt from the discussion shows. I asked Syd whether he felt that his truth, trust and teamwork had stood the test of time. He replied:

> 'It's only been three years, so I don't think it is long enough to say you've embedded it and tested it, and had the rigours of everything against it.'

Syd said that the approach had stood the rigours of three difficult years in which the top management were turning a business round. During those three years none of the management group of the business had received a bonus for the last three years, and R&SA was the only FTSE 100 company that hadn't paid a bonus for three years. In response I asked him if this meant that the targets were too high, but Syd gave another reason:

> 'No, it's because we've taken a long time to deliver. I think the targets are realistic, but I think we underestimated the turn round, and how hard it was going to be to go from where we were to where we set our targets.'

I asked about the measurement of success and how the company's shareholders felt about it.

> 'I think our shareholders have got every right to feel disappointed. In the same way, if you like, that we haven't earned a bonus because we haven't done well enough to justify that kind of rating, then in capital appreciation terms the shareholder has probably felt the same way.'

As we returned to our discussion on vision and values, we moved on to issues of the work/life balance and the work ethic. Syd acknowledged that R&SA had a way to go here, but there were signs of hope. They accepted that there needed to be a work/life balance and they were trying hard to address the fact that they were not very good at it, and in particular the more senior they were it seems the less good they were.

Syd told me about a group of people in Liverpool, Horsham, Bristol and London who have tried to look at when they get together as a group and when they get together in a physical context.

> *'What they are trying to do is to build it into the concept of work/life balance. If the guy in Liverpool's son has got a school play on the day they're doing the meeting, they'll have it in Liverpool so he can be at the meting and then go to the school play.'*

The discussion then turned to lessons from the merger experience between Royal Insurance and Sun Life some years ago. In retrospect, Syd could see two classic errors in addition to the fact that there were no agreed values in place.

> *'We made two classic mistakes. One was that we kept both CEOs and that was a conflict of opportunity. The other thing was that, as soon as we merged the two businesses, we set about doing what the stock market wants you to do, which is seeing how you could squeeze integration costs throughout the organisation. Virtually the whole focus of the business went on cost-cutting and funding synergistic integration opportunities.'*

Conceptually, cost-cutting in itself was not bad, but Syd was very clear that cost-cutting of itself was not a good enough reason to justify a merger or a takeover.

> *'I think there's got to be something more than that as a rationale. I think increasingly where businesses want to merge with or acquire somebody else simply to get bigger, and strip costs out, then they will be found wanting.'*

Mike Rake of KPMG needed no persuasion that vision and values were core to the business. He actually saw the values proposition[1] as an alternative to internalisation and bureaucracy.

> *'I believe the core to having the ability to move the organisation to succeed lies in some fundamental tenets around the values proposition for the organisation as a whole.'*

Mike argued that, without those 'soft side' issues being prevalent within the firm, they wouldn't succeed because they would lose flexibility, lose their ability to have what might be called the antennae to the outside world. Otherwise, large people businesses turned inwards on themselves and become bureaucracies.

> *'I think that, in order to achieve, the real challenge is to have a proper sense of sustainable values. That is something we've worked really, really hard on in the last few years. We've been trying to re-establish, root and branch, a whole values charter that all our people can operate. Now we're moving into a whole project of re-*

engineering the whole organisation to eliminate unnecessary
bureaucracy, to have fewer rules for people to apply, and really to
unleash the potential of our people, so that they can move more
quickly and automatically react quickly to situations.'

In a not too dissimilar fashion to Alan Smith, former Group MD at
Anglian Water and Chris Mellor's predecessor, Mike came to this
policy after a 'sabbatical' period at Harvard. He had spent some time
in the summer studying organisations, people issues and thinking.

'I concluded that the problem we have is behaviour, values, and
principles. That was why we got something like 2,000 partners
together for three days. We went away and did some work on it, and
put together some value propositions. Once finalised it has really
made a difference to the way in we've collapsed the whole
organisation into one. The result was good. People then said 'Why
did we ever fight this?' The turf wars were over and so you realised it
works.'

One of the key products of the value propositions and the re-
engineering project that became known as Project Darwin has been
the integration of separate 'silos' that have been there since the days
of merger. Mike explained that when he took over, in the UK KPMG
was a combination seven different regional partnerships that had
grown up over the previous twenty years from one partnership
approach, and thirteen different profit pools.

'People were doing all sorts of different things in different ways. We
wanted to bring all of that together and at the same time to integrate
our European operation, but we couldn't do that unless we merged
the UK operation. It struck me that somehow, in the culture of the
organisation, while the firm had been quite successful it had gone to
the point where everyone did things in different ways. It was almost
as if the Birmingham office was more intent on beating the London
office for a project (and vice versa) than beating is competitors.'

(This is very reminiscent of my own experience at Rolls-Royce IPG
in the 1990s, where we had five transformer factories world wide with
overlapping product lines. See *Beyond World Class*, chapter 4 pp56-73)

Mike confirmed that the KPMG document 'Our Values Charter'
was much in evidence in the firm's offices.[2]

'We'd established these values, and you see them everywhere. There
even on the wall over there. They're part of the induction
programme, they're talked about every day, and they're a tenet by
which we work every day. They are a tangible, simple thing.'

He described how KPMG had launched Project Darwin, which was
a complete re-engineering of the firm based on the tenets

underpinning the values. It was saying that they want an organisation which was fast, practical, fulfilling and fun to be in. Mike said:

> 'We want to eliminate hierarchy, bureaucracy, and have a simple number of basic rules that we all accept are necessary. The challenge for us is how we get this tight/loose balance right – some things tighter, some things looser – and move it forward on the basis of a set of values and behaviours that allow you to do that. I believe our whole success in separating ourselves from our competitors is dependent on these kinds of behavioural issues.'

I asked Mike if these values had been seen as relevant by KPMG staff. He was quite clear that they had:

> 'Absolutely. For every one of the last three years we've done a values survey of all our staff. At the very beginning 95 per cent of our people understood the business case for the values proposition. Secondly, increasing every year, they have been more and more convinced that we mean them, and that this is beginning to have an impact.'

Going deeper, we explored the issues of work/life balance and the relevance of the KPMG values. Mike highlighted the real tensions that were involved. He reported that the work/life balance was an area where only 45 per cent of staff believed that KPMG had things correct.

> 'What we try to do is to get our people to understand that there is no business value in getting guys to come back from six weeks on the other side of South Africa, and send them straight away to Afghanistan or wherever. You lose the people.'

But Mike also recognised that there could be times and situations with people working on major projects who felt so motivated and where the team leadership was so strong that you couldn't pull them away.

> 'We've had one hundred people involved in a major airline working twelve weeks, seven days a week. You couldn't have torn these guys away, because they were trying to save the airline. They were emotionally committed and they liked the teamwork.'

However, Mike agreed that occasionally you do have to tell people to go and have a day off, because otherwise they do become inefficient.

> 'I think the most difficult thing to get right in what we're doing is the work/lifestyle balance issue. Frankly, our people consistently have to work harder than many of our clients.'

So, I asked, were the values durable through bad times as well as good? Mike said this was very interesting, because back at the beginning in 1998, when KPMG launched the values, people did ask whether this was this just for the good times.

> *'We said, absolutely not. The values are about bad times as well as good times.'*

Mike explained that in bad times, a firm really has to be agile and on its feet to survive. Therefore the principles were even more important in bad times.

> *'It requires a level of honesty and directness. But the flatter the organisation you have, the more the workforce rallies to what you're trying to do. They've seen the issue and identified with you, and trust you and work with you to achieve it. This enhances for example your agility.'*

Something that is also interesting in the KPMG story is the way that the values proposition was used, many years after the substantial mergers, to unite a workforce, gain focus and break down 'silos'. Mike described how he sees the results:

> *'It's been dramatically successful. If you ask people, it was like a war at the beginning, trying to remove powers and change it to one partnership with one profit pool, a common HR policy, and remove all those things that had grown up over the previous twenty years. Most partners would say it was all complete nonsense – we must have been smoking something in the past!'*

Sometimes, propositions like this come as a shock to the Board!

> *'When I first came back from Davos, about a year and a bit ago, and I told the Board I wanted to blow up the whole organisation, they were all terrified. But finally they all understood it. They said 'You're absolutely right', but of course without the values we couldn't even have thought about doing this.'*

Todd Abbott at Cisco saw the propensity of many companies to change their vision too rapidly. as the problem area within vision and values:

> *'I think far too often companies come up with a new vision every year. Today the imperative isn't about shaking up the world. It is about validating what we have. We've spent a significant amount of time during this downturn in the market, in developing and evolving our strategy. What I find our employees need, because this is going to be a multi-year recovery, is a period of constancy or consistency from a vision.'*

The constancy comes from a vision that only needs 'tweaking' for varying conditions. With Cisco, the values come out when we talk of work/life balance for employees.

*'What we're saying right now is that we want work/life balance
because you're a better employee when you can see the forest for the
trees, and you see that when you have balance. When you're so heads
down, work focused, you lose sight of the big picture.'*

Todd explained that work/life balance was critical to Cisco, and they
were driving hard to bring consistencies to their employee base, and
tools and other things to make their jobs easier. Then:

*'They can focus less time on the tactical, bureaucratic and procedural
things and more time out with customers on the intellectual stuff.'*

This has training and development overtones. As Todd realised, when
a firm was not bringing additional people into sales, then
development became even more important.

*'A lot of companies make the mistake of cutting training when
they're in expense cutting mode. We actually work the other way
around. We actually increased our training budget in the last twelve
months and will do it again next year. You've got to have the
commitment to the employee from a development standpoint, because
career opportunities are not as dynamic as they were.'*

The merger and acquisition policy of Cisco is renowned. Even
though, with the severe downturn, the acquisition strategy has cooled
off somewhat, the value-based policy remains.

*'When we look to acquire, perhaps the first thing we look for is the
technology and skill set. The second is the culture. If the culture
doesn't fit, we won't buy them no matter how good the skill set is, or
because the people will walk out the door. If the partner doesn't have
a culture to partner, no matter how much effort you put into it, it's
never going to fly. So we spend a lot of time looking at the culture of
the potential partner and asking can we make this a win-win?'*

But there have been failures, as Todd admits honestly. Not every one
of Cisco's partnerships and acquisitions had been 100 per cent right.

*'We've had some very public investments in partnerships with other
companies that sounded good at the top, but didn't make sense out
on the streets. If there's not a win at the salesman-salesman level, if
the culture is not a win-win, then it's a waste of time no matter how
much it makes sense on paper at the Executive level.'*

I asked how Cisco tested this issue of culture down the organisation.
Todd replied that, now more than ever, the partnerships were
'bottom-up specific'. One of the big mistakes Cisco had made during
the period of rapid growth was that they stopped listening as closely
as they needed to the customers, and to the market and to their
potential partners in technology.

'It became a silo mentality, and we've spent the last twelve to eighteen months pulling that back together so it's much more 'field' driven. As a 'field' leader, that's exactly what it should be.'

From her experience, Sally Vanson of MCL/The Performance Solution perceives that there is a growing desire in business to evolve values based philosophies. Visits to the US in the wake of 9/11 have convinced her that there is a trend towards a concept of spirituality in business. One of the biggest of their activities is executive coaching, working one to one with senior people in blue chip companies. Sally observes:

'There is much more of a values base to what people do in business. They're tired of living the corporate life, the corporate greed, tired of the big bonuses and the big bucks. That doesn't mean they believe that people shouldn't get them, but they believe people should be rewarded for working hard and achieving, not just because of their status and their hierarchical position.'

So, I asked, is the world in a state of flux? Sally said it was. So what, if anything, is constant?

'The flux is what's constant. The sooner people learn to live with that constant state of change, the happier they're going to be.'

In this, Sally is in tune with Syd Pennington of R&SA. As we have seen, Sally is now in the training and development business. She has had to coach MCL employees, familiar with the cradle to grave philosophy, towards something more entrepreneurial. The focus is on gaining skills for employability. She told me how she usually talks about this to people:

'First of all, forget working with the Japanese, forget the cradle to grave mentality of a job for life. No business is secure. Your only security is in yourself.'

Accordingly, the firm's philosophy was that they would train and develop people, spending a lot of money on the training, because actually it was keeping up-to-date and learning new skills that was keeping these people marketable. And then, instead of doing all the 'sheep dip' training that lots of companies did, on things like brand values and so on, they would talk to people about the strategic objectives, what the company stands for, and what they as human beings stood for. The discussion was about:

'How can you fit your values with where the company is trying to go, so that the two are aligned? That for me is a much more honest way of dealing with it. If then you have to make people redundant, you haven't raised expectation.'

This programme has no official title. It is more about cultural shift. Sally says.

> *'I don't like to call it a values programme because it's not an official thing. I would say it's a coaching programme.'*

I asked about the results. Sally said that the only bottom line evaluation they had of all the activity was actually in Mazda.

> *'Although the Mazda transition was an upheaval, for the people who have gone across to Ford it's been a very successful transition. It wasn't a war, it was a partnership. It was a very easy transition.'*

III PUBLIC TO PRIVATE

The context for this area in fact was the start point for this book. Could its experience tell us whether, in a world in a state of flux, there is a move to find something constant and consistent? The leaders of organisations in this category saw the change from public to private as an opportunity to link the purpose of the enterprise with individuals' needs for meaning and purpose.

Chris Mellor, Chief Executive of AWG, put it this way:*

> *'Boiling it down, what I think vision and values is all about, at its most simple, basic human need, is a sense of purpose and direction. Everybody in the organisation needs to feel that it is going somewhere, and has a purpose they can identify with emotionally as well as intellectually. This company has a certain way of doing business, a certain set of values, that it will always endeavour to adopt when it moves into any business, or when the going gets tough, or whenever change in circumstances comes about.'*

As we saw above, Chris makes a direct link between the issue of values and behaviours, and to almost a spiritual dimension (chapter 4 page 47).

Tony Ward, Group HR Director of BAA also saw the need for something constant:

> *'If you dive in from standing in a rubber dinghy, you're not going to dive very far. But there is a difficult dichotomy involved with putting a stake in the ground around a vision, if that means being so definitive as to lock you in and then make you inflexible and lacking in agility. That's a difficult balancing act.'*

However Tony recognised, as many others did, that while the vision may have to change over time, the values should be constant. The constancy comes in the process of revision and renewal. There has to be a degree of continuity in how strategy and strategic change is

* For detail see Appendix II

applied. For instance, Tony believes that sustainable companies have to be selective about when they go in for transformational change. He argues that you can't have revolution, followed by revolution, followed by revolution.

> *'The customer loses out every time, so you've got to strike that balance.'*

Like many companies associated with Tomorrow's Company, BAA endeavoured to follow an inclusive approach to evolving its vision and values. They engaged the business at all levels to gather perspectives on what was important, with the Executive signing off the result. However, Tony is realistic about the limitations of such an approach.

> *'I think 'ownership' is often a bit strong. It is rather a high expectation for people who are consulted and included then to say they have ownership. If you ask if there is a relatively high awareness then, yes, there is. Is there some scepticism? Yes, but overall I think there's a fair amount of understanding and awareness and quite a good level of ownership.'*

The approaches that are being reported, together with the insights we are gaining into the basic philosophy of our interviewees, are reminiscent of the Collins and Porras work Built to Last. In this, they quoted Thomas J Watson Jr, the founder of IBM, in his booklet A Business and its Beliefs:

> *'If an organization is to meet the challenges of a changing world, it must be prepared to change everything about itself except (its basic) beliefs as it moves through corporate life… The only sacred cow in an organization should be its basic philosophy of doing business.'*

Collins and Porras go on to say:

> *'We believe IBM began to lose its stature as a visionary company in the late 1980s and early 1990s, in part because it lost sight of Watson's incisive caveat.'*

Collins and Porras talk about the need to 'preserve the core and stimulate progress'. Again, this is something to which BAA is committed.

> *'Yes, it's as the business evolves, grows, changes. You need to re-check whether you were appropriate in your previous vision and mission statement. Also, the language changes a bit. For example, our understanding of working with the local communities is different to how it was five years ago. So the language has been shaped to reflect that.'*

Sir John Egan (a former CEO of BAA) is clear about the role of the Chief Executive in communicating the vision:

'They have to understand it. So, if it's big enough for you as a CEO to start concerning yourself with, then you have to explain why you're doing it. For example, I was always quite clear that night flying at our major airports was unacceptable. That was one of the reasons why we really wanted Terminal 5, so we could get more planes through during the day. It seems pretty obvious, but it was very difficult to do that kind of programme when some of our customers like British Airways were adamantly against it.'

At the time Sir John was Chief Executive of BAA, this vision was:

'We were going to be the best airport company in the world and concentrate on the safety and needs of our customers. We also said that we would make all the processes in the business world-class, and we had to know what they were. Thirdly, we wanted our employees to bring their brains and enthusiasm to work. Lastly, we eventually brought into our ideas the notion that we had to grow our airports with the support and trust of our neighbours.'

Bob Mason, formerly of BT, reinforces the issues of constancy of values.

'Values are by definition unchanging, and so very important. Secondly, they have to be written in a way that relates them to human behaviour, in some way that personalises them. Values are something that people, rather than organisations, hold.'

In a similar way to AWG and BAA, Bob Mason believes that in changing circumstances the vision needs to be revisited from time to time.

'In a changing world it is difficult to know that your vision is sufficiently ambitious, challenging, and I think periodically just reviewing that vision is well worth doing.'

In discussing vision and values, Jeremy Long, CEO of GB Rail was concerned about how any statement of vision and values from the top gets translated into action in behavioural terms at the customer interface. It was about consistency, and the 'I know what they in head office would do in my circumstances' type of vision.

'You do have to be clear what it is you are going to emphasise. Communicating vision for me is like asking 'What do I think he'd do in the circumstances?' and you've got to get that across as far down the organisation as you can. They've got to feel 'What would I would expect them to do at Artillery Lane?''

In terms of communicating the vision and values, Jeremy saw the value of standing up in front of mass audiences. However felt that the off cue communication was more effective and real:

*'I think it's a bit like in watching TV. You watch people's least
expected replies, and you believe more of that than the stuff played
most to camera. So I think you have to do all of the 'big bang' stuff,
but at the end of the day that is probably the stuff that carries least
credibility. People will watch a management team more for the
unplanned, the unpredictable events.'*

Vision and values and the work ethic

All interviewees in the public-to-private category, without exception,
felt that in general people were working harder than even five years
ago, and certainly harder than the regime of ten or twenty years
before. They also felt that the tensions of work/life balance were more
acute than ever. However, they were also convinced that the old
solution of 'compartmentalising' work from home and vice versa was
not real. Several leaders felt that the reality was one of more
integration, and that balance could be struck in this way.

Chris Mellor was particularly sensitive over the pressures on
people, which for him was a fundamental issue which transcended the
workplace and many aspects of life these days.

*'I've worked for this company for over twenty years, and there's no
question about the pace at which people are being asked to work. The
level, the output is hugely greater than it was five years ago let alone
ten or twenty years ago.'*

Chris talked about dealing with emotions and that this also had a
number of social consequences. There was a high degree of
correlation between the amount of hours, and general strains and
stresses, of corporate and business life these days and a lot of the
social ills that are being seen. He encourages people to get the balance
between life and work correct, because he believes that a healthy body
equals a healthy mind.

*'I think the notion that people can compartmentalise their life into
'this is work' or 'this is home' is nonsense. People at home are
thinking about work, and people at work are thinking about home.
You cannot switch off from one to the other. So if either one isn't
happy then, one way or another, it's going to impact on the other.'*

When asked whether, in those circumstances, the vision and values
helped the individual who struggles with the balance, Chris
responded:

*'I can see from it that, first of all, there is a sense of pride and
belonging to the company that they work for. I think that's very
important, and also that there is a supportive culture that enables
people to get the best out of themselves and the company to get the*

best out of the people. I think the payback to the company is when
that person comes back and feels that he or she should put something
back into the company.'

This puts me in mind of the story of the CEO of Cantor Fitzgerald
(Howard Lutnick) who was supporting his child at a school event in
New York on the morning of September 11 2001 when so many of his
colleagues died in the World Trade Centre.

Tony Ward saw the supposed decline of the work ethic as being a
polarisation between the haves and the have-nots.

> *'I think you've got two polarisations going on in the world we're in*
> *now. I think a lot of young people, certainly in advanced western*
> *countries, are in a position to question whether or not they wish to be*
> *slaves to the desk and the shop floor. Then it polarises because there*
> *are people who are very driven, who are going to go the extra mile*
> *all the time. They set the competitive standards, so if you want to do*
> *that, you've got to be like them.'*

This polemic of Tony's is similar to that of Richard Donkin in his
challenging book *Blood, Sweat and Tears*[3]. He asks whether, on the one
hand we are totally slaves to work if we are in employment or, on the
other, alienated from society if we are out of work. It is the issue of
people who are either time poor and cash rich or time rich and cash
poor. Tony Ward saw a different way of expressing this issue:

> *'We can see very clear, contrasting, examples. You can work very*
> *conscientiously and very hard for your lifetime, and come out with*
> *very low disposable wealth. And you can work for very short periods*
> *of time in financial capital, the City, and make huge gains*
> *instantaneously.'*

Bob Mason of BT also reflected on the issue of employee choice in
terms of work/life balance:

> *'The talented people of today are increasingly asking this very*
> *question, and don't necessarily want to give life and soul to an*
> *organisation 24/7. They want to feel they have a challenging job, and*
> *an opportunity to make a difference at work, but also have a life*
> *outside work. I think, though, too many companies still pay lip*
> *service to this. They identify it as an issue and find all sorts of ways*
> *of not confronting it.'*

Vision and values and major disruption

The last topic within this heading we needed to explore was whether
the vision and values statement (if there was one) had been affected
by any major disruption within the organisation, or by a merger or
demerger. In general terms, interviewees found that the hard won

vision and values had stood the test of time, often even being reinforced at times of disruption. The most testing times appeared during the experience of mergers and acquisition and/or demergers. In 2000, AWG acquired Morrison Construction, so adding to the UK workforce of 6,000 a further 3,500 people who had had very little exposure to the original vision and values introduced in 1997.

Chris Mellor saw the challenge in these terms:

> *'At this stage a fair amount of vision and values is trust. There are questions about two parts of the organisation and what each one means to the other. To some extent, we have to recreate that trust and sense of purpose and direction, and revisit the values and get a consensus. The way we've behaved, true to our values, has created a huge amount of goodwill.'*

The question then comes, with a newly diversified group, is it appropriate to have total consistency? Chris saw the different tensions that this situation brings:

> *'If you're not careful, you turn them all off. So getting the overarching sense of togetherness, pulling in the same direction, is important but so is celebrating and respecting the differences.'*

There are some interesting contrasts here, particularly with Cisco who insisted on compatibility of culture between the constituent parts, particularly following acquisition. Tony Ward of BAA, reflecting on the acquisition of new airports, saw some issues affecting commercial returns in sticking to a firm line over values:

> *'We've had good and bad experiences. In our core airport business, a good example would be Naples. Transformation originates from our basic values and missions. Where we've moved away from some of our core airport management, then it has been much more difficult. We're not prepared to risk our reputation and undermine the core things that work for us.'*

On demerger issues, from BT's experience of devolving into different business sectors, Bob Mason had a view:

> *'I think that at different times companies have to do apparently conflicting or paradoxical things. They split themselves up, but they still want to retain this kind of integrated feeling and work well together. I think that tensions are inevitable, and there has to be that healthy debate.'*

IV PUBLIC SECTOR AND PFI

For the public sector, vision and values again are about meaning and purpose. However, they are linked with constancy and performance but not necessarily with sustainability. Often the values are inherent, and have been assumed and unexpressed until of late. Professor Sir Liam Donaldson, Chief Medical Officer at the Department of Health, summarised this trend. He saw that having vision and values was probably a way of creating stability and continuity, but they might not necessarily be apparent to everyone in an organisation.

> *'The values have tended to be implicit over the years and because they've been implicit, they haven't been obvious to everybody delivering services. So for example when we talk about being patient centred, some people would say 'that's ridiculous, obviously we're patient centred because we're delivering care to patients.'*

Sir Liam argued that people did seem to like hearing the patient-centred objective made explicit, so it became a value. He agreed that the vision has changed from time to time, and in the NHS the vision is often expressed in a goal or an aspiration, such as 'better quality care for patients', but it was often tempered with a style of delivery which varied from time to time according to the political philosophy of the day. He reported that, at the moment, devolution was a favoured way, so:

> *'The vision statement is often bound up with some sort of expectation of how the vision will be delivered.'*

Sir Liam raised an interesting point by asking when 'something' becomes a value. It is a point that affects a number of organisations in this study. For many of the start-up organisations, it originates with the philosophy of the founders. With large corporations with a great deal of history, it is often unspoken and evolving. Sir Liam talked about this process, and said that you could argue a bit about when something does become a value.

> *'Is it like sainthood, where you have to go through certain stages before you're canonised? I think you would say that 'free at the point of delivery', equity and patient centredness are very clear values. However, if people choose to conceptualise some of these things and start talking about dignity, respect, empowering the patients and so on, then these will become values too. Is it a value that we will run our service in a locally sensitive devolved way? Or that our management style will not be to control from above. Or isn't it a value? People will use the term 'values' very, very loosely. In the sense of conceptualising values, I think the NHS is a bit loose and slack about how it does it.'*

This lack of clarity and vagueness about the 'corporate' values has given rise to the predominance of strong 'professional' values. These are often in conflict with what others feel the NHS is all about. Sir

Liam suggested that, particularly for doctors, some of those things have not been properly debated before.

> 'I heard a doctor at a meeting recently get very indignant with the discussion about NHS priorities and goals. He said very indignantly, "I do not work for the Government". Given that we've got a state health service… I can understand what he meant. On the other hand, it is a strange organisation where people feel that their biggest affiliation and loyalty is to a set of abstract values, and behind that would come their loyalty to their local employer, if the local employer in their view was adhering to those general values, and then their third and least loyalty would be to the State run service which pays their pension and everything else.'

This comes to the essence of the frustration at each end of the gigantic NHS system. The doctor who is trained to give pre-eminence to his or her own judgement on clinical need, and regards the issue of money as an enabler and management as potentially an interference, is at one extreme and at the other extreme, are government ministers who regard the system as a 'black hole' and out of control. To successive governments, who emotionally support the original values of the NHS, it has become an insoluble problem and one of enormous frustration. Is difficult to show progress overall to voters, even following the provision of additional resources, as the current administration knows only too well.

To the doctor, the independence that was once sacrosanct is further and further under attack. This generated the suspicion that led consultants in England and Wales to reject the new consultant contract in 2002 that had been negotiated between ministers and the doctors' union, the British Medical Association. Liam Donaldson reflected on how, over time, there had been changes concerning the expected length of tenure for consultants.

> 'In the old days, it was appointment to a ward in a hospital. That would be your ward. It was before the days when emergency admissions were so high that doctors had patients all over the hospital. You would come in to see your thirty beds, and those would be your thirty beds for the next thirty years.'

Speaking from the viewpoint of the local management of the NHS, Malcolm Lowe-Lauri focused on the gap that needed to be bridged between the 'push' of the national professional bodies and standards, and the local 'pull' of rising expectations and an increasing number of constituencies with whom the hospital needs to work in partnership.[4]

> 'As expectations rise so the gap between the reality of service delivery and those expectations widens. It is a complex and multi-faceted

service, which is not fully understood by the population at large.
Hence systems are required for "emergency" and (elective) or
'scheduled' services which have to work in tandem but
independently.'

Malcolm also describes how the system external to the locality and
the hospital struggles to keep up with what is needed locally.

'There are a number of stakeholders, not least the outside professional
bodies and organisations, whose culture may not yet be in tune with
the changes that are needed locally.'

He believed that it was necessary to build links and common vision
and values both outside the Trust, for instance with primary and
social care, and patient groups, as well as inside, with the differing
professional groups. The methodology used has been to communicate
the vision for the wider health system in Greater Peterborough,
making sure issues and successes are well broadcast and celebrated
where appropriate. He accepted that there would be resistors, and
Malcolm was adamant that much effort needs to be put in to win over
the disbelievers. There is little doubt that Peterborough Hospitals has
moved from a 'victim culture' where there was a feeling in the mid
1990s of being 'out of control' with little hope, to a very much 'can
do' culture now, which is demonstrated in successful achievement. (In
2001, 2002 and 2003 the Trust was designated a Three-Star Trust.)
As Chris Bottomley found in interviewing Malcolm, a lot was down
to strong and consistent leadership.

At One NorthEast, John Bridge is convinced of the need for
defining what is constant, in order to facilitate change.

'We do need constancy when we're involved in a state of flux. I think
vision and values are absolutely critical. It's all about buy-in. It's
about people understanding what the problem is, whatever that
problem happens to be, and also buying into the solution. But
actually I think actually it's the first point that is more important
than the second. It's about buying into the problem.'

At Arts Council England, Peter Hewitt knew what the vision and
values should be, and appreciated how important it was to achieve
them. However, he explained that the organisation needed to change
before the vision and values would take root. For Peter, the internal
thrust needed to reflect the external priorities.

'This is deeply unresolved. If externally we are responding to a global
need to adopt a more people-centred [the artist and the arts public]
approach, then internally we must adopt a people-centred approach.'

At the Patent Office, Philip Johnson was familiar with their mission statement.

> *'We stimulate innovation and enhance the international*
> *competitiveness of British Industry and commerce. We offer customers*
> *an accessible, high quality, value for money system, both national*
> *and international, for granting intellectual property rights. We*
> *develop staff to meet this mission.'*

However, Philip didn't feel that the most had been made of the opportunity. The potential of vision and values was not recognised. While individuals took pride in their work, it was the individual's work not the corporate product. He felt the end product was good but could be so much better. He was critical of the whole way of working:

> *'Silo mentality, individual office-closed doors, minimal face-to-face*
> *communication, and dozens of e-mails.'*

What was missing seemed to be getting passion and motivation into a traditional civil service culture. Overall, despite an apparent air of stability Philip described an odd sense of paranoia within the organisation. There was a worry about privatisation, from looking at other government agencies (eg Post Office), and concern about the potential widening of the EU Patent Office remit. So there are some issues about flux, but no handles to grab hold of for stability, such as a 'vision and values'.

This shows that either of the extremes, of complacency through stability or instability through potential threat, do not of themselves create the perceived need for defining and aligning an organisation behind vision and values. The issue then has to be one of a leadership that perceives what is needed, intervenes and confronts.

Mike Walters at Bovis Lend Lease took a pragmatic, no nonsense, view that was about what the original Bovis stood for and how they had gained alignment.

> *'Having a stated vision and values gives that framework on which*
> *you can build your processes, procedures, and the way you do things,*
> *and unifies everyone globally. They are there to give focus, and mean*
> *that the person at the top has 'set out their stall' saying what is*
> *needed. They are then lived all the time through the way decisions*
> *are made.'*

The experience of merger with Lend Lease gave Bovis a potential problem of two sets of vision and values. Mike tells the story.

> *'When we were just Bovis, we had a set of values that would see us*
> *through, and we created a vision and values booklet for all*
> *employees. When Lend Lease bought Bovis, we had to merge two sets*
> *of vision and values. To achieve this, we ran workshops to work the*

two together. However, there were many similarities so this was not so onerous a task. Our vision is 'Providing the best real estate solutions for our clients globally'. We now have just five values – integrity, respect, collaboration, excellence, innovation.'

V 'BUILT-TO-LAST' ORGANISATIONS/'STEADY AS SHE GOES'

The organisations included in this section are ones that have stood the test of time. At Shell, Mark Hope feels that the issues of philosophy, at both company and personal level, are very important. If corporate vision and values do not resonate with individuals, you are unlikely to get high performance. Shell as an organisation is enormous, of course, and the key thing is to be relevant at operating level.

'Shell has its General Business Principles up front. They include all the things you'd expect to be there. Perhaps the greatest current challenge is to get to grips with sustainable development. I think this has to be the umbrella under which everything else fits.'

Mark sees the crucial outputs in terms of behaviours and how those are seen.

'Shell Expro has been doing quite a lot of work on values and behaviours – getting different parts of the business to articulate what those values are, and then considering what behaviours demonstrate the values. We now have mandatory 360 degree appraisal, so every year, before you have an appraisal discussion with your boss, you have to consult a number of your peers and subordinates about both your performance and your behaviours.'

I asked if such openness was making a difference and he felt that it was. He recognised that we live in a rapidly changing world where none of us have all the answers. Therefore we have to depend upon other people and learn fast. Both of these are difficult but:

'Everybody can help each other. If one can create a supportive/learning/coaching atmosphere, the rewards can be very large – a highly motivated team which is challenging and fun to work in.'

Work/life balance is explored in some depth in Shell. Where possible, it takes a very flexible attitude. Mark himself has a four-day week, and tries to put all the community work to which he commits on the Friday of each week. For him personally this often means sixty to sixty-five hours a week – *'a bad example to my staff!'* But the flexibility is also there for his staff.

'I try and encourage flexibility whatever that means. Of course it can mean very different things to different people. Anyone can have

a PC at home if they wish, and connect into the Shell network. This suits some people but feels like an intrusion to others. So within my team, we try to understand what work practices are best for each of us. Our team currently has one person who works two days a week and two people who work part-time to fit in with nursery hours.'

Should there be any difference between home and work in vision and value terms, I asked. Mark thought that many people did put distinctions between their home life and their work life. He used to do the same himself, but for him the distinctions have become less and less meaningful.

'My current view is that you can't actually have two different value sets, one for home and one for work. You can, of course, behave differently at home compared to work if you choose, but if that means contravening your values in the workplace that's not good for you and, ultimately, not good for your employer either.'

The issues of Brent Spar and Nigeria have caused Shell to revisit the issue of their values and how these are lived. Mark explained:

'If you just put stuff in words somewhere, and don't spend time talking to people about it, you would be better off not to have bothered at all. I haven't been with Shell very long, but I imagine there's been much stronger engagement over the last decade (not least with our own staff) about what does this really mean for us, and do we really buy into the engagement/listening concepts or not. I can start to see things happening differently now, but this is a very long journey – listening remains a hugely under-utilised skill.'

This story is one of a mature organisation that has learned from knocks and challenges, and one that takes vision and values seriously into practice.

Lawrence Churchill at UNUM is a strong believer in the importance of vision and values. In UNUM these form part of the contract with all employees.

'The value set in the US Company is the same as within the UK one. I believe that when it comes to values, most organisations would express broadly the same issues. What matters is the way in which they are used and integrated into individual and corporate behaviour.'

Lawrence believes that the value set is essential to sustain company performance. He uses a neat description of a virtuous circle in which values drive the vision, which drives the behaviours, which drives the culture, and thus can make this approach work.

The words of the Burall philosophy, which is in Appendix I, according to David, took a long time to hone. He said he was really quite proud of it.'

> 'It was probably ten years ago it was put together. It was quite
> widely discussed through management teams, and there were a lot of
> contributions to the structure of it. A lot of staff who joined us in the
> 70s and 80s and their families committed to the company –
> husbands and wives. In a place like Wisbech there is not a great pool
> of talented labour to be drawn on, so you have to look for something
> else. What there is, is a lot of indigenous common sense and loyalty, if
> you deserve that loyalty. I think by demonstrating that we were
> interested in long term employment, and sharing the growing wealth
> of the company, we earned the loyalty.'

This shows that such deep values and trust are a product of
relationships developed over long periods. The House of Hardy has
been through many structural changes but craftsmanship and quality
have been the hallmarks of sustainability. Richard Maudslay explains:

> 'Is it necessary to focus on something constant such as vision and
> values? Yes. We make the top quality stuff and we've got to continue
> to do so. The other thing that is absolutely constant is we've got to
> where we are by a process of constant innovation. If we forget to
> innovate, or lose the ability to innovate, we won't survive. It is
> innovation built on tradition.'

However, based in Alnwick, Northumberland, House of Hardy is not
a business that would have gone in for flowery language in expressing
its vision and values:

> 'If I went into Hardy and said I'd got a vision and values
> proposition they'd say ... well, they've already accused me of coming
> from the deep south, and I thought that was a reference to my
> upbringing in Sussex until I realised they meant Newcastle!'

The (unexpressed) vision is simply to make money by satisfying
customers.

In common with House of Hardy, Gardiner & Theobald is a very
traditional business, where the importance of quality is understood
but generally unspoken. Similarly, the values are implicit, despite the
worldwide coverage and separate businesses.

> 'Valuing people; Strong ethics; a very strong sense of incorruptibility
> that comes from professionalism. Quality, of course, is expressed in
> the Quality Assurance manuals, but it is also about doing the job
> properly. Even if we lose out financially from it, the job will be done
> properly. That matters. Quality is also about being an agile business
> ready to meet new challenges, and working in different markets to the
> same high standards.'

With a lot of 'out-posted' staff who work as Gardiner & Theobald professionals in other organisations, they can become somewhat detached.

> *'Some people say, 'I've been out for so long I don't feel I belong' and will say, 'I want to come in for a bit', meaning coming back to Gardiner & Theobald offices and working for new clients.'*

The partners make the effort to get round to keep in touch.

> *'For example, one partner responsible for one group of out-posted staff spends a lot of time going round seeing people, and arranges evening seminars followed by an enjoyable and relaxed dinner. Others come into the Gardiner & Theobald offices for lunchtime seminars and, of course, for social events.'*

John Cridland at CBI felt that vision and values are foundations, but that they do not solve the issues of managing change, which are about implementation.

> *'Vision and values are always important. I'm not sure how far they help though. I suppose what I'm saying is that I don't think they are sufficient to tackle the problem of a world in flux. Vision and values should be self-standing if they are genuinely to last. Therefore they won't in themselves act as a bridge of finding ways through managing change.'*

However, clearly, they can give constancy. John quoted the case of Shell, corroborating the points Mark Hope had made in his interview.

> *'You need to be quite lateral in the way that you look at risk management at a time when the world is in flux. This is best illustrated by things like Shell and Brent Spar. It can be the external things over which you have less control that can catch you unawares.'*

The CBI finds it has to be pragmatic, as it represents its members, practically based corporations:

> *'Our course is determined by events. There is an extent to which it is a lobbying and representational organisation, but actually we have to be flexible to respond to what others are doing. Our destiny's less in our own hands.'*

In discussing work/life balance, John feels that this is related more to how employees are treated.

> *'My own view is that the work/life balance stuff derives rather more from the fair treatment of the individual rather than organisational purpose. I think work/life balance is in danger of getting somewhat hyped. In a well run organisation, line managers are sensitive to addressing individual needs.'*

At Ashridge, according to Leslie Hannah, vision and values are at the heart. We both believe that profit and shareholder value are by-products of the way vision and values are lived out. First, it's the people business

> '*We recruit tutors from business. A typical tutor is recruited at thirty two or thirty five after ten years' business experience and perhaps an MBA. Those people are essentially coming here for work/life balance and the values of the place which are very related to human resource type values; respect for people.*'

Second, it's about what gets you out of bed on Monday morning

> '*I really do believe in the Jerry Porras, Clive Morton, John Kay sort of story, that people who build great businesses do not wake up in the morning thinking, 'I'm going to create shareholder value today.' Bill Gates gets up and says 'I'm going to make a damn good computer programme today'. They set creating shareholder value as a by-product of vision and values which are broader and more purposeful.*'

As with many aspects of management speak I was expecting a wide variation of opinion over whether 'vision and values' was seen to be central to the organisations studied. What is surprising is the degree of unanimity over the role of vision and values as a means of gaining consistency and 'glue' in 'pursuing goals in a co-operative way'. (Richard Hicks, AIT)

The enthusiasm for vision and values has been a reaction or balancing force to the systems led approaches of TQ and Business Process re-engineering and has been reinforced by the evidence from researchers such as Collins & Porras in *Built to Last*.

The 'snowball effect' has also been aided by the stakeholder philosophy adopted by the many organisations that recognise that single axis goals such as profits and satisfying shareholders only is short term and often counterproductive. Hence it is a necessary reaction to the increasingly complex world that organisations find themselves in. Interestingly the not-for-profit sector leads the way on recognising the need to measure progress in stakeholder terms. Alan Bartle of Lymphoma Association talks of the need to measure success in terms of outcomes for a wider range of constituents – not just against objectives for the Lymphoma Association. Bill Penney echoes this in the quotation highlighted at the beginning of this chapter 'helping individuals or organisations realise more of their potential'.

Similarly the common theme of vision and values related to meaning and purpose shines through. Peter Smith of The Strategic Partnership reflects:

'Vision must encompass the values and relationships with stakeholders. Boards cannot do this on their own. At the end of the day, employees want to work for someone whose values link to their own.'

For the large organisation often in a state of flux, vision and values has a great role in alignment and making sense of complex, confused situations.

The lessons highlighted by Syd Pennington of Royal & Sun Alliance over the post merger experience are salutary. Not just the organisational confusion or the overwhelming emphasis on cost cutting but critically the lack of agreed vision and values led to failures.

The discussions on work/life balance were illuminating. Several interviewees made the counter-intuitive point that it wasn't about separating work and home life but about integration. Peter Ward, Telos Partners:

'I don't think there is a work/life balance, and as soon as you start thinking in terms of work/life balance you've probably missed the point. It's work/life integration. You shouldn't need to make choices if you're working with an organisation that believes in your beliefs.'

Lastly the issues around leadership neatly link to the theme of our next chapter, in particular the conclusions of this chapter in the context of vision and values are that leadership is about perceiving what is needed and then intervening and confronting key issues to 'pursue goals in a co-operative way'.

Notes

1   For details see Appendix II
2   See Appendix II
3   Donkin, R *Blood, Sweat and Tears* Texere 2001
4   For details on the Transformation Project at Peterborough see Appendix III – extract from NHS Modernisation: Making it Mainstream March 2003

Chapter six

LEADERSHIP AND ENTREPRENEURIAL ABILITY

I want now to turn to the topic of leadership and the development of leaders. Over a period of time I had developed my own ideas about the development of leaders, which I had encapsulated in four statements. I believe that effective leadership requires:

- the ability to know yourself and others
- an understanding of the role of emotions and emotional intelligence
- the effective understanding of individuals and teams.

I also believe that one of the major challenges of leadership is about effectively dealing with and resolving dilemmas. In my conversations, I therefore asked people to comment on these four statements. Specifically, I asked them 'What place do the following have in developing leaders?' and I asked both about their personal experiences, and how their organisations handled these issues. The questions were:

- Knowing yourself and others – is this deliberately encouraged?
- The role of emotions and emotional intelligence – is this explored?
- The individual and the team – what understanding and what adjustment is there?
- If leadership is all about effectively dealing with and resolving dilemmas (for example, short-term vs long-term), can you recount how your organisation dealt with a crucial dilemma? Did it demonstrate leadership?

The discussions produced some fascinating insights, and revealed a number of common themes. As before, we present the information in the familiar categories and sub-categories.

I   START-UPS/ENTREPRENEURSHIP/PHOENIX

A   NEW START-UPS IN THE FIELD OF TECHNOLOGY

Richard Hicks of AIT needed no introduction to the ideas. His response was immediate, and he saw that leadership, and an understanding of it, was crucial. :

> *'If you try and engage people's hearts and minds, then you have to be aware of the issues about knowing yourself, the emotional engagement of people, the individual and team and the relationship between them. We take those points as a given.'*

In particular, Richard commented that this was important in a knowledge based organisation, which had to depend on peoples' commitment, agility and imagination, and where you were not just asking people 'to run down a pair of tracks as fast as they can'. I went on to ask Richard how AIT dealt with resolving dilemmas. He said that dilemmas frequently were dealt with by consultation, and that AIT had set up a structure called 'T group Systems', which was not dissimilar to John Lewis' staff council.

> *'The big issues of consultation were around things like floating of the company. What we got back was a huge range of issues that just needed better communication. It's very easy for people running organisations to forget other people's relative ignorance about things that they take for granted.'*

The link between Richard's different answers reinforces where, I believe, the connection lies between the first three of the Leadership 'bullet points' above and the issue of handling dilemmas. So, if Boards of companies are familiar with exploring the first three amongst themselves, then the fourth should be easier. Differing views will be taken into account early, rather than being submerged and possibly only emerging after the event!

For Keith Moscrop at BioFocus, leadership was all about dealing with anecdotal situations, and intervening when relationships looked rocky. He felt that, as clever ex-Wellcome scientists, his colleagues resisted 'HR type systems'. In the past things had been 'done to' them by such systems without good effect. But Keith's approach marked him out as someone who did things differently:

> *'I'm considered to be a real oddball because I operate intuitively. When a difficult situation arose, then I'd bust in on the discussions. If people want to dump, then they could dump on me, and it gave them an excuse to consider all the possibilities.'*

When systems were applied, Keith observed, there tended to be little feeling used. He reflected that the founding directors must have been fairly good as a team, because they reached goals that had been set for them that they were not expected to reach. But it was the people issues that caused him particular difficulties. He also recognised that sometimes, although people were doing things 'by the book', they could fail to deliver results.

'The sleep that I lost in the first four years was over worrying about individuals. Try as I might, they were not very keen to take advice. One person was particularly awkward, and that helped unify the others. Another member of the team was most diligent at applying his HR training with regular appraisals. He spent time with key individuals, and yet the outcomes were not particularly fruitful. Others were good at encouraging staff but lacked ability to build management systems.'

When we went on to talk about resolving dilemmas, Keith gave a concrete example of how the team, unspoken, had buried their misgivings and pulled together.

'The first time we ran out of money, some of us had big mortgages. However, five out of the seven founders didn't take salary for four months. We got to within a week of having to declaring ourselves insolvent. Dave and I did all the rushing around, trying to find money from various places. We didn't have to spend a lot of time communicating with the people that weren't at the meetings. They saw customers to keep the company going. So in a sense the teamwork at that level was very trusting but effective.'

This anecdote reminded me of the expression the Japanese use, of 'tummy speak', to describe situations where all the team understand without the need for explanation.

It was clear that the process Keith described worked well because the caucus knew each other. However, with the coming of plc status, the Board imposing more structure and formality, and less knowledge of new incumbents, the organisation entered a different, non-entrepreneurial, phase.

'Yes, it was a very collective leadership. It became known as a collegiate, and in some circles this attribute was despised. It's over now, of course, because the board has changed and a number of the founders have stepped down. We are going through a fair degree of pain, trying to rebuild with the formal corporate governance approach. And I think that's the end of most of the entrepreneurial drive.'

Keith recognised the necessity of a more formal approach and the changes he described are typical of the growth pains of a start-up, but he mourned the perceived loss of entrepreneurial spirit. He accepted that now the organisation had built up to 2,000 people it needed to mature, acquire some proper systems, and become more stable.

> *'The fly-wheel effect of the company being that size carries it*
> *forward, the reputation has gone up, and the company can live off*
> *it's reputation while the new organisation is being created.'*

An interesting postscript to this conversation is that Keith
confirmed his decision to retire in 2002. He is not now part of the
rather more systematised, formal future he was describing. Since
this interview in 2001, The Morton Partnership has been working
successfully with the top team of BioFocus on individual and
collective development during this transition to plc corporate
governance. It has seen the arrival of a new Chief Operating Officer,
Geoff Macmillan, to support Chief Executive, Dr David Stone. Now
the team does not need a 'Keith Moscrop' to intervene to be the
catalyst over people's feelings. Hopefully they know sufficient about
each other to value their individual and collective contributions.

Duncan Hine, then Chief Executive at The Generics Group, had
devoted considerable time to thinking about issues of personality
and leadership. He described how he used Belbin type classifications
to think about it.

> *'It is a very unusual company, because I would say a good 80 per*
> *cent of the staff are 'plants'. That's a very odd mixture. I think in*
> *typical companies, 4-5 per cent (of plants) would be good. So, of*
> *course, many people are very creative, very innovative. You don't*
> *have to encourage people to invent things, or think of new ways of*
> *doing things, because they do it completely naturally. On the other*
> *hand, of course, 'plants' are not usually 'completer/finishers' or*
> *'shapers' or 'evaluators'. So we do struggle a little with internal*
> *processes and management issues. We're a place where people can*
> *make personal progress without having to be a manager.'*

Generics are conscious of the tensions involved when 'plants' are
given free rein, but also of the opposite effect if they are immersed
in hierarchy. As a result, Duncan explained, they. have the minimum
amount of structure that just allows the business to function. He
also told me that Generics had very wide salary scales for people
who were currently doing the same job, because these reflected the
quality and the amount of contributions. Duncan commented:

> *'People build an enormous initiative from the bottom of the*
> *organisation. If they've got something that's compelling, and starts to*
> *be reinforced by the market, they can ride that wave as far as it will*
> *go.'*

Generics made quite a lot of use of peer group processes. Duncan
said that many of the firm's investments and intellectual property
were managed by a peer group of a dozen people who were very

experienced in the technologies and the commercial aspects and who were not managers.

In Duncan's view, Generics struck the balance in relation to commercial reality by proper debate between the creative and business disciplines:

> *'I think one of the clever things here is that people can flip backwards and forwards very easily between the creative, sparky and open strength thinking and the actual, and then saying, What would the business case look like?'*

This style is reflected in Generics' recruitment policy concerning what Jon Sparkes, who was then Group HR Director, called 'polymaths', or those who showed ability in discrete areas. As Duncan Hine expressed it:

> *'Generally we won't offer jobs to people who are just creative. They've got to be showing business disciplines, project management disciplines. It's a function of the environment, the nature of the work, which gives a chance to develop all of those things at the same time.'*

On dilemmas and leadership Duncan saw the issue as providing a framework corporately within which people could act in order that dilemmas are resolved further down the organisation. Clarity is important here.

> *'I've rarely seen black and white situations. The interesting thing to me is whether the framework is sufficiently clear that people understand it before things happen, or before they present you with the dilemma. When we're investing money, it's our money we are investing, so people shouldn't be suggesting things they don't think are a brilliant idea.'*

Apart from delegating decisions downwards, and avoiding ideas being turned down, Duncan believed people in Generics are far more in control of their futures than they are in a production line dominated environment. There are two obvious routes people could get experience and development:

> *'You can get experience inside the organisation, doing something for us, but you're ten times as likely to get it outside the organisation doing it for a client. So the response to people who say, I really want to work in this area, is, Well, just sell an assignment to somebody and you can do it tomorrow.'*

In our conversation, Dianne Thompson, Chief Executive at Camelot, made the link between the earlier discussion of vision and values and leadership. She did this by recounting the experience of the first management conference Camelot had held for five years, which happened after the news about the second franchise period had come through. As she said, it was a very, very upbeat event.

> 'Basically, I was sharing the new vision with them and saying that, to achieve our goals, we have to be more creative, more innovative, more proactive, and agile. To do that, I've got to empower you because I can't do it all. Of course we'll make some mistakes. I don't mind, that provided we learn from them. Right at the end we did an interactive keypad thing, effectively asking them whether they were up for it. And they all were!'

Agincourt comes to mind!

When I asked her about managers and their continuing commitment, Dianne was uncompromising.

> 'This programme is for all managers, and they will have some hard conversations at the end. Either you're in this or you're out. There's no room for somebody who's not going to buy into this.'

Looking at the first three leadership bullet points, Dianne was candid. She felt that, although the 'Winning Ways' programme had delved into the first and third (knowing yourself and others, and the individual and the team), the second – emotional intelligence –was a mystery.

> 'I'm not sure we've thought about emotional intelligence particularly, to be honest. Knowing yourself and how others see you is very much the core of how we're going to change people's behaviours. We think that is absolutely critical. It is all about leadership behaviour. The individual and the team are very critical and one of our six values is about teamwork. One of the things I've tried very hard to do is to get far more cross-functional working.'

On reflection and discussion, Dianne felt the knowledge about emotions would come out in the workshop processes.

> 'I think perhaps in many ways we are an emotional company. The day that we lost, 400 people or so gathered this floor for Tim Holley (the previous Chief Executive) to tell them that we'd lost. People were in tears.'

The question about relating to a leadership dilemma struck home, including an element of work life balance:

> 'We lost on a Wednesday; we re-grouped on a Thursday afternoon. We couldn't meet on the Thursday morning because that was the day my daughter was getting her GCSE results. I didn't take her out to lunch to celebrate, which I would have done otherwise, but at least I was there for the moment. So we met here at 12.30pm and debated what we should do. We took the decision that afternoon that we would fight, not with any real hope of changing it. It was just so

unfair, so our decision was easy then. There was nothing to lose
–apart from 800 jobs –if we didn't have a go.'

Dianne went on to talk about her misgivings about taking over from
Tim Holley, her predecessor.

'A lot of the people who were here at the start are still here. They all
had a very special relationship, because all they were doing was
writing the bid, and Tim was there all the time. One of the things
that used to frustrate me when I first came was that people said, Oh,
we never see Tim any more. It's not like the good old days.'

Diane used to reply that people had to look forward. It was never
going to be like that again, with only seventy-five people. Tim now
had all sorts of things to do with running the Lottery, not just
writing the bid and floating out and about. But, she went on:

'There is a real pool of affection for Tim here and justifiably so. I was
actually slightly worried when I took over as CEO designate quite
how I was going to make my mark on this company and follow Tim
as the leader. In fact, the fight that we got into did it for me because
suddenly, although I was still only the CEO designate, I actually led
the fight and the people thought I almost single-handedly was
fighting for them.'

I reminded Dianne of her quote in the media, *'Although I am a*
woman I have steel balls'. She agreed she would live to regret that.
But the staff had seen her as their potential salvation and therefore
the leadership thing was very easy to do then.

'I think what happened then for me as a leader was, because I was
so high profile and the story was so high profile and there was so
much of me around, they felt they knew me really well. So I would
pass somebody on the stairs and before I knew it (because I'm
northern and I'm friendly) I'd say, Hi, how are you? and they'd say,
Fine thank you, and scurry off. I'd now say, Hi, how are you? and
they'd say, Hi, I'm great thanks and how's Jo doing with her A
levels? because they'd read so much about me. Some really nice
things happened. One Friday when I came back into the office, on
the table was a bottle of Bolly with a computer-generated card which
just said, Dear Di, have a drink on us this weekend. From your
friends on the hotline. They'd had a whip round that morning to buy
a bottle of Bolly for me so there's lots of little things like that, some
great emails. When we actually won I got an email from a girl up in
Aintree, and this email said, Thank you for leading the fight. Thank
you for saving my job. Thank you for saving my home' and for a lot
of them it was as important as that. I was very lucky in hindsight
because that sort of catapulted me there.'

This interview with Diane left me feeling somewhere between Henry V at Agincourt and Good Queen Bess at Tilbury and somewhat sorry for the regulator!

B　NOT-FOR-PROFIT/LYMPHOMA ASSOCIATION

Alan Bartle has had to reverse a bureaucratic structure in the tiny Lymphoma Association. Consequently, he felt that aspirational issues of leadership were some way off.

> *'In keeping with many organisations of our size, particularly in the charitable sector, I think it's an area we at which we don't do well. Possibly, we compensate for that in some ways by a caring atmosphere within the team. When I took over my current role about fifteen to sixteen months ago, I inherited a situation where, although we are a small team, we had an incredibly hierarchical system where effectively only one person in the staff team actually knew what was going on. One of the things I've attempted to do is to have a flat structure, so that hopefully we are now more of one team rather than three very small teams. Some of the people that are working in our organisation have got emotionally draining or challenging roles, and they need support and opportunities to increase their skill levels in dealing with callers.'*

All of this seems to be a good pragmatic solution through team building to the problems facing the Lymphoma Association. The positive results have since shone through. When we talked of dilemmas, Alan Bartle recounted the issue with which he had to grapple taking over as Chief Executive. It was the issue that prompted the departure of his predecessor.

> *'I guess the biggest dilemma was within the last eighteen months or so, when we were facing effectively a deficit budget for the forthcoming year. At that stage, the then CEO proposed some very harsh cuts in terms of our service provision. For instance, his proposal was that we should reduce the newsletter, which is our quarterly publication and the most valued part of what we provide, from four issues per year to two. That caused a lot of angst amongst the staff. We knew if that happened it would severely impact on what was going on. That was all part of what happened with the previous CEO leaving.'*

The solution demonstrated the difference between blinkered cost cutting, leading to a depressed workforce, and trading out of deficit in a positive fashion.

> *'What we actually said was that, if we have got our targets right in terms of meeting the needs, then we believe that we have got a very good product to sell to funders. That is precisely what we did. We said*

to the fundraising team, now go out and sell it.'

As a result, Alan said, instead of having the projected deficit of £70,000 for the year, the combination of this and the previous hard work resulted in the Association actually being something like £70,000 to the good.

> *'I believe there was something about the positive responsive atmosphere and message, and the fact that the whole team —as opposed to the three separate teams —was motivated and was willing to move forward, that meant that we struck success.'*

I feel this is a brilliant example of leadership in the 'glass half full' category. The end result was that the fundraisers felt they had something to sell. The external circumstances were the same, and yet the organisation went from deficit to surplus and the newsletter was retained. Alan was sensitive to the potential effect on morale:

> *'Had we gone ahead with cutting the newsletter to two issues, the person who edits the newsletter would have had her hours reduced significantly, so she would have been less motivated.'*

Leadership is all about having the right person for the right time, situational leadership. Just as Dianne Thompson of Camelot was the right person to pick a fight with the competition and the regulator; Alan Bartle can see differences in style between him and his predecessor. He referred to our earlier discussion of being extrovert and to the antennae concept.

> *'Without being unkind, to my predecessor, the reality was that he rarely went out of his office. Now in an organisation like our own, I am only in the office for about 50 per cent of the time. The rest of the time I'm out and about. It is a question of creating opportunities to promote the organisation and also motivate people as team members.'*

C   'PHOENIX' ORGANISATIONS

For Bryan Jackson at Toyota, leadership is not about dealing with crises and critical interventions but much more about encouraging leadership amongst a wider population. Hence the basis is a well thought out system. There are some twenty defined leadership competencies, relating to measurable objectives. The process of developing leaders is to assess for competence and then train for improvement. The underlying ethos is to create a blame free culture – it's OK to make mistakes. Hence the bosses' attitudes are crucial. If those being trained for leadership positions are afraid to make individual decisions then there will be an erosion of confidence in their own competence. Just as at Komatsu and Nissan, there was a good grounding in 'Nemawashi' (or transplanting ideas) and 'Hoshin Kanri' (or catch-ball with ideas) – all of which are Total Quality products!

Bryan's definition of the role of the leader is to develop people by making the company a pleasing place to work, and to make things happen through mutual respect.

Having got such proven systems in place, Bryan admitted that they were finding the issue of emotional intelligence a new subject which they were starting to explore. Turning to leadership dilemmas, Bryan felt that at times strong leadership was required. This needed to be forthright and direct in order to give clarity and gain understanding. Essentially, he saw leadership as being about bringing the team with you and recognising the differing skills required. It was not about dogmatic initiation of others.

In Unipart Automotive, Paul Forman took a characteristically individual stance. His useful insights included some in particular which stressed the link between good management and the acknowledgement of limitations.

> 'It's as important to know what you are not good at, as well as what you are good at, as a manager, and complement those skills with others around you. There is a strong correlation between people who are good general managers, and those who are able to openly acknowledge their limitations.'

On the topics of emotional intelligence and teams, Paul said:

> 'If you can empathise with other people, and can or do have the emotional intelligence to understand, then there are a multiplicity of styles you have to adopt with people.'

D   CONSULTANCY/OUTSOURCING

Tim Watts of Pertemps takes a personal view on encouraging leadership qualities.

> 'Most importantly, we need to sell ourselves and not let arrogance get in the way. I place great importance in our Induction Programme, particularly to get across the message, I will invest in you.'

Bill Penney thought that, although he had learned a lot about himself and the issue of emotional intelligence, this was not universal.

> 'Certainly I think knowing myself is very important. I reflect on that, and I have had help reflecting on it, and I think I have learned a lot. I'm not sure that other members of the team see that as a priority for themselves, and I don't think I've done an enormous

amount to help them do that, if I'm honest. I think there is a lot of emotion that is suppressed.'

Peter Smith of The Strategic Partnership felt that there was a fundamental need to change the way boards are appointed.

'The whole basis on which boards are managed needs lot of attention and rethinking. The Chairman and CEO relationship is a difficult one and not enough thought is given to that relationship by both parties.'

Lastly, Peter Ward of Telos takes the trouble to define how the leadership style works in his firm:

'To know yourself and others is fundamental to our business. We are a band of independent people who have inter-dependency rather than a co-dependency. That only works if you are independently minded. So there is a huge amount of self-knowledge, and Telos people are encouraged to discover even more.'

Asked whether you have got to know yourself before you can lead others, Peter thought that probably you did. I asked if there was there anything special about good leaders. Peter said that Telos was greatly influenced by the idea of 'Level Five leadership' (Jim Collins).[1]

'(It is) the quiet influencers, pushing people, encouraging people, working through people. I think leadership is about consistency and constancy. It is about allowing the purpose and values to determine what you will do in all situations. That's why your purpose has to be unchanging.'

This takes us back to vision and values. In the corporate context, Peter cited the example of Sir Stuart Hampson, Chairman of the John Lewis Partnership and the way he dealt with news reports calling for the flotation of John Lewis.

'In an environment that was demutualising anything that was standing still, he made it quite clear that the constitution would not permit such a move. And this is an era where nothing is sacred and constitutions are there to be changed! I'm a great believer that any legal agreement, foundation agreement, articles of association can be overturned if you have the will to do so. But Stuart had the courage, the leadership to say, 'No'. It's quite wrong to change.'

Peter went on to express the opinion that we will need to reinvent mutuals in order to re-create financial institutions with heart and soul. He wondered how long it would be before someone had the courage to do so. No more need be said!

II   M&A/DEMERGER ORGANISATIONS

Syd Pennington of Royal and Sun Alliance totally agreed with the first point. He had found from his early experience as a manager in Marks and Spencer that unless managers were able, in his words, to 'solve their own personal equation' they would not be effective at managing and being responsible for other people. He explained what he meant by this:

> 'Before you can look after somebody else, you've got to be clear who you are, why you are here, and what you want from life. I think until an individual can clearly say all that, they are ill-equipped to manage other people.'

He related this concept to the later experience in Royal and Sun Alliance of needing cross-functional working, and the values of Truth and Trust and Teamwork, we described in the previous chapter.

> 'I started to think there was some real credence to the fact that you need to know yourself and others, but I don't think it is encouraged anywhere, in general. What I am convinced about is that the rate of change is such that a business will only be successful if it can marshal cross-functional teams to address the really difficult issues it needs to address, because of the complexity and speed of change, and different technology.
>
> That's why I think truth, trust and teamwork are so critical. If to start off with you can be open and honest with each other, you've got a chance then that you'll build trust. If you've got trust you can have a team and operate as a team.'

Syd was not so sure about the concept of emotional intelligence, although I suspect this may have been more because of the terminology. .

> 'Where we're not so sold on some of the modern concepts is this issue of emotional intelligence. I'm quite a touchy, feely manager, and quite an empathetic manager, and pretty good at managing people, but I think quite a lot of the conceptual stuff around emotional intelligence has kind of vanished.'

However, Syd used the proposed definition of leadership in dealing effectively with dilemmas neatly to put the business case for diversity:

> 'One of the things in which we are struggling to be effective as an organisation is in being able truly to develop a real diversity in its widest sense. Why does a business want any kind of diversity? Because a business should reflect the ethnic nature of its customer base.'

Somehow this financial services industry doesn't attract ethnic minorities in any real quantity. It goes beyond searching for a mix, disabled people, and gender mix. If you want to manage dilemmas and resolve them, I think the more diverse a group you've got, the more effective you will be at resolving dilemmas.'

The discussion went on to the necessity to have a balance of personality types in order to 'think outside the box' as well as deal effectively with day-to-day operations.

'There's a lot of evidence that people who can think outside the box are the last kind of people who make very good operational people, but they're important to businesses because of their particular ability. Einstein didn't pick up his theory of relativity while he was in the office or when he was in his work place. He was on a boat out one afternoon, if you like, enjoying himself, apparently when the thing came to him.'

In terms of a dilemma that demonstrated leadership, Syd pointed to the support he had had from the top of the organisation in pursuing the long term cultural change while all the pressure from shareholders was for short term results.

'I think that one of the really key dilemmas for which I've admired them is that, over the three years of the turn round, when the huge pressure was on short term results, they have supported me in all the cultural change things that I wanted to do.'

As Syd went on to say, this included investment in the development of a corporate university.

'I've been able to receive investment to develop a corporate university to continue to upskill people in the organisation. When I arrived and started to look at this, we found there wasn't any substantial investment in people. What's also clear nowadays is that if you're not continually upskilling your people, they will leave, not because of not getting enough money, but because they're not enhancing their skill set, they're not widening their CV.'

So, I asked, what results were looked for from this investment? Interestingly, Syd reported that RS & A were not looking to measure them in any direct way.

'Just a real, natural, belief that it is worth the investment and that this core of people, and what they can do, and what they can achieve for the organisation, will be important to the long term viability of the business.'

This is somewhat of a step of faith, in the face of short-term pressures.

In putting the same set of questions to Mike Rake of KPMG, he thought the propositions did ring true, but he started his response by separating the issues of developing managers and leaders.

> 'Put simplistically, you can train people to be managers but I think it's very difficult to train good leaders. I think you can bring out the leadership qualities within people, and give them the opportunities to see whether they have those leadership qualities. But I think real leadership is about an extraordinary balance between sensitivities, self-confidence, emotional intelligence, communication skills, all of the sorts of things in which it is really hard to train anyone.'

So if leaders are in such short supply, I asked, how do you develop them in KPMG? Mike replied that they tried to create an environment where people are given opportunities to push themselves, and develop their skills. The firm had all the practical help they might need right the way through their careers.

> 'No one can become a partner in the firm unless they have 'out of box experience', that is, they've gone to another country or they have gone on to government. It is what we are doing on the way through that really allows natural leaders to come through.'

Again, like Syd Pennington, Mike recognised the need for the balance of personalities in the team.

> 'You can have what the Americans would call, good cop/bad cop with the visionary and the guy who gets things done. That's often the best team in any organisation.'

In terms of dealing with dilemmas Mike saw this in terms of taking risks, which, at the time, were greeted with scepticism but subsequently were seen to work.

> 'I think in a number of key areas we have exercised leadership, and taken risks, which people have seen have worked. Going to one single UK firm, and launching the values, was a big risk. Most of our partners thought I'd lost it completely, and they couldn't believe it when it worked. They were astounded. The integration of our European practices, which people couldn't believe we'd do, has been amazingly successful too. We've accomplished that off the back of the values, and relating it to people. So I think people now believe that the senior leadership of the firm have not only set a direction but tried to live by example and are completely determined to keep their systems and never to give up on it.'

Another example Mike described was the hard issue of redundancies, and how to handle them. Mike had a perspective on how it was done a decade earlier.

'For example, we did have to get rid of 300 consultants because of the real, dramatic cutbacks in the IT sector. We handled that in a way based on the values, which gave us no backlash at all. If I go back, as a person caught in the middle of it, to the way in 1990 or 1991 that we handled the need to fire 700 people, we were just firing ten people at a time and wheeling them out the door. We then destroyed, for years, the whole relationship and trust.'

Mike sees the way KPMG handles these situations today as a product of the culture change, values, trust and communication.

For Todd Abbott of Cisco, leadership development processes should be present on a formal basis, with a concentration on the top echelon. He explained that Cisco spent a lot of time highlighting and identifying who is in that top 15-20 per cent of the organisation. There is a different development cycle for them than for people in the middle 50 per cent.

'There is a tiering of investment, and a tiering of development, from a formal and from an informal perspective. But we spend a lot of time helping people to think outside the box, knowing themselves, and developing and identifying weaknesses or areas for improvement. We are putting together custom curricula to help people through their own development.'

However, turning to the relevance of 'Emotional Intelligence', Todd says that this is considered a more informal, ad hoc, way, individual by individual. It could do with more systematic application.

'I tend to think that it should be a formalised element of the process, but at present it's not a formal element of what we had focused on. The individual and the team starts with the team first and then the individual, not the other way round. You absolutely have to be part of the team.'

For Todd, the test of a good leader is how the team carries on when he or she has moved on, and how future leaders are developed.

'Our view is that you can always tell the strength of a leader during the six months that they leave a job, because that's pure momentum, that's how well they have developed the team below them. Does the team think without them, be empowered and to run the business.

The number one thing that we look for in leadership is development of the future leaders. It's developing their talent to think outside the box, and take risks. I tell my guys that, as a director and above, 80 per cent of your job is people. Everything you do, jumping into deals, jumping into critical accounts, never lose sight of the fact that there's got to be two or three guys running along with you that are willing and able to do it.'

Todd believes in constructive confrontation over these issues in developing leaders.

> '*I never have an issue with somebody making a mistake, as long as you are willing to own your part... If you're going to give excuses, if you're going to try to hide, if you're not going to face up to it then, we can't have a decent discussion to accelerate the learning process.*'

Todd saw leadership dilemmas in terms of strategy and determination:

> '*Going through the depression of the telecoms consolidation over the last twelve months has been the biggest dilemma, the biggest challenge, I have faced in my career. The process that we went through, over about six months to develop a strategy which could combat and to respond to the challenges was a very strong collaborative effort.*'

I asked Todd what the approach to his leaders had been about this.

> '*We're going to get through this and, you know what guys, I don't have all the answers. We've got to figure it out together. We did that with a lot of emotion and passion, and we came out of it with a strategy that makes sense.*'

Sally Vanson at MCL/The Performance Solution felt that they had used these specified methods of development, but with varying degrees of success. She saw this in terms of culture and generalisation.

> '*I'd hate to generalise, and it's probably more about our culture, but first of all, all of our directors and managers apart from me are male (that's the motor industry). I would say development has generally worked with anybody under fifty-five who is not a senior director. At main board level it very definitely does not work. There's something about it that once you're at main board level, you've made it. So why would they want development it because they've got there anyway.*'

I seem to have heard this before – 'if you're God you're not trainable'! The contrast Sally paints is far too typical of the difference in reception of these ideas at different hierarchical levels in organisations.

> '*Divisional directors tend to be younger in years but also younger in years of service to the group since they've come in from other companies, with much more openness, much more willingness to explore themselves, their own attitudes, their beliefs, personality, emotional intelligence. We've recently talked about the use of intuition in business. There is a lot more interest, and it's much easier to work with them and they are willing to explore on an individual basis, or*

with the team. For example we took out one MD and his three other directors that report to him. He was very willing to chat, he was one of the group, and there was no status. He then invited me to join the team, because obviously I pop in and out of these teams. They were all very happy to talk in front of me and allow me to join in. It was a very much a sharing-looking at each other's strengths and weaknesses and so on, as opposed to our main board. There we brought in consultants, who worked with them for eighteen months, only for the team to decide they didn't like each other, there was no way they were going to give, share, talk, they didn't have any weaknesses and the whole thing just folded. It's sad, it's fear...'

It was obviously not for want of trying! As Sally explained,

'They've been through personality profiling, they've been through Belbin, they've been through 360 degree feedback. They're very happy to tick all the boxes and get the feedback, but it's an intellectual exercise. They don't own it. It's not theirs. One even refused to have had the feedback. He was very happy to do the tests, and for me to have the feedback, but he wasn't interested in knowing. One other, who could do the personality stuff, couldn't take the 360 feedback because that involved his direct reports. I was halfway through the feedback and he said 'I can't take this any more, I don't want to hear another word about it, go away'.'

Sally commented that the effect of this was to delay the change programme, because the CEO had to find another way of dealing with the individuals concerned.

'We started this change programme five years ago, and we could have been so much further on if these people had got behind the CEO, put personal issues to one side, and worked as a team. Instead of that, he's had to adopt a strategy where he works with the people as individuals, which therefore delays the progress of the business.'

As an example of dealing with a fundamental dilemma, the CEO clearly made an intuitive decision on when to get out of the old business. He then used his leadership skills to take the Board along with him. Sally reflected on another dilemma, the issue of having to give up Mazda to Ford.

'On the one hand pride was involved, the fact that our company started out as Mazda, so there was the barrier about loss of face. 'We've always been lucky, and if we hang on we will get through it this time'. Opposed to this was the fact that we were losing so much money on every car that we wouldn't have a company if we'd kept it. So the dilemma was, what do we do? Do we wait and hope, do we find more creative ways of selling cars –we looked at selling online and so on – or do we just go with the flow and let Ford take it. That

decision was made very quickly by the CEO as the leader rather than the Board. Then, having made the decision, it was beautifully managed, which meant it cost us the absolute minimum to get rid of it, Ford got what they wanted and everybody won.'

It is all about how you deal with the dilemma, the processes you use, not necessarily the decision itself.

III PUBLIC TO PRIVATE

All of the businesses in this category see themselves in transition. In many cases, the transition is from 'managing' to 'leading'. In their pre-privatised form, the focus of these organisations would have been on managing assets in a risk-averse way. The important things in the public sector pre-1990 would have been issues of consistency, ability to escape criticism, a focus on administration, and 'engineering' solutions.

It was a command and control structure where survival by 'keeping your head down' was the order of the day. I can recall this from a brief spell in a predecessor of AWG – the Essex River Authority, where I was Works Engineer between 1970 and 1974. Whenever an issue came up that had to be reported to the governing body (The Committee) of the Authority, the first question always was, 'What did we say to The Committee last time?' Consistency was the order of the day.

Post privatisation, these organisations have all made deliberate efforts to change the culture of management towards one of leadership, although often for very different reasons and priorities.

For GB Rail, the priority has been customer service. I quoted Jeremy Long in the last Chapter as pinning the priority on front line staff knowing how their leaders would react when faced with certain situations at the customer interface. It is about developing a level of confidence, where customer-facing staff can use discretion. Jeremy sees the same factors in developing leaders. He believes that the issue of 'knowing yourself and others' also depends on confidence.

'Knowing yourself and others, you can only do that once you've got a certain confidence. It's like any group, whether family or friends, you can only start being rude about your best mate! If you can be humorous at the same time, so much the better.'

Sir John Egan saw the issue as both knowing which leaders would be good in certain situations, and at the same time balancing skills in the team.

'Firstly, you actually have to know yourself, know what you're good

at and, particularly, what you're bad at. The reason is that, for example, it could be that some people are brilliant in a crisis, and tend to emerge with solutions which are fundamentally better. The second thing, of course, is the team of people that you've got around you, because there's a limit to what you as an individual can do. You've got to make sure that if you're bad at something, you've got somebody in the team who's good at it, so hopefully one of you can actually do these difficult things.'

Bob Mason, formerly of BT, recognised the tensions in the 'soft skills' approach to leadership but saw their inclusion as vital, a point that was often not understood.

'How can any leader, or person in a position of responsibility run that organisation without a good dose of all three of those things? Yes, he might be ultimately the best equipped person to read a balance sheet, or understand the financial engineering of the business, but if he can't motivate a team or express himself, communicate his ideas, all of those things, he's not in touch with the feelings of the organisation. I think that hard-edged business acumen is going to take someone only so far.'

Then there are the internal tensions:

'I've also seen the reaction when the business tries to develop greater emotional intelligence and people wade in wielding the bottom line stick. 'Never mind all this soft stuff, show me the results'.'

Also, there is the need to justifying this approach to the City:

'I think that the other people that haven't wholly bought this yet are the City, in valuing businesses. I don't think they spend enough time looking for these qualities in the executive teams in which they're going to invest their money. They'll pay scant regard to the emotional intelligence of the senior team, and ultimately it will be that which will have an impact on their investments in the future.'

This tension, described by Bob, immediately put me in mind of the dilemma that faced BioFocus in succession planning for new leadership, and in thinking of the internal and external view of leadership.

For BAA, the progression from management of assets to leadership has taken the form of defined competences. Tony Ward saw the tension that Bob Mason identified, and his solution was to limit spend by focusing on immediate business priorities. However, he admitted this didn't allow enough depth to get to what he termed 'the shared leadership concept'.

'We have introduced several programmes which create self-insight in some depth. We've had to target that, because of how much you can

spend on it, but nevertheless it's still quite significant. The emotional intelligence dimension comes through very strongly around judgement, enabling others, future focus, learning from others, working together, stakeholder focus, providing meaning.'

For Tony, the stakeholder focus was not seen as transitory with intermittent priority, but central to business needs.

'What I'm talking about is a model of constant balancing the different stakeholders. Because we are a public service company in the private sector, our shareholders are very important. The government is very important, our local communities are critical, our employees are equally critical, and so are our business partners, because we don't manage a lot of the offerings we provide and the Government license us to operate and grow. So we've got a real balance of stakeholders in the business. That is the business case for us.'

Chris Mellor saw these three bullet points as fundamental to development of leadership in AWG. They were the means of translating the culture from one of command and control and risk aversion to risk taking and being successfully entrepreneurial. He saw the process through which the AWG leaders had gone so as to tap into Emotional Intelligence as instrumental in reinventing the business. Talking about knowing yourself and others, Chris said:

'I think that's essential to being a good leader. You have to have an awareness of what sets off reactions in you, some of which are irrational, and you have to learn to control them rather than let them control you. If you can't do that, you won't develop the trust that is required. We sympathise with something that we call projection and reflection, whereby the reflections that you get back from people, or their perceptions or reactions to what you say, are very much literally a reflection of the way you tell it.'

His comment on Emotional Intelligence was:

'We're human beings, and we've got two parts to our brain. I've seen so many examples that demonstrate that you don't get very far until the whole brain is engaged. At the very best, you only get half the result you were looking for.'

He also commented on individuals and teams:

'At senior level, we have done a lot of work trying to put together teams in terms of how they think and their basic psychology. All our people participate in psychometric tests, so they understand their basic type and preference. As a conscious factor in developing the team we try to ensure that we have a good mix. Then we have tried to study team dynamics, how people interact with one another, how

*people think in different situations, and how people's different skills
can be used in different stages of decision making.'*

Chris took a personal view on what this meant in terms of the role
for himself.

*'I think leadership, certainly at the top level in a company, is mainly
about managing relationships. Sometimes I think my job is really
about trying to create the right perception of the company in the
outside environment, and the Executive is really just managing the
top team, confronting the issues as they arise, and trying to set the
right example in terms of how we should behave.'*

In reflecting on how different this is today from the pre-privatisation
days, Chris can take a very personal perspective of then and now,
having been with AWG and its predecessors for over thirty years:

*'If there was a serious problem, then it invariably became the source
of simple friction between senior people as one person sought to cover
their backside by laying blame on another. Now, we sit down
together, we try to say honestly what's our part. Everybody has a
part, and nobody at a senior level can say 'It's not mine, it's nothing
to do with me'. So we try to own our part. We have got to a level of
trust, where people express their emotions; it might be anger or
sadness, the whole gamut. I think it's just that initial process that
clears the way, clears the air. Then we move forward and try and
address what the issue is. In the past we promoted sticking plaster
solutions that weren't long-term solutions, weren't facing up to the
issues and, from the commercial point of view, promoting extreme
risk aversion. Now we're in business to take risks. You don't grow
and reap rewards without taking a few risks – you have to manage
those risks.'*

Chris described the pay off from the investment in leadership
development in changing the culture of AWG in these terms:

*'It's created the environment in which we have really started to
create some growth, and maybe we are more of a risk-taking
organisation now. In another organisation that didn't have our
heritage and our roots, that might not have been as necessary, but we
had to kick start getting into a different gear. Creating that licence to
take the risk within that supportive framework of trust is very
important.'*

The contribution that Chris made to leadership development in
AWG was immense, but regrettably it was not recognised by some
shareholders and others with short-term objectives and he was
forced out of office in March 2003.

Leadership and Dilemmas

Our leaders agreed that leadership could be defined as effectively dealing with and resolving dilemmas, although this was perhaps only one definition amongst many possible. Jeremy Long saw the good leader anticipating the dilemmas by spotting the inconsistencies, relating several sources of information on what is going, on so that major dilemmas are headed off or avoided. It was about listening and not dictating: -

> *'The days of the autocrat in business are finished. It's not a question of whether they fail; I think it's a question of when they fail. The chances of the autocratic business being sustainable, I think, are non-existent.'*

John Egan saw the way to deal with dilemmas as through going back to the fundamental mission and vision of the business, a definition of constant purpose.

> *'Whenever you're into a dilemma and into a crisis, you go back to what you fundamentally believe in as a business. You try to act as closely in line with that mission and vision that you have for your company. Although it might not be the most short-term easy thing to do.'*

John then went on to talk about the event on the Heathrow Express project that came out of the blue, and has been seen since as the turning point and the catalyst for decisive partnership.

> *'When we had our huge tunnel collapse at Heathrow, the first thing that most people normally would have done was to get the lawyers in to see how we could take it out on the contractors. The contractors had already gathered in evidence to say that ground effects had made some contribution. The courts could have spent a good couple of years over it.*
>
> *We did a very rapid analysis amongst the team, the two possible directions, and it was pretty obvious that if we wanted a railway, and if we wanted to recover the project, we would have to do it our way. I was helped, strangely enough, by knowing the Chairman of Balfour Beatty. By the most extraordinary piece of luck, he used to be my next-door neighbour in Leamington Spa. I phoned him up and said 'Bob, this is a tough one. Why don't we just talk it over and decide what to do?*
>
> *We met, and I believe I said, 'I have no idea whether it's your fault or my fault but I know we have to get the job done. Let's co-operate as much as we can and let's share the costs of putting it right 50-50.' We shook hands and we also said, that, if in future any really big problem comes up, and they don't know how to answer it, you and I will settle down and we'll reach an agreement ourselves.*

We put in a partnership process on the whole supply chain. Do you know, we trebled the productivity of most processes, and we actually put in a preliminary service, not using the tunnelling system but stopping at a station short of it, but actually on time. When you think that nothing happened on site for a whole year, you actually realise we gained seven months back. If we had gone to war, I'm sure it would have been a 100 per cent overrun. Instead, we met with only a 15 per cent overrun.'

This example shows how leadership can deal with dilemmas based on a great deal of trust.

In interviewing Tony Ward, who is currently on the Executive at BAA, it is clear that the focus on mission fostered by Sir John continues after his departure. Tony's reply about dealing with dilemmas was that it goes back to the mission: 'We focus on our customers' needs and safety'. As a result:

'Providing a healthy and safe working environment and security is the highest priority at all times. So that's the managing of a dilemma. In many situations, we are faced with a cost versus safety, or cost versus security, issue. We make it very clear that safety and security are our highest priorities at all times, to try and simplify it for people.

For example, we have the balancing act of security and customer convenience. You've got business dilemmas and you've got process dilemmas. An example might be security queuing, which can irritate people having their bags and themselves checked, because they're always anxious at that point in their journey. They want to get through into the departure lounge and we try for customer service reasons to keep those queues short (although we don't always achieve it). We continue to invest in improved forecasting and planning, but our airline partners have operating difficulties and traffic jams occur, so we can get hit at the wrong times, but we try to manage to give customer service, high security and both at a reasonable cost.'

This has meant that BAA has sacrificed short-term profits for sustainability and looking after the interests of all stakeholders, not just one set.

'It does depend on what you pursue. If you don't start off with a balanced stakeholder model, then you'll get it wrong, for example, if you focus only on certain of the stakeholders, or if you don't recognise that safety is your first priority in this type of industry, but it's high risk. This is why for some years we have put safety, and getting that right, as our number one priority. We have quite strong discussions with our business partners, who are not used to working to the safety standards we operate, and we have to enforce that.'

BAA is not a total monopoly provider. It started with the core
airport facilities at Heathrow, Gatwick, Stansted and Glasgow and
since then has grown by acquiring more facilities, as the business
has been able to afford it.

In contrast, on privatisation, BT started with a total 100 per cent
monopoly of UK telecommunication services (with the single, and
small, exception of Hull). With privatisation, and with the regulator's
plans to introduce competition, BT was faced with a different
dilemma. Bob Mason explained:

> *'I think leadership and business, certainly large corporate business, is
> all about resolving dilemmas. I suppose, over the last ten years, the
> classic dilemma for BT I suppose over the last ten years has been
> that you start off with 100 per cent of the market, you've got a
> regulator who's determined you'll end up with a lot less than 100 per
> cent, but you want to remain a competitive and growing business.
> How do you do that?*
>
> *BT has met the challenge through strategies which ultimately grow
> the market. Certainly in the UK consumer market, and to some
> extent in the corporate markets, the market is now much, much
> bigger than it ever was, and BT's revenues are much bigger than
> they ever were, despite their smaller market share.'*

The growth of the business was managed by the same value set as
was the reducing monopoly business.

> *'What's also important is that that competition is dealt with and
> managed fairly. It's back to ethics. The company has always
> maintained a very principled, ethical stance on the way it will
> compete. Some things are written into its licence, but it won't
> predatory price, it won't disparage competitors. It would sell its own
> features rather than disparage its competitors.'*

Earlier in this chapter, Chris Mellor was quoted on the contrast
between the historical way, under the old regime, of dealing with
issues, and the new culture, which avoids blame and encourages
learning. This meant that dilemmas in AWG were not the province
of one leader at the top, but were shared by a wider group who
knew what strengths they could bring to resolving those dilemmas.
They were then able to embrace managed risk.

IV PUBLIC SECTOR AND PFI

The public sector sees itself as continually being held up to X-ray
examination in terms of efficiency and effectiveness. It is not really
sure where its salvation comes from. Is it from the top, where

leaders are in prominent and 'public' positions, that is ministers with a political stance for public sector delivery? Or can leaders be produced down the organisations, as distinct from managers of a resource that have to operate at the interface, between the grand design from the top and the rough reality at the 'coalface' as Nonaka and Takeuchi[2] put it or, for the enlightened, 'the customer face'.

Certainly ministers in UK's New Labour administration have verbally gravitated from a desire for central control (since, after all, the centre provides the money) to recognising that, without local autonomy, many centrally led initiatives are akin to eunuchs. The problem is how to achieve effective autonomy that produces global or at least national results. The NHS is a perfect example. Unlike many government departments, it starts with a degree of local autonomy and local leadership. As we saw in the previous Chapter, doctors have retained a considerable degree of independence since nationalisation in 1948. Also, the creation in 1990 by the previous Conservative administration of NHS Trusts enshrined further corporate autonomy, at least in theory. The policy did not guarantee success at local level. It depended on successful leadership. The same applied to the Training and Enterprise Councils (TECs) that, in the view of the Labour administration, ended up with very 'patchy' performance.

Even with localised success, governments end up with another problem. How do you spread success? How do you transfer best practice from one part of a silo organisation to another? At the other extreme, if from the centre you take a 'sheep dip' approach to ensure consistency, then you're unlikely to encourage leadership, ownership and an entrepreneurial attitude in the outlying sub-organisations.

In our conversation, Professor Sir Liam Donaldson recognised that the NHS has come to leadership development rather late but was catching up fast:

'I think the NHS has come to the concept of leadership development late. It's starting to take off now, but until now I think the assumption has been that leaders are born and not made. We've tended to rely on that. We've now got a lot of initiatives in place. We've got a Leadership Centre, which is within the Modernisation Agency. With clinical leadership, most Medical/Clinical Directors have not had any formal training, or not very much. We haven't invested enough in the past and that's recognised now. I think the other side of it is that some of those modern ideas like 'emotional intelligence' and so on haven't impinged yet at all. I think the other

thing about leadership in the NHS is that we're in a culture that's very risk-averse, so the opportunity for the entrepreneurial manager is much more limited, because the penalties of failure are very high. I think that boxes you in to certain styles of leadership. I think it's very much a steady style of leadership. Obviously you need motivational and inspirational people, but you can't depart too far from the technical task.'

However there was still a difference in perception between the management streams and clinical specialties.

'I think management is closer to understanding true leadership. I think a lot of doctors think of it as management training. Within their medical training they're never told how to manage staff or manage budgets and their first thought is about the practicalities. Help me to read a budget statement. Help me to understand what to do when I need to discipline a member of staff when they're not turning up for work, or so on and so forth.

As for teaching leadership, Liam Donaldson believes it is difficult in the medical field to create situations for learning.

'I think that, on the whole, too many big decisions are taken in isolation. It's difficult to create the opportunities to allow people who are developing lower down the line to watch the process of deliberation on some of those big decisions. They are often taken rapidly. They are often taken in crisis-laden circumstances. I'm sure there are ways of replicating that, but in busy, reactive organisations it is quite difficult to document things so they can be used as case studies.'

From the perspective of the individual NHS Trust, Malcolm Lowe-Lauri takes a slightly more optimistic view. He argues that

'Front line managers have an increasing amount of empowerment, and teams are led well, with emphasis on socialising and team development. Individuals are taken through development programmes. I am convinced that people want to get a good job done.'

Malcolm felt that there was no doubt about the quality of so many of the NHS employees and management, particularly in terms of academic and professional capabilities. However, he acknowledged the impediments of the structure: -

'(The NHS is) a series of highly individual and powerful corner shops, complex, with individuals having various citizenships. Who is the employer? Who does the individual work for? Those who are stable and long standing, see the 'employer' moving around with the many reorganisations (politically driven), which have taken place

over the years. So the core is constant, but it is the core which needs constantly to change and respond to the new demands.'

John Bridge, looking at leadership and learning from the One NorthEast viewpoint believes that:

'Companies and individuals work best in open and rich information environments. So it is a bit like the plankton-rich sea. You get all sorts of people that thrive in it. So perhaps, in the past, individual companies felt that the possession of knowledge, and the retention of that knowledge amongst a very limited number of people, actually provided them with significant power – but only for a short period of time. The really clever organisations should share that knowledge in the very early stages of its acquisition, so that individuals operate in a very rich environment.'

This is a strong argument for travelling from the belief that knowledge is power (the mark of the protective manager) to knowledge shared (the mark of the perceptive leader). John and I shared views about the development of his Board, and the importance of such leaders agreeing on shared values.

'If all your Board are coming in with a very different view about where you're trying to get to, then that's going to be extremely difficult. Now the shared values come through the regional economic strategy – that's where we cracked it. We literally took the Board away over two forty-eight-hour periods and sat them down and, in effect, we ended up asking three questions. The first question was, Where are we now? given the paucity of regional data. And then the second question was, Where do we want to be in ten years time? Of course, the general answer to that question is income from very, very different sources than now. The third question was, Where are we going to do whatever we're going to do? – and that told you a lot about location.'

This accords with my experience in developing other boards and what we do with our clients in Board Performance Ltd. It is necessary to give time to share where board members are coming from, and to use this process to decide upon strategy. I am convinced that the similar process we went through for the board at Peterborough Hospitals gave the opportunity and focus for radical change below⋆ – it set the tone.

For John and his board, progress has been far from straightforward. In the early 90s, after the demise of much of the indigenous manufacturing, the high technology future showed much promise. Siemens established a state-of-the-art silicon chip plant at North Tyneside at a reported cost of £50m. However, due to the

---

⋆ For details on the 'change below' see Appendix III

later worldwide glut of these products, it was closed within eight months of opening. John explained this experience from the perspective of transitions.

> 'Siemens is actually a very interesting bridge between the past and the future. If you look at them in the past culture, Siemens is a solid manufacturing building block. It's a bit like shipbuilding, like steel, allowing the licence of language, a bit like all these traditional industries, it's a new traditional industry which has come and it will stay. It's actually telling us is that we as a region are never, ever going to be in a steady state. We're actually going to be in a constant state of flux, and we'd better get used to it. We'd better plan for it, and we'd better get people understanding that.'

This in fact is the essence of this book. I argue that this constant state of flux needs to be recognised as the norm, together with finding out how to deal with it. For John and his board, this calls for radical thinking and action. It is not about tinkering or minor changes in direction.

> 'If I was able to say to people in the north east, looking at the regional economy, 'As far as we can see, from a deep analysis of the situation, 95 per cent of the north-east economy is working extremely well', that would be an immensely comforting message to give out, because 95 per cent of the people would say 'It's nothing to do with me.' That's not the message. The message is that a very high proportion is in need of substantial change. Therefore we are involved in a very, very radical change within the regional economy. That doesn't go down at all well, because it suddenly tells people that the vast majority are in the wrong place, doing the wrong thing, at the wrong time.'

The prognosis is a challenge to complacency, and it applies to the majority of sectors we are studying.

For Peter Hewitt, at Arts Council England, a large slice of leadership is dealing with emotions and being frank about weaknesses.

> 'I personally don't have difficulty being open about my weaknesses; I recognise that I need to deliver emotional intelligence to the senior management team. If it could it be achieved it would be ultimately beneficial.'

From the Learning and Skills Council's viewpoint, Jenny Clarke can perceive the leadership issue from the corporate perspective, and she sees the tensions between following the leader and the brand.

> 'In my experience, it was not always the leaders who resolved the dilemmas. The best organisations were those who empowered the

*people. Teamwork in delivering results was critical, as was the ability
to develop team dynamics. That sometimes required both internal
and external coaching.*

*The Council has recently worked with Call Centres where team
loyalty was in evidence and was strong. The tension became evident
when loyalty to the team leader became stronger than the loyalty to
the customer or to the brand.'*

Philip Johnson again sees the tensions between what he sees as
leadership practised by clients of the Patent Office and the Civil
Service mentality within it, where there is little incentive to be
innovative or to challenge or question. Philip believes the successful
and entrepreneurial business leaders must inspire and give people
space to succeed. He sees his role as a change agent (and therefore a
leader in my book!) but recognises that senior management will
have to lead the culture change towards customer focus. At present
there is too much emphasis on 'conformance' issues from the top,
for example statistics or web site hits, rather than 'performance'.[3]

In Bovis Lend Lease Mike Walters faces the almost diametric
opposite of Philip Johnson's experience. Whereas the theme for the
Patent Office is constant (and consistent) administration, Mike and
his colleagues deal with a steady flow of changing project-based
business, and often a steady flow of people. So the emphasis at
Bovis is to train senior teams in leadership development and to have
clear succession planning.

*'At Bovis there is Leadership development for senior teams.
However, it is more strategic development rather than the soft issues,
although these do come up as part of the modules. We have a very
extensive training and learning programme. The Directors also
went through a 360-appraisal system and receive personal
development. There is clear succession planning to identify future
leaders. We have Springboard courses to bring together people from
all over the world and develop their leadership as well as 'Uniting
Europe' courses.'*

Mike did not recognise the issue of dilemmas, probably because to
the construction industry it is meat and drink, in that they always
have to be swift on their feet.

*'I am not sure how to answer this, as we don't experience dilemmas
as you describe them. We are very nimble anyway, and known for
being innovative. Our business planning is shifting and moving all
the time. The nature of our work is fluid.'*

V 'BUILT-TO-LAST'ORGANISATIONS/'STEADY AS SHE GOES'

Those included in this section are organisations that have stood the test of time. Mark Hope echoed a familiar view that now 'jobs for life' had disappeared, the picture is different.

> *'The idea that you have a portfolio of skills at least, and you improve that portfolio over time, that's all important and I think understood and valued by people.'*

Mark felt that the first three elements of leadership development felt were axiomatic to Shell's policy and practice. On leadership being defined by dealing with dilemmas, Mark agreed in part but added:

> *'For me, the key is motivating and inspiring, by which I mean making people feel really valued. Only then will you get the best out of them.'*

Maturity has brought the realisation, as Todd Abbott said, that ears have double the capacity of the mouth!

> *'I try and say less, and listen harder every day that goes past, which is terribly hard because when I was twenty I used to know the answer to everything. But actually, skilfully listening and really hearing people, and then helping to create the group environment in which people flourish, I think that's hugely challenging.'*

With listening and a great team, Todd says:

> *'If I've got the best people, then with my team around me I can, or we can collectively within the team, or individually, resolve dilemmas.'*

Lawrence Churchill of UNUM commented:

> *'I fully subscribe to the importance of these bullet points. I am a strong advocate of the need to have these elements in the development of individual leaders. A leader must understand 'himself/herself' and how 'you' interact with others. Understanding your own profile and the profile of those you lead enables effective interaction.'*

So how can you acquire such skills?

> *'Learning from peer groups, but importantly from your (past or present) boss is key. Eliminate the bad points, and manage your team in a way that is different from poor examples you may have experienced.'*

Regrettably of course, there are those who become 'abusers', having been 'abused'.

Interesting Lawrence is sceptical about entrepreneurship in large organisations.

'The concept of entrepreneurship is overrated and it does not really work in large organisations. The structure, the reporting lines make pure entrepreneurship impractical.'

In contrast, David Burall saw his job in leadership training as developing entrepreneurs!

'In a sense, in establishing separate operating businesses within a holding company, we worked to create the opportunity for people to become MDs and FDs. I could afford to take the risk of letting other people have their heads, and I was really trying to create lots of little entrepreneurs. Other people could be entrepreneurial within the company and as a result of that, create wealth for the company.'

However, David had early experience at dealing with dilemmas and demonstrating leadership. He describes the situation he found as a very young man with the incumbent matriarchal society. His Aunt Kathleen ran the business, and when he was Managing Director she was chairman. David described one of the difficulties he faced at this time, concerning the fact that there were quite of lot of aged geriatric part-time employees around.

'Aunt Kathleen couldn't bear to see anyone retire who wanted to work beyond the age of sixty-five. I did a deal with Aunt Kathleen that we would enforce sixty or sixty-five retirement, but in return we would offer a programme of pre-retirement. Six months before they were due for retirement, they would take Mondays off, a couple of months later they would take Fridays off, and for the last two months of their working life they'd take three days a week off and we would encourage them to do something vocational. I thought it was pretty grim that on reaching the age of sixty-five, on the Friday afternoon, you handed them a cheque and thanked them for 'n' years' loyal service, and they'd wake up on the Monday morning wondering what to do. I think that was my first step towards solving a minor problem but in a fairly imaginative way. We still run that pre-retirement programme. I'm very proud of it.'

I asked David where letting people decide for themselves fitted. His example was the question of what to do with the profit share:

'I turned to the Works Council and said, The Company is putting in this sum of money monthly, and we will pay out quarterly. You sit down and decide how we should share it out. About half wanted the same for everybody, and the other half wanted it according to gross earnings. And this was not going to resolve itself. So, in a stroke of genius, the obvious solution was to divide it into two. We paid half out equally, and the other half according to gross earnings. It's still, to this day, done that way. It's stood the test of time – in excess of thirty years.'

The product of this process included improved communication and a commercially aware workforce.

> *'Every month, I would meet the day shift on the factory floor and with the aid of a flip chart tell people how we were doing. I told them pretty well everything. It was an education process also for our workforce. As time went on, month after month, we explained where we were being successful, where we were failing, and what the financial numbers meant. After a number of years we had a very commercially aware workforce. It was quite surprising.'*

Profit sharing in 1990 progressed to share ownership in 2001, when employees achieved 56 per cent ownership of Burall Ltd.

Richard Maudslay at House of Hardy had to make somewhat of a fresh start when he took over as Managing Director. As a result he sees the issue of leadership development in the context of recruiting the right team and ensuring alignment.

> *'What I've done is to bring in experienced managers. There has been some development, but it was really a question of going through the recruitment process and getting the right people in. We've got the team all facing in the same direction.'*

In terms of resolving dilemmas, the issue for Richard is change and alignment with the rest of the team.

> *'I suppose the big dilemma that we had to deal with was whether some of these people are actually going to change or not. Do we have them as second line managers or do we get rid of them? We've got rid of quite a few because we've concluded they will not be able to change.'*

However, he quickly recognises the downside of 'you change the people or you change the people'.

> *'We'll get somebody coming in with a different attitude and that is then regarded as these outsiders coming in and kicking all of us old timers out.'*

John Cridland at CBI candidly admits that the organisation has taken the amateur road to leadership.

> *'We have taken the sort of amateur rather than professional road to leadership. This is because people are our main competitive advantage so we've put the emphasis on the professional and technical skills that people bring. We've not put as much emphasis as we might have done on their leadership skills, which is why I characterise us as the amateur school of leadership.'*

However he does believe it warrants constant reflection and learning.

'I've never been entirely convinced that it lends itself to being put into models. I'm a bit of a sceptic about models in this area. I think it's almost too intangible, but that doesn't mean that I think we can afford to leave it on one side. I think it's a matter of constant reflection.'

The defined CBI role prevents active encouragement of such matters within their member organisations, but the organisation does support areas of research into leadership.

'We haven't tried to second guess what others are doing, so for example we've looked at what the Council for Excellence in Management and Leadership is doing. In a sense we've outsourced that bit of the work to them.'

Undeflected, I explored the issue of leadership being about effectively dealing with and resolving dilemmas. John agreed with this definition and added one of his own:

'I think there is a parallel stream which is about personal leadership. I tend there to focus on the role of the leader as team coach. I like the notion of mobilising the work of others, rather than too strongly leading the work of others.'

It was no surprise to find that Leslie Hannah enthusiastically embraced the concept about leadership.

'We live this. The Ashridge Leadership Programme is the prime leadership course in the country. It runs about fourteen times a year, compared with Cranfield's four and LBS's three or whatever. It really is the market leader. And it does tell participants about self-knowledge and emotional intelligence.'

In terms of facing dilemmas, Leslie recounted one that has faced an increasing number of organisations, that of over-generous and under-funded pension schemes.

'In the past, we have had a very, very generous pension scheme, which it emerged as soon as I arrived was very, very seriously underfunded, like a lot of others. I just had to bring that to an end. We've ended up with a perfectly reasonable scheme, which is equivalent to all our competitors. So that was the only big crisis. People saw the Ashridge scheme as a statement about Ashridge values, valuing people, but I said, 'Look, we'll respect vested interests, not change it for anyone already here, but all new appointments will be on different pension schemes, and we've done that.'

However, because of the escalating costs, staff had to choose between a salary increase and saying in the existing scheme.

'They were getting a 0 per cent salary increase because of the

pension fund. They were clamouring to end the pension fund as soon as we made that clear.'

This seemed to focus the mind. Unfinished business concerns profit share and performance reward. This is the typical dilemma of whether you manage performance through monetary reward or 'performance management'.

'That's a real dilemma for me, because I can see some of the arguments for performance related pay. Some people here are coasting and others are contributing much more to the organisation. Some of the latter are getting fed up about some of the former, but I believe the right way of dealing with it is performance management not profit-related pay.'

It was pleasantly surprising to see how deeply our interviewees had thought about developing leaders, and in a systemic way. I suspect that just ten years ago we would have obtained very different answers. That was certainly before the term 'Emotional Intelligence' had been coined. The issue of using emotions and what we now term the 'right hand brain' was not in common parlance. Nobody taught it or much valued its use against logic, rationality and systems thinking.

Further the issue of leadership would have been about 'do as I do' role modelling not systemic approaches which can take all these factors into account.

A common theme has been how do you deal with specialists such as scientists, technologists and doctors in the context of leadership. This crystallises around the most common dilemma of leadership – as Richard Hicks and Todd Abbott recognised – 80 per cent of the leadership role is about people, engaging, inspiring and creating agility whereas virtually none of the formal training concentrated on this area. People instinctively go back to their roots, where they know they'd be successful – usually in the technology, the art, whatever the specialism.

As Mike Rake summarised, *'real leadership is about an extraordinary balance between sensitivities, self-confidence, emotional intelligence and communication skills…'*

The value of interventions comes out strongly. The Camelot Queen, Dianne Thompson, who effectively said 'up with this I will not put' when it came to the crunch over the re-franchise.

The charity sector shows the way in dealing with dilemmas – Alan Bartle's example that there is a viable option to cost cutting when such cuts can destroy longer-term morale. The growth engendered within Royal and Sun Alliance by the emphasis on learning provided the foundation for the recovery the market has seen in 2003.

The role of sensitive leadership was well illustrated by Sir John Egan in the story over the Heathrow Tunnel collapse. What's interesting to me is that the partnership solution was not only the right pragmatic solution at the time, it was also right for the future of large scale project management. As John says it saved time, money and energy. It also formed the emotional link for John in pushing for the reforms in 'Rethinking Construction'. It was about thinking and connecting outside the organisation, which brings us to our next chapter – The Extrovert Organisation.

Notes

1   Collins, J *Good to Great* Random House 2001

2   Nonaka, I & Takeuchi, H *The Knowledge Creating Company* Oxford University Press 1995i

3   Garratt, R *The Fish Rots from the Head* Harper Collins 1996

Chapter seven

THE EXTROVERT ORGANISATION:
LOOKING AT THE OUTSIDE WORLD – RELATIONSHIPS AND SUSTAINABILITY

OUR INTERVIEWEES HAVE ALREADY EXPRESSED their general views about the topic of the 'extrovert organisation' in chapter 4 when they were discussing the basic premise. Now, in this chapter we go a little deeper into this topic. In doing so, we will link 'extrovertness' with the closely related issue of relationships, and also explore how both affect sustainability.

I START-UPS/ENTREPRENEURSHIP/PHOENIX

a Start-ups/Entrepreneurship

We heard in chapter 4 from Richard Hicks of AIT that the firm has had a very active community affairs policy, and that this was linked what happens inside the company. It is founded as an act of faith and is based on trust relationship. I asked about the sort of results that the policy brought. Richard explains:

> 'We have a relationship with our customers which, hopefully, is an open and honest one in which we are all trying to be clear what we are trying do. We bring an openness, an honesty and a clarity which does us good with our staff, and it definitely does us good with the community... Does it help anticipate external change? I'm not sure. It's not a diversion. It makes the internal community feel good about itself, and it makes the external community feel good about us. That's not the explicit end, goal but it does happen. Everybody in Henley is always putting the word about getting a job in AIT.'

Talking about how important internal and external relationships are to AIT, Richard delves deeper into the thinking behind trust and integrity. He quotes from Putnam's *Bowling Alone*[1] in which he describes two types of social capital.

> 'There is –'bonding capital', by which people with a shared interest and a very inward looking view of the world go through a process which makes them stronger and bonds them together. Then there is 'bridging capital', which creates links between your group and, let's call it, your community. I suppose, at one extreme, if you have no co-dependency at all in the outside world you might have a very powerful organisation, but a very separate one. There might be

substantial risk, because you're not connecting with the outside world sufficiently to understand what's going on. But if you bridge too much, then you do end up co-dependent. So it's a balance.

Does one have a policy on it? I think that is the essence of being in business. . An entrepreneur's 'nouse' is to understand it, to some extent, and manage those relationships. You manage the balance at a macro- and micro-level. You manage at a micro level with your customers.'

In hindsight, I suspect Richard may be wishing that there had been a way to build a similar level of social capital with the City before investors took fright, by judging AIT as an out of favour technology company about to renege on its promises.

When questioned about the advent of distance-type relationships through technology, Richard described an experience where bright talent can be connected with organisations intellectually rather than socially. This sounds not unlike the relationship Generics encourages with its 'intelligentsia'.

'Technology changes the nature of relationships, doesn't it? We had a really great software engineer who worked for us for ages. He was an exceptionally inventive and clever engineer. Eventually, he got himself an electronics shed at the bottom of his garden. The earlier relationship with him was that we provided a warm and comfortable, efficient, place to come and do what he did. When he built his electronics shed one could see a severing of that connection. To him work wasn't a place that he went to, it was something he participated in. Interestingly, he did maintain his connection with the company. So what was holding him in, what kept him connected? He was connected intellectually rather than socially. It changes the nature of the relationship.'

This line of thinking of Richard's neatly connected into our discussions about sustainability. Richard reflected that there were three different facets of sustainability, economic, social and environmental. The arguments were not the same in every case.

'There is absolutely no argument that in a big environmental sense, we all live on the same planet. There is a single 'community of use' of Planet Earth, and there isn't an opt-out option. So there is no argument about sustainability, and we all have our part to play. You can get into the George W Bush argument about whose job it is and how you go about it. But there is no question that the human race needs environmental sustainability environmentally. That's what I'm trying to say.'

When it came to the social dimension of sustainability, Richard did not see that necessarily this was required.

> *'I think we are becoming accustomed to the idea that sustainability is not required in a social sense. There's all the talk of portfolio careers and mobility of labour that gives the idea that it's a question of whether we want sustainability socially, whether we want to be part of the same groupings socially. Sustainability socially is probably a good thing, but I'm not sure. Whether it's a good thing or whether we should just be looking to reinvent all of our economic groupings, depends on what the economic unit is'*

Richard also brought the role of the nation state into question:

> *'A frontier in which anyone who can write software will emigrate to the South of France and live in small communities of like-minded souls will call into question the very nature of nationhood.'*

This might lead to the raising of barriers to migration. Richard cited a recent example:

> *'In the papers there was a piece about somewhere like Kurdistan, where the new self-elected president has declared a $30,000 tax payable to the state on anybody marrying one of the local women who are skilful in weaving carpets. His argument is that he doesn't want anyone marrying their skilled women and taking them away to weave carpets for them.'*

Lastly, Richard raised a very valid question for debate.

> *'At AIT, we're bringing people into the UK from India, highly educated people who can earn a substantial salary by working over here. I think the national picture of mobility is going to be reflected in a global picture of mobility. Charles Handy has asked what a company is for. There's a theme for government in the future, which is 'What is a country for?' What is the essence of the shared interests that we have that keeps us together?'*

As I write, the new Archbishop of Canterbury, Dr Rowan Williams, has shown some keen interest in this issue. He quotes Philip Bobbitt, strategist and historian, and author of *The Shield of Achilles*. Bobbitt postulates that, because the nation state is unable to meet expectations, we are seeing a shift into a new political mode, the 'market state'. In this, the function of government is to clear a space for individuals or groups to secure the best deal in pursuing what they want, irrespective of boundaries and moral concerns. The Archbishop is concerned if 'government is free to encourage enterprise' but not to protect against risk; to increase the literal and metaphorical purchasing power of citizens, but not take for granted any agreement about common goals and social good. The Archbishop clearly sees a role for the church in filling the vacuum. I would also maintain that business has a similar responsibility in this new 'market state'.

For Keith Moscrop at BioFocus, the issue of external relationships has to be customer focused.

> 'Customer-wise, it is hugely important to us. Basically, all of our selling, or 99 per cent of it, is done on a relationship basis, so making friends with the people you're working with is very important. One of the reasons we've done so well is the type of people we've been able to recruit who we have put in as team leaders on projects for different customers. People have enjoyed working with them.'

Keith explained that BioFocus extend the thinking to contracts, where they have encouraged a very transparent, honest, approach.

> 'All research is tarred with failure, so we tell the customer as soon as possible if we know we're failing. We take the attitude 'early rather than late'. It is much less disappointing, and also the customer can be involved in the solution. I've only had one feedback from a customer about it. He's just so grateful to find somebody that he thinks he can trust. It just shows you how bad many of the others are.'

But Keith also drew attention to the dangers that there are in the organisations becoming too close and co-dependent. One reason concerns potential difficulties over intellectual property, although in practice this has not yet been a problem:

> 'Some customers have been a bit concerned about confidentiality between projects for different customers, where there could be leaks. The reason is we're getting into such a close relationship with the customers that people understand everything about what is going on with them.'

Keith recognises that sometimes the risks involved in knocking down the barriers pay off. He illustrated this by referring to one of their customers from the USA:

> 'We told them how we operate and they weren't going to use us. They'd got two other companies lined up in the USA because they were nearby. We said, "Give us a try, and we'll give you a discount." This was a bit of a surprise because usually you don't buy your way into these situations. But this time they were looking for discounts.

> Actually, they ran us alongside two other suppliers. We insisted on visiting, even though we were in the UK. We took our project leader over there and introduced him to all the scientists, and we paid for that ourselves. So out of this discounted fee, we were putting more into it. We produced a report, a nice scientific report, at the end of six months, which they said was the best they'd ever seen. Neither of the other two American suppliers had visited site, and none of them had had this close working collaborative relationship. So, on that basis, we

were able to spread over all the world, and beat the competitors to the draw, even though we're way distant. It's all around this relationship idea.'

For Keith and his colleagues, the issues of sustainability did not loom large. The worldwide growth in the drugs market, the continual upheaval of mergers and acquisitions amongst the big pharmaceutical companies, and continuing demand for what BioFocus could provide, means that the issue is not high on the agenda. As Keith put it:

'I think when you're in a rampant stage of growth, you don't spend a lot of time thinking about it.'

At The Generics Group, although in different technologies, the similarity to BioFocus is striking. Again the key relationship is with customers. Community interest is there, but it is led by individuals, these 'polymaths' with a wider range of interests who are willing to get involved of their own volition. Duncan Hine remarked:

'We have people who do a very catholic range of things, in the full sense of that word, in terms of sport, hobbies, other relationships, and so on. I think they would do it anyway. It's part of the recruiting and selection process, I think, rather than something that has developed.'

Like many Board directors, Duncan found the cross-board involvement very useful for networking, connections and benchmarking. The issue of connections with spin out companies is interesting.

'The relevance comes out fairly naturally from the process of having spinout companies, which eventually become distant. They have directors who we've never seen and who have never worked here, but people from here are still on those Boards and in touch with those people. I've seen that work well, certainly in my own case where I'm a non-executive director of a PLC somewhere else, in a different industry segment, computer services. I'll often sit through those Board meetings and hear them do something about driving the budget for the next two years, or renewing a piece of strategy, and I'll think, Ah, we should think about that. However, you can't just bring it back and do it. You must adopt it and deploy it.'

In a parallel with BioFocus, Duncan believed that, judged in terms of the scale of relationships, Generics were at the extreme of co-dependency with their clients.

'The reason is that our key relationships are with customers of which there can be 120-150 at any one time. When you're rolling the

history, we probably have pretty strong relationships with hundreds of companies. That's actually one of our assets, because it's often very important in individual assignments to involve other past customers.'

Duncan gave the example of a client who might want to diversify into automotives. They would find it really useful to be able to ring up, say, three top automotive companies and get an opinion about the acceptability or otherwise of their proposed new product. As Duncan said:

'Part of our service is being able to do that. We have a major government department here tomorrow and part of the service we're providing them is to bring in ten industrial mentors for the day to interact with them. While we can do that easily, they can't. This is profound, because we're offering real interaction with customers as equals.'

This therefore is a design factor for Generics. When it comes to spinout companies, co-dependency aids co-investors.

'The other reason for being at the extreme end is because the other key relationships we have are co-investor ones. If we spin out a company, it's very important to get four or five other people to invest in it. Often, at subsequent rounds of investment, more new investors come in so you end up with very complex networks of people.'

When we discussed sustainability, Duncan focused on the sustainability of customer relationships. In our conversation we concluded it was about 'sustainability of the process not the content'. In other words, although Generics may have many repeat clients, the content of the contract was likely to be different each time. It was a difficult issue for a business like Generics, and Duncan spoke of a number of competing or conflicting forces

'Essentially, what we do is new business all the time, even if it's for a company for which we've already worked, They don't pay us to do anything routine, so even if we're working regularly with somebody, usually we'll have to do something radically different every twelve to eighteen months. Otherwise the relationship will just come to an end.'

As Duncan explained, the attitudes and aspirations of Generics own staff also had an influence here. The type of people they recruited did not want to undertake routine work.

'In complex product development, it may take two years to take something all the way through to volume manufacture in China. People really enjoy that the first time. The second time they are approached, I tend to get the reaction, Er, there's a lot of detail involved in this. I know how to do it now. They certainly don't want to do it a third time.'

Generics were fortunate in having enough people to go round, so this was not a real problem. However, one of the reasons people liked working there was that there was not much routine work. This implied there would not be a lot of work which involved doing the same things for a long time. In summary then, for Duncan, the sustainability issue was about the sustainability of relationships:

> *'A lot of the sustainable arguments come around long-term relationships. We do lots of repeat business but it's all different.'*

As Dianne Thompson made clear, in the quotes in the previous chapter, Camelot's focus in the first franchise had been on demonstrating that the lottery was run in an 'inclusive' fashion, with stakeholder interest being integrated with the business. Over time, Camelot's Social Responsibility Panel, together with 'activist' Sue Slipman, ensured that this was not just rhetoric, but something of real substance. Dianne viewed this progress with some satisfaction. She came up with a phrase to treasure here:

> *'I'm not sure it helps us anticipate external change, but it helps us anticipate where we will have to change in the future.'*

In terms of the scale of relationships, Camelot is striking a balance between being too co-dependent and achieving uniform negotiations with suppliers. On a scale of one to ten in terms of co-dependency, Dianne thought Camelot was at six or perhaps seven. The GTECH experience had taken its toll.

Readers may recall that in Spring 2000, shortly after Camelot's bid for the second lottery operator's licence had been submitted to the National Lottery Commission, Camelot faced a major challenge. At that time it came to light that Camelot's lottery systems supplier GTECH had, without informing either Camelot or the then regulator OFLOT, in June 1998 discovered, and in July 1998 corrected, a software error. This error had, between 1994 and 1998, caused Camelot's systems to record a very small number of duplicate lottery entries, resulting in slight overpayments and underpayments of some lower tier prize amounts for the lottery draws affected. In view of the National Lottery Commission's concerns about GTECH's handling of the software error, Camelot radically restructured the lottery systems supply components of its bid, proposing a technology transfer in respect of GTECH's UK operations. In due course, Camelot's bid was adjudged the one most likely to maximise the proceeds of the National Lottery and it was awarded the licence.

Dianne explained that Camelot had a risk register, and one of the risks assessed is in relationships with suppliers. As she admitted:

'This obviously comes out of the GTECH issue. Fingers got burned, and so our attitudes to our dealings with some of our suppliers has changed as a result. I don't think we'll ever get to a situation where we're so co-dependent that we couldn't take independent action.'

Dianne said that Camelot did believe very much in profitable partnerships, and that they tried with all their external stakeholders to have long-term relationships. With their key suppliers, whether it was the advertising agencies, the technology hardware and software suppliers, or the firm that did their scratch cards, Camelot had contracts for three years, with break clauses, or for the life of the licence, depending on the firm concerned. She commented:

'We try very hard to have win/win negotiations with everybody. As a company, we are a bit of an interesting conundrum. If you like, we have a set of creative tensions, because we're in a gambling market, we're there to raise as much money as we can for good causes, yet we've got to protect players from excess. We're a commercial organisation making profit, but not too much profit.'

This, we recognised between, was a classic leadership dilemma. For good measure, Dianne added another, internal, dilemma about performance management, which many leaders will recognise.

'It is the same here in terms of having a balance of good, ongoing, mutually beneficial relationships with all our stakeholders. It is true inside as well. I want Camelot to be a great place to work. I want my people to feel happy, safe, secure and well rewarded, but I won't tolerate poor performance. It is the same thing, isn't it? I'm happy about work/life balance, but the day I catch you swinging the lead and taking the Mick out of it, you're in trouble.'

Camelot's licence is only ever given for seven years, which puts issues of sustainability in a slightly different context. However, even given this, Dianne thought it was achievable.

'When you've only got a seven-year life that, by definition, at one point in time will force you to look at the business in a different way. You're always hopeful you may win the third licence, but you tend not to focus on the long term.'

Dianne explained that they had tried to find a different way of achieving sustainability. They had explored the possibility of floating the lottery, in which case it would genuinely have become the people's lottery. But they were told by several financial advisers that they would not be able to do this, because they only had a seven-year licence. So, Dianne concluded:

'I do believe in sustainability and durability and it's terribly

important for businesses. It's just slightly less important for Camelot than it probably would be for lots of other organisations.'

b Not-for-profit start-up/Lymphoma Association

I had half expected that this area of enquiry would not be seen as relevant in the charity sector, so Alan Bartle's responses surprised me somewhat. The Association tapped into external views, which came from trustees and through links with the medical profession. But in addition he saw a new window of opportunity opening up. He described how, in addition to providing information to the forum, the Association would also become an advocacy/lobbying service on behalf of patients, in particular in terms of the funding of research and clinical trials. Alan commented:

> *'That immediately that takes us into another field. We then get into the larger arena of politics. We are already involved in this, in that for the last eighteen months or so we have been involved with the National Institute for Clinical Excellence (NICE) in two of their drug appraisals, one of which has become very contentious and went to appeal.'*

Alan explained that the appeal had been allowed and the drug had been reappraised. The Association had been partially successful in achieving a more positive outcome than was previously envisaged. But this success had also created new expectations and pressures:

> *'I think seeing that has opened the eyes of both the staff and the trustees. But I also think it has raised expectations within the membership that it is something that we ought to be doing more of.'*

This would have other spin offs in terms of image. Alan said that it would become an extremely important additional arm to what the Association did, because it would raise their profile quite dramatically. This in turn would drive an increase in contact from patients:

> *'If we're engaging with people at that level, then the name of the Association is going to increase. The more publicity we get, the more people will be aware of us. This increases the potential for us to contact even more patients.'*

There are occasional concerns, Alan said, at Trustee level over the Association's closeness to pharmaceutical companies. However, he balances this against the entitlement to apply for Department of Health funding.

> *'One of the key areas to which I would apply that is in the area of funding. That is one of the external factors with which we are involved. We have been successful in getting a reasonable amount of*

*Department of Health Section 64 funding. At the same time we
have, on occasion, been able to get donations from some of the
pharmaceutical companies. Certainly the question is asked at Trustee
level, We're not getting too close to a drugs company are we?'*

Alan said that, currently, his answer to this was that the Association
was getting three times as much in Department of Health funding
than from all the drug companies put together, so he was quite
relaxed about the issue.

*'We would have to get an awful lot more from the pharmaceutical
companies before it would ever be seen as undermining in any way
what we are doing, or compromising our independence.'*

The Lymphoma Association similarly is cautious about political
involvement. Alan said that in the future the Association would have
to look at whether it engaged in lobbying. But it was clear that it must
not engage in anything, which was party political.

Finally, Alan underlined his priority on relationships. For him, the
internal relationships were the more important:

*'I think the internal relationships are absolutely vital and crucial.
The external ones are important, but I believe the internal ones are
the more important.'*

When we turned to the subject of sustainability or durability, Alan's
reactions were the total opposite of those from all the other
respondents. He thought that in the charitable sector there was no
such thing as durability.

*'Actually, no-one would be happier than me if tomorrow we ceased
to exist, if it was because we'd met our objectives! If we felt that all
patients diagnosed with lymphoma were getting the information and
the support they needed at the point of delivery (the hospitals), if
there was sufficient funding for clinical trials and for research into
lymphoma treatment and the disease, then I would be a very happy
man. In that sense I don't think durability is either necessary or a
good thing.'*

Of course, this was not an argument against the concept of durability
while the purpose or mission still existed. Alan was simply stressing
that durability needed to be pursued for the right reasons!

c Phoenix organisations

Unsurprisingly, Bryan Jackson of Toyota had thought through very
clearly the relationship and sustainability issues. He commented that,
as a business, Toyota could not afford to operate in a vacuum. He
described three principles that applied:

- employees came from the community

- the community provided the customers
- the business needed to know the views of the community, and to have an active voice so that its resource improved the community.

Bryan described how Toyota in the UK took an active 'institutional' approach, by being involved with Government organisations (for example the Training and Enterprise Councils and the Learning and Skills Council, employer organisations (for example the CBI), industry organisations (for example the Society of Motor Manufacturers and Traders) and networks. Together with this were the usual and expected level of delegations, visits, benchmarking activities that are de rigueur for Japanese implant companies. When I asked Bryan to rate Toyota on the scale of their relationships, he did not shy away from the top end of the scale.

> *'I estimate nine out of ten on your scale. This comes back to the Toyota credo of 'making better cars for more people at lower cost'. Suppliers have complete access to the Toyota Production System, which is about taking cost out of the process whilst increasing quality and using innovation. Hence there is a strong policy towards partnership.'*

Our discussion about durability was very much focused on a stakeholder philosophy. Bryan saw the foundation for durability as the strength of the company and its people. But he recognised the potential danger of complacency. In terms of what motivated the Board, Bryan thought it was the moral case with overtones of the business case. The moral case is about minimising the impact on the environment. Managing the balance with the business case was the art of the possible, having strong ethics and delivering what they believe in, a stakeholder philosophy.

Unipart Automotive has spent an enormous amount of time over the last decade on developing productive relationships with customers, suppliers and the community. Paul Forman gave some indication of how seriously this aspect of the business is treated. He explained that Unipart was one of the prime exponents of the stakeholder philosophy. The firm was involved in local sponsorship, and in local charities. A number of their employees would act as business councillors, and get involved in things like Business in the Community and the Oxford Partnership. Historically the firm had been proponents of what was called a model B supplier philosophy, which was predicated on working with people to achieve mutual benefit rather than anything else. Implicitly this meant greater involvement.

> *'Yes, we do work closely with customers. John Neill's (the CEO) philosophy is about long-term, shared-destiny, and partnerships. If you look at our relationships with Jaguar, or Vodaphone, the whole Unipart group philosophy is about that kind of partnership. There is no doubt that closer supplier relations are a massive advantage in helping the business. It doesn't mean that as a customer you have to be soft and cuddly and a pushover. The fact that Model B demands global competitiveness from your suppliers doesn't have to be contradictory. In fact it can be mutually supportive.'*

Paul does see that, if the partners aren't careful, the fundamental objective of making a profit can be lost. He saw a danger in too close a relationship with a customer.

> *'With a balanced score card, you can almost forget the fourth quadrant, finance, because you're too busy saying how nice we are to each other. The customer is thinking, Ah, I'm getting much better terms here. I'll stay with this. I'm not saying we go down that route, but it is a potentiality.'*

Paul recognised many benefits resulting from this policy, including contributing to the local reputation of Unipart as a company for which people would like to work, thus aiding recruitment.

In terms of the importance of internal and external relationships, Paul rates customer intimacy highly, so that Unipart as manufacturer and supplier must 'eat, sleep and breathe' the needs of the crash repair body shop. With suppliers, the relationship is practised in depth with the 'ten to zero' programme for continuous improvement in suppliers' product lines being clearly codified.

However, even with the concentration on these external areas, in summary Paul feels that internal relationships are paramount.

> *'Internal relationships are more important, than external relationships. If I had to choose a good relationship, I'd rather have it with my team than a particular customer or supplier. A lot of people pay lip service to this idea. But most people's default setting is naturally to gravitate to the customer. I spend more time with my people than with customers.'*

d Consultancy/Outsourcing

Tim Watts at Pertemps is strong on partnerships, both internally with employee ownership and externally with a range of stakeholders.

> *'We see everyone as partners in our business and having these links is central to the way we operate. We invest heavily in community projects on an ongoing basis, and have done this for years.'*

I asked whether this helped with the business. Tim had no doubt that it did, because the stakeholders, suppliers, and people in the community are Pertemps' prospective flexible workers. Tim said that everyone was encouraged to contribute to the firm's antennae.

> *'We encourage external involvement and if someone has a suggestion or idea it is encouraged.'*

Talking about sustainability or durability, Tim painted a clear mental picture:

> *'The picture I have is of someone on a tightrope. The tightrope leads into tomorrow (the vision), but is often in the dark, so you are trying to balance on a thin line when you cannot see what the future will hold. At the same time, you are not alone on the tightrope but have to juggle different groups of people who are different shapes and sizes, which is not easy. By this I mean your employees, shareholders, the community begging bowl, suppliers – you need to be a magician to be a leader.*
>
> *The only way forward is to have a magic wand, which is your communications wand. You go forward into the darkness through sensing and feeling your way. You need to create partnerships, and have a sprinkle of magic dust - mine is bullshit! - to help. I have 211 team leaders, who are all different and who bring different magic dust, to enable us to continue to juggle and go forward on the tightrope.'*

This is certainly a very different, but very real, way of seeing how to 'deal with dilemmas'!

Bill Penney sees that 'extrovert organisation' in a very self-interested way. Deliberately and strategically, Ashton Penney has built up relationships with the Chartered Management Institute, the CBI, and the trade association for interim management, to get both their industry and themselves on the map. Partly, the purpose of this is to build up the network, but the great success has been to gain the endorsement of bodies such as CBI and CMI for a new form of management cadre.

For Peter Ward at Telos the place of the 'extrovert organisation' was central. He felt that they spent all their time and energy outside the business:

> *'We try to make the internal process and management as straightforward as possible. We find that when we turn into ourselves, Telos de-energises. When we're out there, it energises. We work with interesting and stimulating organisations that are not always financially driven. It helps educate us and keep us real.'*

Peter explained that currently Telos was doing some leadership work with a sports body and they were trying to do some work with voluntary organisations to look at the effectiveness of that very important sector.

'*The people who want to work with us include a lawyer, a vicar, HR professionals, accountants, planners, and strategists. It is this sort of diversity that's very stimulating. My job is actually to ensure that the external antennae are always out there. My job is to make sure that Telos is stimulated by external things all the time.*'

Peter uses a philosophy propounded by Arie de Geus, but recognises there is a distinction between 'business' and 'campaigning'.

'*Arie de Geus, in his Living Company[2] book, talks about being in the middle of your world and understanding the context of your business and how it fits. We think we've got an understanding of where we fit. Are we campaigners? No. Do we sometimes have to resist that? Yes.*'

Peter gives an example of where this works to influence, or be influenced by, other Boards.

'*We've got some views on governance and senior remuneration which might lead us to write and article or two, but we're more interested in developing practical experience, using our thinking to stimulate our approach, and looking for contact with like-minded people. For example, we will invite a few people around to talk about whether Boards should actually be paid on the basis of their personal contribution, rather than what a remuneration consultant says the sector should be paid. We've got some quite significant people saying that is an interesting question. So is that influential? Maybe it will be, but it will influence us.*'

Another topic in development using this external process has been diversity, but this is an 'integrated' activity and not necessarily just for straightforward business development. Peter explained:

'*I want to be diverse, because diversity can stimulate our creativity. It also enfranchises you to deal in places and organisations that you otherwise could not access. If I've got people from a particular background, their contacts and their way of working will make it much easier for us to make contact. So as an extreme, if we want to get a room full of bishops, I've got my vicar who can arrange it. And if we are about a different cultural response to a particular situation, then we will want a contact that can make it happen for us. We have been talking to an organisation that is set up to work with new ethnic minority-run enterprises, purely to gain more experience and to learn. Will it develop the business focus as well? Are we doing that to develop the business? Are we doing that to be diverse? Yes. Am I doing that to learn something? Yes. Are we doing it because that's going to educate our future decision-making? Yes. So is it business development or is it something else? It's an integrated activity.*'

Peter saw the emphasis placed on exploring cultural issues with clients as a great business driver. Talking about the scale of relationships, Peter saw Telos as tending towards inter-dependency.

> 'We would be towards inter-dependency because that is part of us. We naturally keep in touch, and maintain the relationships, with people that work with us. This isn't about managing a relationship just for the sake of generating transactions. It is about keeping in touch because we are genuinely interested.'

As Peter described it, this approach was not about exploiting the association. It was more about a long-term relationship, and a journey of discovery. Not surprisingly, given these views, Peter saw sustainability and durability as axiomatic.

> 'We wouldn't be doing what we're doing if we didn't believe it was achievable. We've set up the business for a particular purpose and with the intention of being around for a very long time.'

Peter described how, although Telos was a young organisation, they had already put in place provisions to ensure the business could never be sold to outside shareholders.

> 'We have built in a formula which will always favour buyers, so a new entrant to the business can buy in reasonably advantageously. We believe it is important that our intellectual capital controls this business, and so we will not set up a potential conflict with external shareholders.'

This leads into a business perspective on the future. Peter had an interesting view about timescales of perspectives:

> 'My belief is that you can only have a future perspective for about as long as you've been around. I've been around fifty years; I might have a perspective on the next fifty years. Telos is only three years old. It can only realistically talk with any authority about what might happen to it in the next three years. So we can have long-term aspirations, but our perspective on life is only as long as we've been in business.'

So, I asked, where do ideas of 'creative destruction' fit with this? Peter's response was:

'If you're in touch with your external antennae, you'll know when to start to develop the next business model'

II   M&A/DEMERGER ORGANISATIONS

Syd Pennington, of Royal and Sun Alliance, was a little unhappy with the term 'extrovert'. He thought it might appear in personality terms a little frivolous for the serious business of insurance and financial services. However, this reservation masks the reality of what they actually do.

'We've got lots of involvement at local levels with community events, but at a macro level we've done a deal with the Red Cross and the Red Crescent. We sponsor them for £1m, and in every part of the world we work with them to achieve key objectives. They indeed work for us, as well as benefiting them.'

Syd explained why this is seen as a win-win arrangement.

'By nature, we are in the business of assessing risk and forecasting risk (particularly over global warming). They are the people who pick up the pieces when something goes wrong.'

R&SA had been working with the Red Cross in American schools, to educate on fire risks in the home, and the policy has paid off. It had actually led to new business. Syd explained:

'We actually won a piece of business from a company called Chicken Fillet, which is a huge burger-type place like KFC or McDonalds, but regional in that part of Carolina. When they were looking at people who were quoting for business, they asked 'What's your community involvement?' We were able to show them our deal with the Red Cross, and we got that business.'

I asked how deep the different relationships were. For external relationships, Syd felt that the inevitable atmosphere of conflict and legislation over insurance claims inhibited the depth of relationships. However, there were long-term relationships with major clients, and one of the constituent parts of R&SA (Sun) had been in business for over 290 years!

The R&SA Board could be motivated by both the moral and the business case. This is illustrated by the example of R&SA sponsoring the clean up of 800 tonnes of rubbish in Antarctica. Robert Swann, the explorer, inspired R&SA to commit major resources to the project.

'He spoke about the fact that this was the last great unspoiled wilderness in the world. Governments had to decide by 2041 whether or not they were going to continue with the agreements they had made not to exploit Antarctica, and not drill for minerals and oils. He wanted to mount a major exercise to ensure that the next generation were aware of this, and were going to be environmentally tuned to stop anything happening. At the same time, he had personally looked to find the kind of sponsorship and support to remove from Antarctica all the rubbish that had been dumped there.'

I asked Syd what the business case was.

'There's a hole in the ozone layer above Antarctica, and the environment is gradually being impacted by a whole range of different things. Global warming means floods, which are bad news for insurance companies.'

KPMG policy about involvement in the community goes back a long way, and Mike Rake found more and more reasons to support it. He was interested to ensure that the policy on Corporate Social Responsibility was not changed.

> 'When I first got involved, I felt very strongly that we as a firm were privileged, and we had to put something back into the community. I quickly realised that all of our people were privileged, and putting them into these communities made them more aware.'

KPMG established a 'time bank' to support community work, established so that people's line managers could not stop them from doing such work.

> 'I then realised that the more I gave them opportunities, the more they really enjoyed and benefited from it. That's actually attractive to recruitment and retention, and so you have a business case. I was Deputy Chairman of Business in the Community and I then got involved in the corporate community investment group. You quickly realise it's easy to put together a strong business case which creates a sustainable proposition and which is stronger than the will or desire of the current CEO.'

I asked Mike if this proposition was supported by the peer group and managers. There were some real tensions, as Mike related:

> 'In any organisation, you get resistance. There is a balance issue, for example. Obviously, when you have a large business, you have to pay attention to the utilisation of your people, and the allocation of resources. You have to hold people accountable. Of course the initial reaction of your line resource manager is 'Thanks very much. One day I'm getting an email about resource utilisation and the next you're sending them off on community activities!' So we have to find a way (1) to explain what we're trying to do and (2) to build in systems that take account of that.'

The external involvement has helped with change within the firm. Mike returned to his theme of consistency when we talked about sustainability and durability.

> 'Consistency, with a base of values, is vital to the success of a firm in being able to adapt to its environment.'

In KPMG, the values shine through over the environment.

> 'Getting this message across about sustainability and the environment is hard work, but I believe it's right. There's a strong business case, and it is becoming a huge issue for businesses which they ignore at their peril.'

However, Mike stresses that durability must not mean inflexibility.

'I think durability could mean inflexibility. I'm not sure that's right. You have to be really agile. Look how fast this recession hit us.'

When I talked with Todd Abbott at Cisco, he told me that, for them, extrovert means listening intently to press, analysts, partners, competitors and customers. As he put it:

'God gave us two ears to listen twice as much as we talk. So, at any opportunity I get, I ask for validation. Does it make sense, is it consistent with your vision, Mr Customer?'

However, further down the organisation this isn't quite so easy.

'Our sales guys want to sell, and I think selling is all about talking and pitching and not about listening. It is a typical weakness in sales guys. I think we've come a long way when we think about having to sit down with customers and really understand what their pressure points are.'

The picture from Cisco then is one of a focus on execution, with continual validation along the way. Given, in particular, the nature of the industry in which Cisco operated, and their involvement with information and communication technologies, I asked Todd about the place of virtual relationships in the scheme of things. From the unique standpoint of an Internet infrastructure provider, Todd confirmed that virtual relationships via the net do need a physical or social foundation!

'I think the virtual relationships work well after you've developed a foundation. You've got to meet the guy, and spend some time with him. The tools make it a very efficient and productive relationship. I can't point to a single example where I've had a relationship of any meaningfulness with somebody over the net without having first set up a couple of key meetings to establish the foundations thereof.'

We talked about durability of the economic model around the Internet. Todd saw huge opportunities for overcoming the digital divide in developing countries.

'When you look at India as an example, they've used it as a vehicle to get tremendous economic development and growth. It does offer an ability for developing countries to get access to information and efficiencies that otherwise they never could have.'

I questioned Todd about what motivated the Board in cases where the economic justification was slight or non-existent. He ascribed it to a combination of all three motives, the moral case, 'Society biting back', and the business case.

'If you're a company that's in survival mode, the only thing that really matters is the business case. When you're a company with as

much financial strength as we have, I think it weighs more heavily on the moral and the social cases.

We spend a lot of time helping developing countries or charity organisations to utilise the net for development. We've put in networks in Afghanistan after the new government came, in and there's no business that's coming from doing that in Afghanistan.

We don't try to leverage that with advertising. In our view it is much more of a moral, social responsibility. As a company that's as successful as we are, we have a responsibility.'

For Sally Vanson at MCL/The Performance Solution, the idea of the extrovert organisation operates at three levels. The CEO is a great advocate for the values in the business, and is a sought-after speaker, Mazda worked with charities such as Barnardo's, but very much on the car selling side of the organisation. Thirdly, there was employee development where there was some input from employees to a charity. However, Sally believes this last must be down to employee choice.

The depth of relationships is affected by the transition from the co-dependency of the Mazda era, which reduced scope for decision making and responsibility down the line, and now to risk assessment, valuing people rather than cars.

'In The Performance Solution, it's a virtual business. It doesn't have employees, it has a network of associate consultants and so on. So it purely exists through partnership and co-development. I have a strap line – everyone I meet is a customer, because one day they could be.'

III PUBLIC TO PRIVATE

As with the other groupings, our interviewees' outline views on the subject were given in chapter 4 when we discussed the basic premise. However, this issue is so vital for the 'public-private' sector, in terms of stakeholder relations, it is worth delving a little deeper.

Chris Mellor of AWG saw three dimensions to the extrovert organisation, which he grouped under the umbrella of 'sustainable development'.

The first level: This involved balancing three irreconcilable objectives:
- economic growth of the organisation; whilst
- protecting the environment; whilst
- becoming a good citizen playing a role in the community.

The second level: This consisted of involving those working for, and with, the company in balancing these objectives, so that employees who contribute to, and see the company doing, things for the environment and the community are proud to be associated with them, while improving the overall image. For Chris, this is about being in line with the values (see chapters 4, 5 and Appendix II). Chris also recognises that another by-product of this is the developmental benefit of working in teams outside the organisation, and interacting with people at all levels and from all backgrounds.

The third level: This relied on making the knowledge AWG has into a source of competitive advantage. As Chris explained:

> '*As we develop our business model, what we are trying to do is to do things in a sustainable way. So, when we come up with solutions to the problems the clients have, we're automatically addressing the sustainable development issues that potentially those clients need to address as a company. This is particularly true of the area of infrastructure, in which we specialise. What we're aiming to do is to come up with a solution where the unit cost of operating the asset over its whole economic life is as optimal as it could be.*'

The AWG example is one of maturity. The firm had, for many years, followed the natural path of a water utility with a keen interest in the environment, particularly where it itself had an impact. By using project teams in the community for people development, and almost by serendipity, this broadened out and led to business development.

I have a beautiful example from my time at Anglian Water. The transformation journey, which was in full swing when I joined in 1996, was consistently criticised by my peer group as not attacking bottom-line costs. It seemed that all the 'journey' groups of employees were keen to do things in the community. This was regarded by my peers as a waste.

Four years later, AW had a viable subsidiary selling non-water products to its six-million customers in the UK. This was established after a market survey showed that customers trusted AW because of the work it did in the community. Companies may never know precisely when business benefit arrives as a result of a proactive stakeholder approach, but the evidence is that it will be delivered at some point.[3]

Now, with the addition of facilities management to the portfolio, via the acquisition of Morrison Construction, the previous investment of time and money in developing the 'extrovert organisation' pays off, as Chris Mellor recognised.

As we have already seen, the extrovert organisation cannot be separated from the issue of external relationships or sustainability. Chris Mellor modestly put AWG as half way on my scale from risk assessment to deep co-dependency, with ambitions to move into deeper partnerships for mutual benefit. Partnerships have been essential in Anglian Water International, where a local partner in a foreign country is a prerequisite. With Public and Private Partnerships, often consortia are the modus operandi, and AWG has been building experience in the PFI sector and applying its post-privatisation experience.

Turning to 'sustainability' and 'durability', Chris is pessimistic about many companies' ability to adapt sufficiently to suit today's rapidly changing circumstances.

> *'All companies these days have to keep reinventing themselves. So durability, in the sense that it is an economic entity that continues to survive and prosper, is possible, but durability in the sense that an organisation can carry on doing pretty much what it always did, isn't.'*

Interestingly, despite the pressures of the regulator, NGOs, and other pressure groups on the water sector, Chris Mellor does not see 'society biting back' as the driver for the Board's motivation to act in this area.

> *'I don't think that society 'biting us back' figures too much at all. We live in a society of naming and shaming and fining and governance, and I think that's a very dangerous thing. I am a firm believer that most intelligent human beings respond rationally to the views of partners. Reliance on legislation will simply drive people into not believing in sustainability, or not doing things that otherwise they would do.'*

Further, Chris believes that increased use on business of 'the stick' in the corporate governance sense will drive good people out of business for fear of litigation.

> *'Who in their right mind would want to take the responsibility? It gets ever more litigious, and an adversarial environment where it is 'dog eat dog', and you fight for survival. I think the long-term dread would be that good, able people will say 'It's not for me'. It's one of the reasons why it's hard to get good people as non-executives. Who wants to take that responsibility and have all that exposure? From our board, we try to operate on the basis of doing what we believe to be right because of the moral case, not because of newspaper disclosure.'*

Essentially, Chris believes it is the business case that motivates, within a moral framework.

> *'I think the business case is where we start from. There is a moral dimension to it. I think there's a real sense in the board that there*

are certain things we would not do, they would not be ethical as it were. This is particularly important overseas. There's a sort of moral, ethical, undertone but the goals are mainly business driven. It makes good sense for employee development, and it could be a source of competitive edge.'

Although Tony Ward of BAA disliked the expression 'the extrovert organisation', he saw the antennae issue as paramount. It was an extension of the stakeholder approach that is a hallmark with BAA.

'Our market research is very important, because we do carry out quality service monitoring all day, every day. That's very important feedback for us but, yes, what's going on out there is critical.'

Balancing stakeholder views, and thereby obtaining the scope to grow the business, is vital to BAA. The management of the three London airports, Heathrow, Gatwick and Stansted, as a whole system has given benefits.

'The London system has worked better as a whole than as the individual parts. We're full in Heathrow for most of the year. Where we had capacity, we did market it to attract and encourage people to go. As a result, the low cost airlines have developed at Stansted.'

The antennae provide the opportunity for strategic thinking about where government and the regulator will give scope, and where customers and community needs can be balanced. Sometimes BAA has to adopt the role of quasi regulator:

'Let me give you an example where a dilemma meets the external point. We actually fine airlines for going off track and creating noise outside of the envelope, and we plough those fines back into the community.'

The antennae and the balancing of customer and community needs give 'future focus an external awareness', in Tony Ward's definition. BAA staff involvement in these is a deliberate part of management development, in particular because of the context BAA is in. Tony used the company's airport Managing Director positions as an example. He stated that these roles are something like 60 per cent externally focussed, and 40 per cent directed within the airport.

'Most people in an equivalent general management position would see it as 20-80 or even 10-90, but ours are 60-40 focused in favour of the external world. So we have to select and appoint people on that basis, and we have to inculcate that into the way the business operates. Using our competency framework, we can confirm the importance of future focus in the role of a Chief Executive in this business. The only way you can get a handle on the future is being

out there with an external and stakeholder focus. It is the business of all our senior directors to ensure this, and prevent stakeholder related issues becoming serious problems or obstacles. The ability to form good relationships is a critical competence.'

When I asked Tony how he saw BAA on the relationships scale, his response was that each stakeholder would have a separate measurement, and this would vary over time as stakeholder interests were balanced. BAA's now famous response to the public inquiry about Heathrow's Terminal 5 was that a further runway was inappropriate due to community interests. However, for other stakeholders, Tony commented:

'The airlines would want to see an expanded Heathrow. It is valuable to them. But we have to balance our stakeholders' requirements; and we cannot show any favouritism to any one airline.'

Thus partnership working is an aspiration, but sometimes independence has to be preserved. BAA has found that in such cases they must be prepared to take an unpopular stance.

In this interview, I was able to explore with Tony the influence of e-business and virtual relationships. I asked if this had changed the importance of relationships. Tony thought that it made the 'non-critical' relationships easier, but that it didn't affect critical relationships. Tony saw dangers in using virtual means for important relationships, but there were benefits in enabling those without relationship skills. Tony commented:

'The risk is that people make the misjudgement of using these media for what are critical relationships. Where it is a relationship of influence, then that remains just as critical, no matter what world you're working in. At the same time, for some people, it's actually helped. For some people who don't have the relationship skills to a high degree, they can have a better relationship than might otherwise be the case.'

On durability Tony had an interesting view. He saw two extremes, and used examples of these to explain why he was always talking in contextual terms:

'I think there is a polarisation. I think there are the shooting stars, where durability isn't even a consideration strategically, and nor should it be. It has a time in our lives as it were, a time in society and then bang. But for other things, absolutely you need durability. For example, I think the water industry needs a robust, durable, enduring supply.'

It follows that, under the creative destruction theory, businesses may come and go, and others have to undertake the reinvention within a durability framework.

> 'There are many features of our society that change but fundamentally remain the same. I think that's true of business, and until the 'beam me up Scottie' technology arrives, you're going to need airports. We can predict that will be the case for the next thirty years or so, because technology doesn't get you there in that time frame. So we need to be durable, and that's not an option for us.'

On what motivates the BAA Board Tony was very clear that all three factors played a part:

> 'We are certainly motivated by the business case because that's our future funding. We are a public service company, and we start with that ethos. I think having that purpose is enriching for people working here. Hopefully it gives something back to society. But we're also very conscious that a number of our services can get a very quick media reaction from opinion-formers and other public in general.'

Tony commented that if, when it hit one of the events that drew bad media coverage, BAA was not using a good values approach, the issue could become all the more damaging. As an example:

> 'Stories come out in the press about security breaches. Our security is not perfect, but we get very high scores. On one side the airlines might say that you could sub-contract out your security and you could pay the minimum wage to reduce costs and our charges. They operated like that throughout the States. You're trying to balance all of that, and unfortunately I think we are driven by all of those factors. It's a constant balancing act.'

It is poignant to note that this interview occurred just before September 11 2001. We have seen subsequently that breaches of security within the US have suddenly assumed great importance. I guess Tony would say again that it is contextual.

In summary, Tony remarked that when all was said and done, the fiduciary duty had to be paramount in the production of the business case:

> 'The Board has to act in the shareholders' interests. In BAA's case this is best served by operating ethically and sustainably. But, for example, if T5 at Heathrow is not financially viable, the Board cannot authorise its build. It has a fiduciary duty to act in shareholders' interests.'

For Sir John Egan, the extrovert organisation approach has been a personal journey. He recalls some early experience with BAA:

'I got involved in the leadership thing with BAA when we helped to give leadership training to many of the headmasters of the inner city schools. That was a wonderful project, and I learned a huge amount from it. We also encouraged our own managers to go and become school governors, and to start teaching other organisations process management, process improvement. We've trained some very, very fine managers and leaders, and we thought that they should be putting their time and energy into the community around them.'

As we saw in chapter 4, the benefits to BAA from this were the development of a reputation as a benign and quality neighbour. There were also benefits for the individuals involved, who became more self-confident as they helped to grow the trust between BAA and the community.

Sir John's experience with supply chain development at Jaguar, and the subsequent 'unintended consequence' of the Heathrow Express Tunnel collapse, inspired an ongoing 'external to the business' involvement with construction that has revolutionised the way clients and contractors can view major projects. 'Re-thinking Construction Mark I' and moving to the so-called 'Mark II', in which Sir John has been the prime mover, is all about involving the supply chain from day one, and planning the project using all the available knowledge. This delivers projects faster and to cost and quality. In doing this, Sir John is very sure you have to be detailed about the necessary steps.

'Re-thinking Construction Mark II is trying to say, Now we know this works, and this is the right way to do it, how do we get all the industry to embrace it and not just 10 per cent of it? That's the next step, and of course it's relatively simple. However, somebody was saying, Surely we don't have to tell them how to do things, only what we expect of them? I said, No, if you want revolution, you actually have to tell people how to do it, as well as what they have to do. Don't expect revolution easily in this industry because they're only just starting to learn.'

Another aspect of doing this, of course, is the need to involve all the professions and disciplines, encouraging them to work across barriers in line with the supply chain philosophy. This train of argument translates into the area of relationships.

In terms of the effect of e-business, Sir John believes one of the biggest revolutions, supply chain co-ordination through the Internet, is yet to come. When it does, the savings in waste will be huge. It was already pretty obvious that you could have paper-free transactions, co-ordinated design processes, and co-ordination of deliveries that would not have been possible before the Internet. Sir John argued that the Internet revolution started in the wrong place.

> *'If it had started in supply chains then you would have had the revolution yourself straight away, and not the ephemeral things of creating businesses that did things that people didn't want, that nobody could make any money out of. We need to embrace all suppliers and for that you need the Internet.'*

Speaking of sustainability or durability, Sir John saw the issue as one of anticipation.

> *'As you go deeper and deeper into it, you will find more and more how it impacts on you, and what you have to do. I think you simply need to make sure your antennae of predictability are there, because if you don't, it will catch up with you.'*

BT has had a long tradition of community involvement. This has helped its image with customers, and assisted the massive change within its workforce as the number of employees has shrunk over a decade from a quarter of a million to less than half that figure, while the volume of business has risen through new products and diversification. BT invests an enormous sum in the community, and Bob Mason sees parallels between BT and other prominent names such as Tesco. He explained that BT is a member of the Percent Club, which means it guarantees to give a proportion of its profits to community activities. Currently, the firm invests £15m pa in community activity, supports schools with the Internet, and has a positive impact on education. Bob commented:

> *'I think that the impact on reputation and, ultimately, on brand is really important. I think the companies that grasp that enhance their brand accordingly. An example is Tesco's computers for schools initiative. It is fantastic. They're giving vouchers out at the checkouts, Mums and Dads and grandparents are collecting them. Tesco is seen as providing computers for schools. It's a grocer for God's sake! It's not exactly the logical company! That builds into the company's reputation and the Tesco brand is enhanced. So I think there are some really strategically important reasons for doing it.'*

Bob graphically described the effect on employees, with considerable feeling. He explained how BT had become involved in some mentoring schemes for thirteen to fourteen-year old kids at school, in underprivileged areas of the country, where there was low parental interest and high truancy levels. BT offered each of these schools a 1:1 mentoring relation with one of their employees. Bob said that the initial temptation had been to use managers to do this, but although they did use some managers, basically the scheme was made available to any of their employees. People who typically were doing quite routine jobs, telephone operators, technicians, call centre people, had the job of spending a couple of hours a week speaking to young people on a 1:1 basis. BT had anticipated a difficulty in getting volunteers, but the in fact the opposite was the case. As Bob told me:

> 'We were overwhelmed with volunteers and the real pay-off came when our people came back to us and said, 'This is fantastic, we feel we are really making a difference. We feel not only that our other skills are being utilised, but we are learning how to use those skills more effectively'.'

As Bob commented, to talk to a young person about why it is important to do their homework, to come into school on a Friday, or to explain why the teachers do have a point about this, that or the other, requires a level of social interaction which is rarely tested in the workplace.

> 'They were getting fantastic personal development. The kids were getting adults that they could communicate with, rather than authority figures, and it was a tremendous win- win.'

Bob sees these efforts as part of a bigger picture. They are not just benefits to employees, but are also impacting on corporate reputation, if not brand. And as he said:

> 'When you're talking about brand and corporate reputation, I'm not sure about brand, but certainly corporate reputation is going to become increasingly important.'

In terms of the scale of BT's relationships, Bob saw the firm towards the upper end of the scale in terms of relationships with suppliers, and customers. As an example, Bob cited BT's diversity policies both within the firm and externally. He explained that BT had increasingly developed their equal opportunities policies quite heavily to think more in terms of a diversity challenge for the whole business. He commented:

> 'We did not just provide equal opportunities to our employees but focused on how we were managing the diversity of employee/customer/supplier issues. To what extent did we use ethnic minority small business suppliers, rather than placing all our contracts with large corporate organisations which were nationally based? This required us to think about our supplier relations in a very different way. I think that was very much a part of BT's approach.'

Where Bob saw a struggle was in terms of internal relationships, and in particular the tensions about central control versus autonomy of the newly spawned business units. He asked:

'Do these business units co-operate with each other? We never felt
that the internal co-operation was as strong as it should be. We used
to measure that through our attitude surveys, and our people didn't
think it was strong, yet the whole business relies on that internal co-
operation. At a very basic level, how do you install a telephone line
to a customer's premises? You need a sales person to take the order,
you need someone to line up all the exchange equipment, you need
someone to do the work in the house, you need someone else to
provide the telephone equipment or the switch, or whatever it
happens to be. There's this whole series of different bits of the
organisation, which need to come together at one time to fulfil what
is a very simple order. We struggled with that.'

This experience has been a very common one for the newly privatised
utilities. From my personal experience at Northern Electric, similar
tensions emerged in the early 1990s as the concept of customer focus
grew. Previously, projects had been organised sequentially, rather like
a baton being handed over in a relay race. Similarly for Anglian Water,
now the challenge is to co-ordinate different businesses to produce a
customer focus. An issue for this is the applicability of vision and
values across the organisation.

When we moved on to discussing business sustainability, I asked
Bob about the business reversals in the first years of this Century, with
the aftermath of the bidding for mobile network licences and the
legacy in terms of debt. Bob said he had thought about this a lot,

And he had come to the conclusion that the strategy at the time
had been the right one. Also, relationships were not really the issue.
BT had all kinds of different relationships; strategic alliances, joint
ventures, and all kinds of different partnerships around the world, and
it managed these with a degree of sensitivity. He did not think this was
the root cause of the firm's difficulties. He explained:

'I genuinely think the firm was caught between a rock and a hard
place. Should it have not bid for the mobile licences? That would
have been ridiculous. How could a major communications company
not operate a mobile network? Did it pay over the odds? Absolutely
but, there again, so did all the other companies. It was quite
interesting that many of the Asian countries did not issue licences in
the same way, and maybe their companies will benefit as a result, but
I'm not sure that it was relationships that got in our way.'

In discussing sustainability or durability, Bob took the reinvention
route. He felt that the companies that would survive and would be
sustainably delivering wealth into the future would be those who
almost continuously reinvent themselves. He went on:

'I think durability is not about remaining the same, it's about *remaining fit in the long term. That for me is the concept. If it's the kind of corporate organisation, 'durability' is - Does it continue? Is it a 'built to last' type of organisation?'*

Bob said that, for him, the organisations that have succeeded are those that have constantly challenged themselves to become different. For example, 3M was originally the Minnesota Mining and Manufacturing Company. Today it worked in coatings and heaven knows what else.

'The companies that will succeed in the long term are those that will constantly challenge what they're about, and do things differently. So I don't think sustainability is just rhetoric.'

Asked what motivated the Board, Bob was very clear that in BT it was the business case for ethical behaviour that would give a competitive edge.

'I think there's no question it's a business imperative. Business has suddenly woken up to the fact that, worldwide, it has to pursue its endeavours in a socially responsible way. I think some companies have had some very close shaves in recent times, in terms of the way they've carried out their business in certain parts of the world.'

Bob was sure that what would be attractive about companies in the future would be whether they were ethically sound.

'It's about having a social conscience. It just makes sound business sense. Companies who feel they are being pushed into this for social reasons, for environmental, or for moral reasons, will come unstuck because they'll be seen as not genuinely believing in what they're saying.'

Bob's comments show clearly that the business case must be backed by ethics that are owned, rather than being forced into the stance of adopting others' morals or else it will be a case of 'society biting back'.

With GB Rail, Jeremy Long saw the 'extrovert organisation' as an opportunity for gaining ideas from other consumer services businesses.

'We're a consumer services business, having to run a railway, but as far as I'm concerned, it's not just about going and looking at other railway companies. There can be ideas from other consumer services businesses. It's not just about what is the best direct marketing campaign for a railway company that we can find. We'll be asking what other direct marketing campaigns are there run by other organisations.'

The other reason for being extrovert, Jeremy thought, was to build relationships:

'I do think that the other thing that one tries to do is to build relationships for when things go wrong. In other words, build the key supplier and community relationships. If I meet a Local Authority CEO or a CEO of Railtrack, what I'm trying to do is leave behind at my peer group a sense of trust, or a sense of wanting to work together which, however weakly, percolates down the two organisations.'

In the adversarial climate of the railways post-privatisation Jeremy takes a refreshing view of partnership. He said that, for some time, he had taken the view that supplier relationships were most fruitful when they were constructive rather than adversarial.

'I happen to take the view that the more you work with suppliers, the more constructive and beneficial are the relationship for both parties.'

On sustainability and durability Jeremy takes a deterministic view. It is what you made of the situation you were in. 'Is this business sustainable?' is not a question you were coming at day in and day out.

'The way you approach it is to say 'These are the assets, these are the skill sets, this is the management team we've got.' It is more a question of coming at it constructively, to ask what more could we be doing with these, against where the opportunities are. So you create your own sustainability as you go along, as opposed to saying, What are we going to do to be sustainable?'

Another strategy is ensuring good relations, so that business may follow as a result. Jeremy reflected:

'You'll do things for the local community because you think that, if you do a good job today, when you go to that council in a years' time and say, Will you now support us with money for a new service? they'll say, Yes, we will, because we've seen what you've done for us in the last year.'

IV PUBLIC SECTOR AND PFI

As we recognised in chapter 4 when we were looking at the 'basic premise', the public sector generally has a problem with the features and goals of the extrovert organisation. After all, it is often not in the interest of these organisations to attract more business, especially when resources to meet demand are limited! This forms an important distinction between the public sector and the others, which we will return in chapter 9.

The issues for policy makers in the public sector are more often whether they know what it is like to work for the services for which they are supposed to be making policy. For the NHS, Professor Sir Liam Donaldson expressed it this way.

> *'If you take the Department of Health's role, the Civil Service is very good at seconding people when they want to be seconded. However, I think an unacceptably high proportion of our policy making people, particularly the middle management, have never worked in the service for which it is making policies. I think that's a big weakness.'*

In terms of the influence of other organisational forms, there is an inevitable scepticism about the effectiveness of the succession of structural reforms on the NHS. Many would say that these have not changed the way people work at all. As an insider who has lived through all the recent structural changes, Sir Liam has an interesting view. He believes that the big structural changes, particularly the ones in the 80s and 90s, produced a situation where people were dealt a completely new hand of cards. They were asked to set up new organisations. As a result, they had to work out what this organisation was for. In so doing, they set some sort of cultural goals and they tried to orientate themselves properly.

> *'I can remember when the 1990 health service reforms came in, for the first time we had to write a mission statement – a vision statement. We had to write a business plan. Nobody had ever written a business plan before. Those are to do with culture, and therefore the reorganisation triggered a change in culture. As a result things did move forward, but it wasn't the structural change that delivered it per se.'*

As we have seen, at local level the NHS, concentrates in 'extrovert organisation' terms on its relationship with local partners. In Malcolm Lowe-Lauri's case, this includes a sensitivity to the place in environmental, social and economic terms, of the hospital as the city's second largest employer. However, this is an unusually broad view for the public sector.

For John Bridge at One NorthEast, the external issues relate to sustainability or durability and, in particular, to the human resource. He argues that durability within a regional economic or social system lies within the people. When there is destruction, it lies in the products and services that are being generated.

> *'If you can get sufficient confidence, and sufficient capability, within the people, then it doesn't matter what's being destroyed because you can always build it up again. The new economy is about saying that individuals have got all sorts of capacities which they can apply to certain products and services at a particular point in time. If the*

*products and services change, that doesn't matter because we're such
a clever, innovative group of people, we can go off and do something
else.'*

Some view the introduction of call centres operations to the north
east as a short-term palliative, before the activities migrate to India or
wherever. John Bridge takes a longer term, skills enhancement view.
He stresses that the development of call centres bring two benefits:

*'Firstly, they create employment and also they generate two very
interesting skills in people. One is computer literacy, and the other is
communication skills. Both are transferable. What we would like to
do is to ensure that we get some sort of positioning in the higher
value added areas, in the areas of distribution services, high quality
diagnostic services, those sorts of things.'*

John recognises that flexibility must ride along with skill
enhancement.

*'I would hope that we are gradually beginning to develop more
flexibility, albeit at a relatively low level. You're trying to do two
things. First of all, you're trying to persuade people that flexibility is
a good thing. Second, flexibility at a higher level is an even better
thing. I think the two work together, and may well come together over
a period of time.'*

For the Arts Council, being an extrovert organisation is its core
business. Peter Hewitt saw the essential business being the connecting
of artists to society. For that, he believed, deep networking was
essential.

*'Being extrovert is core to our operations. We are essentially an
extrovert organisation, or else we would not survive. My time with
the Health Service was striking for its lack of understanding of what
makes partnership work. We have to be in partnership with
broadcasting, the commercial sector, and education. Our capacity is
all based on multiplication of resources and adding value.
Fundamentally, we are about locating artists in society, a task that
means we have to be connected, deeply networked, within that
society.'*

Peter saw the recent changes to the Arts Council as altering
fundamentally the nature of the extrovert organisation. The Arts
Council has fundamentally restructured their operations from a
'federal', loosely governed, organisation to a more centrally co-
ordinated structure. In terms of the effect at regional level, artists are
concerned about differences in relationships with the new structure.
Peter explained:

'It's clear that businesses are moving away from physical territory,

locality and territoriality generally. Our service and function is still related to the regional definitions of the organisation. The weight of politics is against this. The place and the regionality of the Arts Council is seen as a reflection of democracy.'

In considering durability or sustainability, Peter felt that in the Arts Council's case 'creative destruction' was needed to give rebirth.

'The cycle of re-birth/renewal is important in the process the organisation has been through in the past three years. I inherited an organisation that was potentially close to being abolished, and we began a programme of improvements and genuinely threw a lot out to create the renewal we needed.'

As to what motivated the Board, for Peter it was definitely the business case.

Jenny Clarke, from the Learning and Skills Council, observed that their 'pathfinder companies' increasingly saw the value of being extrovert organisations. She said that it was recognised by the pathfinder companies that it was in their best interest to have good community relations. Future employees came from those communities. It was also a means to get the brand recognised, not simply through acts of charity, but more importantly as a reflection of the company's values.

In terms of durability, Jenny felt that the connections between the business case on sustainability and the bottom line value were now being understood.

'I believe that the business case is self-evident. Those companies which do have a community/environmental policy can see the bottom line value, as well as the importance of aligning their actions to the core values of the organisation.'

The duality of thinking within the public sector is shown in the Patent Office example.

Like many other government agencies, the Patent Office had been relocated to the provinces (in this case, Newport, Gwent) to help with unemployment. Therefore the Patent Office is in one sense central to the community. However, as a consumer of public money there is concern over focus and priorities.

'The presence of the Patent Office in Newport is in itself a critical part of the community, but there are currently no structured programmes to become directly involved in the community through sponsorship, engagement with local schemes and initiatives, etc. There is always a 'fear' of being seen to do something 'frivolous' with the public's money. The Patent Office does support the New Deal.'

Relationships with stakeholders are fostered, particularly with professional bodies and education. Philip Johnson highlighted a very positive development of relationships with higher education and schools. The aim of this was the raising of the awareness of intellectual property. They are working too with the Small Businesses Service, since many businesses are not aware that they need help, or of the value which the Patent Office could add.

Lastly, in the case of Bovis Lend Lease, Mike Walters extended the pragmatic, project based, approach to the extrovert organisation. Being 'out there' means Bovis met clients and tackled innovation by assisting with research reports. Judgements were made about what was 'enough' in terms of contribution. The dilemmas were that this can become a diversion. However, as one of the bigger players, Mike considered it was about giving more than taking. This could raise standards, for example in the area of health and safety for the industry, and this could help in terms of raising recruitment standards. Mike recognised the contribution such activity could make.

> 'It does help to anticipate changes for the future. We use scenario planning. If we see something coming, then we can make responses earlier. If you are focused you can get competitive edge out of it.'

Mike also took the enlightened view that all should participate.

> 'Everyone/everywhere in the organisation should contribute to the antennae. This is part of our philosophy.'

On durability, for Mike the starting point has to be the business case, strongly linked with an ethical and moral position.

> 'The business case must be there, but if they are lived the values create the moral case to build social and environmental durability. We need sustainable competitive advantage, and to build more and more in a sustainable way. We are participating in a waste research R & D project to minimise waste. The ethical way is lived through how the Chairman views ethics, and she leads the organisation in a way that encourages that we live this.'

V   'BUILT-TO-LAST' ORGANISATIONS/ 'STEADY AS SHE GOES'

At Shell, Mark Hope took a personal perspective on being part of the 'extrovert' side of the organisation. He has been a Non-executive Director of two very small businesses and he helps run a community arts centre in his spare time. He commented:

> 'I think I'm better than many people at seeing other people's points

of view, because I have regular experience of working at the other end of the spectrum. From an SME's point of view, large companies like Shell are very difficult to deal with. They are compartmentalised, with all kinds of rules that don't seem sensible to a very small business, and requirements which need chunks of work that are unproductive from the point of view of small business. I think the fact that I'm exposed to life as an SME with seven employees and an arts organisation, which is largely voluntary, is very valuable for my own learning.'

However, Mark felt that, as an enormous global organisation, Shell struggled with the issue. He explained that they tried hard at this, and used some sophisticated techniques to support it. They had an excellent process for mapping their stakeholders and seeking to communicate effectively with them. But Mark thought they still fell quite a long way short of any definition of being intrinsically an extrovert organisation.

'Shell is something of a world of its own and many of our staff are insulated from the outside world by our own processes and procedures.'

Discussing relationships and where Shell fell on the scale of these, Mark placed the firm somewhere in the middle. Again it was an issue on which they had done a lot of work and they carried out a lot of consultation, but the organisation was not yet in 'deep co-dependency'. Mark reflected:

'I am not sure to what extent there's a will actually to work our strategy with external stakeholders. In some areas of business, this might conflict with competition law; in others it might be naive.'

This, in Mark's view, was very much in line with how other UK businesses would see the issue.

E-commerce, in Mark's view, is not only changing the nature of Shell's relationship with suppliers, it is also creating different partnerships, which had not been thought of before. Mark described how Shell was already buying well over half its goods and services through e-business, and would be moving toward 90 per cent in the next couple of years. As he said:

'In a few years' time, I suspect that if you can't do e-commerce with Shell, you won't do business with Shell (or many other companies). So it means that suppliers are going to have to get e-literate or go out of business.'

Mark described how new partnerships emerged. He explained that in the United States Shell had been looking at teaming up with dry cleaning people, the idea being that it represented the high value-add end of the chemicals business. There were lots of people in Manhattan flats, for example, who could afford to get all their laundry done for them. Mark said:

> *'Maybe you would make more money out of chemicals if you are teamed up with dry cleaning, say providing a complete laundry service to a block of flats. Five or ten years ago we might have said that dry cleaning has nothing to do with Shell's core business; today we would not be so sure.'*

The same pattern of thought impinges on the issue of durability. Mark asked rhetorically 'Is it achievable?' and doubted if it was, at least in terms of the business as they knew it.

> *'I think Shell's going to have to reinvent itself over the next five to ten years. I guess it's had to reinvent itself over the last twenty years, and the cycle time is getting progressively shorter.'*

Lawrence Churchill at UNUM is a fan of external involvement for business. Essentially, his view is that you cannot sustain Shareholder Value unless you take a Stakeholder view. Like Mark Hope, he believes it gives you a perspective through understanding the views of stakeholders. Lawrence also sees the benefit in terms of staff recruitment, in particular from ethnic minorities. UNUM employees are given paid leave to undertake charitable work. Some 600 volunteer days were undertaken in 2001. UNUM also sponsors awards for companies who, for example, provide accessibility for the disabled.

On the question of relationships, Lawrence sees this in the nature of the business. They ensure that UNUM staff interact closely with their 'partners'.

> *'As UNUM in many instances acts with the 'broker', as the manufacturer of the product, the policy of close working relationships with 'partners' is critical.'*

As we saw in chapter 4, as an entrepreneur David Burall typically took upon himself the mantle of the 'extrovert organisation'. The benefits that came from this were, firstly, seeing other business opportunities, secondly, seeing how other boards work and thirdly putting something back into the community. In David's case, this last is via the Health Service.

David and his wider family have taken a very formative view on durability. Probably more than any of the other cases in this book, they have ensured sustainability for the business (within natural limits) by looking ahead, and deciding to give long-term control to employees through share ownership. David described the situation in 1998, when employees had 8 per cent of the equity and when he himself had decided to retire. He described how he took seven members of the family who between them owned 92 per cent of the business to a local hotel for a weekend. They went through the alternatives facing them. These included selling the company, floating the company, making a trade sale which would have been terribly attractive at that time, continuing as shareholders but without managing the company, selling the company to the employees, or going for an MBO. David related:

> *'We originally ruled out an MBO, because an MBO leads, within three to four years to a trade sale anyway. But in the end we all agreed to go for employee ownership. So now 20 per cent of the shares are in a charitable trust with my two kids and my nephews as trustees. Twenty-four per cent are in the hands of family, so the dilution of the charitable trust in the family will continue. It will probably end up at around 65 per cent in the hands of the employees.'*

The situation in 2001 was that employees owned 56 per cent of the company.

At House of Hardy, in the extrovert organisation sense Richard Maudslay comes from a similar place to David Burall. His comment was:

> *'I've tried to stop other people doing it, because I'm doing enough for everyone else in the organisation at the moment!'*

Joking apart, Richard recognises the value of understanding the world outside. The largest benefit is for staff.

> *'The biggest external thing that's proved useful is in getting people in the first line supervisor level to go and visit another company, because they've never seen another company. They come back and say, they keep it very tidy you know. They paint their floors as well you know!'*

Richard is conscious of the pressure people are under and tries to protect them.

> *'People get very tired, but I'm sure they would get involved in something else if I asked them to. But I've tried to shield them from it in some ways.'*

The focus for commercial relationships is largely with customers and, latterly, with internal relationships. There, unusually for a small specialist manufacturer, House of Hardy won a DTI grant for establishing Partnership at Work with employees and trade unions.

Richard explained:

> 'The great advantage of doing it was because it was a formalised thing. Because the application form had to be signed by both trade union and company, it was an extremely good way of getting in there and saying, 'Come on, we've both got to do this together' and trying to change the type of trade union/employer relationship.'

In considering durability, Richard sees it having three levels:

> 'At level one, it's totally within our control. Unless we get the products better, make the products that people want, and produce them at the price people are prepared to pay, then business is not assured. So from that point of view, the future is entirely within our own hands.'

However demographics and trends are tending against fishing tackle manufacturers.

> 'There are fewer young people learning to fish. As a generalisation, people tend to fish until they are teenagers and then drop out of it and become interested in other things and go back to it when they are twenty-five to thirty. But kids are not fishing so much because of TV games, computer games and also people are so scared of letting kids out.'

Then, lastly, there is the increasing power of the NGOs, which are opposing animal sports including fishing. The industry tries to counter this with conservation arguments, but Richard sees limits in stakeholder relations here.

> 'There is so much evidence that rivers which are fished being cared for much better. We can do all sorts of things with the conservationists, but we cannot do things with the extremists.'

Marion Weatherhead, partner at Gardiner and Theobald, is another 'social activist' like Mark Hope, David Burall and Richard Maudslay. Her commitment to contributing to the community is hers, and not part of a grand corporate policy. She is chairman of Amicus, a large and successful housing association. She does this partly in her spare time, and also in working hours with the support of Gardiner and Theobald. Like Richard Maudslay at House of Hardy, she was active in this area before she joined Gardiner and Theobald. But Gardiner and Theobald value her external work and allow time for it.

> 'In the past, internal meetings have been changed to allow me time to chair an Amicus meeting.'

It helps Gardiner and Theobald's business to have Marion as the head of a high profile organisation in the not-for-profit sector. As she explained:

'When I'm looking for work with other clients, it does no harm that I'm chairman of a very good, best practice company. It aligns with the type of consultancy I undertake. I'm taking Gardiner and Theobald into new areas, as I am involved in some of the softer management issues now being adopted in the construction industry.'

I asked if this had helped with personal development. Marion responded:

'To go to a conference on behalf of Amicus usually means that I gain some new learning. The added value is both tangible and intangible. My confidence level, my ability to present, has got better because of ideas I picked up from people at Amicus.'

Despite Marion's personal and business success, this sort of involvement has not become policy. Marion sees great opportunities for younger people in general, for example becoming involved on a housing association board:

'I think that there is a value to businesses in getting younger people to do a limited time on the board of a housing association or other social business, particularly people who are going to end up at board level within business. I think a time spent on the Amicus board, where we're very supportive, where we're at the forefront of what's happening, we're attuned to the strategic and financial issues, is very valuable. There would be a lot more that a younger person with the basic skills could learn.'

In terms of relationships, and the issues of durability, like its peers in construction Gardiner and Theobald tends to react to the trends and pressures around it.

'There was a time when we would never have entered into a partnership with a contractor, because they have always been at arms length. But, as partnering comes along, some people are working in different ways and we've embraced that and made those changes.'

However, the firm finds itself 'chameleon' like. Marion explained:

'It's very difficult to go from adversarial relationships one day to soft and cuddly the next. Colleagues find themselves trying to wind up a contract that was adversarial while putting in place one that seeks to create a partnership with the same people. It's not easy.'

On durability, history is on Gardiner and Theobald's side in that they've 'lasted over 160 years' and survive by being a reactive follower.

'Does the firm change fast enough? It does actually. Mostly it changes, and adopts management, changes when they've worked elsewhere. There's a lot to be said for tending to be a second rather

*than a first mover in these matters. That's not to say we don't lead
the field. We frequently do in new services, but it's never a wholesale
shift. We always test the water.'*

John Cridland of the CBI puts into the corporate context this
section's emerging picture of the committed individual. To him the
extrovert organisation can be hugely beneficial.

*'It's the corporate version of an individual having some form of
Non-Executive role. I think the value comes from exposing the
organisation, just as it comes from exposing individuals, to quite
lateral situations in which the organisation normally wouldn't find
itself. The organisation gains as much as it offers.'*

As John went on to point out, you cannot measure this in normal
analytical terms.

*'I think that a lot of the value of business education links doesn't
come from trying to justify it on a cost benefit analysis grounds. I
think it comes from the organisation rolling up its sleeves and finding
itself in a primary school environment and realising that actually
there was a whole side of the world, or whole side to a new
generation that it had never appreciated.'*

In John's terms, the CBI is the definition of an organisation based on
effective relationships.

*'I think you have to be, because compared particularly to a
traditional manufacturing business, where 80 per cent of the equity of
the operations internally is within the control of the management; so
much of what CBI does is about collaboration. That doesn't mean
we're particularly good at it. Relationships are hard to get right, and
there are issues of gain sharing and mutual advantage, but we're
dependent on them so we have to be at the top end of that scale.'*

E-business has accelerated this trend.

*'We've been involved in partnership sourcing and supply chain
partnerships for a very long time, but you see the whole thing being
revolutionised by the potential of e-business portals for on-line
purchasing, on-line management of joint ventures, on-line
management of supplying. It is stripping out back offices and leading
to deeper relationships, where independent organisations actually are
able to collaborate regularly at an operational level, as well at a level
of aspiration.'*

Leslie Hannah, formerly at the Ashridge Trust, is also a personal
advocate of the extrovert organisation, and is following the same route
as Mark Hope, Lawrence Churchill, Richard Maudslay and Marion
Weatherhead in that he practised this in previous roles and continues
it in his current role. For instance, he has actively supported the work

of Tomorrow's Company for many years. In Leslie's case, he melds a longstanding Ashridge tradition of integrating 'knowing yourself' with the external 'extrovert' role.

> *'We encourage extroversion, but we also know - because we live by Myers Briggs - that most of our faculty are actually introverts. There is quite significant effort to get people to behave in other than their preferred personality type, because if you are concerned with responding to the market, and your prime product is getting close to clients and doing tailored, then you really have to be extrovert. There is actually much more emphasis here in attempting to get introverts to behave like extroverts than in any university I've been in. Every Ashridge person has one day a week to do consulting, and we encourage people to use that to the full because it gets them out into the outside world.'*

Ashridge also has a corporate social responsibility faculty, linked to the Sir Christopher Harding Legacy Project, aiding business leaders to be effective in this area.

To Leslie, the issue of relationships is vital – internally and externally. Ashridge has found the use its virtual learning resource centre is dependent on the depth of relationship. Leslie commented that one of the things that they had found with it was that the clients who got most out of it were those who use articles in depth within their organisation. Leslie remarked:

> *'The clients who have few hits on the website are actually the ones who just subscribe and say, We'll just tell our people about it. If they invite in our Director of Learning Resources, to share experience of how it works in other places and how to present it to staff, then the hits go up many fold. So there is still a need for client relationship management in a virtual world. It's a lesson we've learned.'*

For Leslie, talking of durability or sustainability is a false dichotomy.

> *'It is perfectly clear that business is about both. If you try to create a sustainable business which ought not to exist then you're going to fail. The British coal industry was an attempt to create a sustainable business, but I actually think it was wrong to send men down coal mines when it was actually cheaper to pension them off and send them on holidays.'*

Ashridge teaches the contrast between Collins and Porras ideas of 'built-to-last' and 'creative destruction'. Leslie argued that it was not always good to create a sustainable business.

> *'The first lecture on the advanced management programme is essentially saying that Porras and Collins are right. But I have to deal with the fact that most of our tutors are saying, 'You'll need to*

destroy your business tomorrow.' I say that there's a very good reason for this, which is that human beings are conservative. We naturally stay as we are, and that leads to not being responsive enough to what's happening in the world outside, and what the competition are doing.

So a great deal of business school teaching is devoted to making you sensitive to the fact that you've got to change. The most effective strategies are those that build on the past. That essentially was what Jack Welch did in setting up GE Capital. He did actually understand that a competitive advantage built in manufacturing could, in appropriate ways, be transferred to financial services. It was not, 'Electrics no good, we'll become the world's global financial services and we'll change overnight'. It was, 'We'll build on what we've got, because the industrialisation of financial services will give us a competitive advantage over banks.'

In listening to clients and using new technology, Ashridge has used emerging trends to complement traditional teaching.

'People can now do in three days plus using the virtual learning resource centre a course which used to take five days at Ashridge, doing the emotional intelligence thing before, and they value that. We're not charging any less for the three days plus the virtual learning resource centre than we were for five days, because the opportunity cost is something they take into account and they're willing to pay for the seamless service. So I think we're on to a winner in seeing them as complements, not substitutes.'

Why do organisations spend time and resource 'out there' when that resource could be deployed or focused on 'internal' activities?

Why are external relationships apparently now more important? Why do stakeholder issues seem to hold more sway on decision-making and strategies?

The first conclusion that I draw from this aspect of the research is that organisations today are more sensitive to the need to be 'out there', listening and influencing. I believe if this study had been conducted ten years ago we might well have found a different result.

Certain areas of 'extroversion' would be always prominent and timeless. The need to listen and talk to customers for instance – these were the actions of the 'confident management team' according to Jeremy Long of GB Rail.

Issues of company reputation have come more into question in recent time, which might explain the keen interest shown by many of our interviewees in activities that helped the brand. We saw examples from BT, R&SA and Cisco together with damage limitation 'insurance' against future situations in the case of GB Rail and House of Hardy. This result is supported by the PWC Survey of 1,000 CEOs referred to earlier. Seventy-nine per cent of the CEOs said that reputation and brand impact extensively on sustainability.

The growth area over the last decade has to be in the concept and practice of stakeholder relations. In analysing these interviews we need to be conscious that the results are influenced by the proportion of our sample that are adherents to the 'Tomorrow's Company' philosophy on the importance of stakeholders. Hence the results could be skewed – however others outside of Tomorrow's Company membership also show that they are convinced of the need to enhance stakeholder relations such as Toyota, Burall and the overwhelming support shown in the PWC Survey for sustainability programmes – 79 per cent of CEOs believing that sustainability is vital to profitability and further that 71 per cent are prepared to sacrifice short term profitability for long term shareholder value. Many of our interviewees saw this work in the context of building their businesses for the future. The category that ended up the more unsure was the public sector – why should they want to attract more business?

What I believe distinguishes this current study from many others I the discovery of the linkage between 'extroversion' and 'agility'.

In many ways this seems like stating the obvious – unless you have good antennae and can read the trends you don't know whether to act. However several of our interviewees saw the 'extroversion' not in the context of defence but the 'anticipation of the future'.

In the next chapter we will be exploring how agile these organisations think they are.

Notes

1   Putnam, R *Bowling Alone: The Collapse and Revival of an American Community* (Simon & Schuster 2001)

2   de Geus, Arie *Living Company* Nicholas Brealey 1997 (see also chapter 9 of this book)

3   Morton, C Newall, A and Sparkes, J *Leading HR* CIPD 2001

Chapter eight

THE AGILE ORGANISATION

AS WITH 'WORLD-CLASS' and the 'extrovert organisation' our interviewees have given their outline views on 'agile, proactive, catching the moment' in their organisations within chapter 4. Here there is the valuable opportunity to drill down on this vital element of sustainability and also to begin to explore the connections between the elements of the basic premise.

I   START-UPS / ENTREPRENEURSHIP / PHOENIX ORGANISATIONS

In many ways agility comes as second nature for start-up, entrepreneurial organisations. We reported Richard Hicks of AIT, talking about agility in chapter 4, saying that the felt that first you needed to 'split people off to be inventive and create flexibility'. Responsiveness comes from diversity – the licence to 'think outside the box'.

In many organisations the perception is that focus in necessary, in order to concentrate on the core business. The implication therefore is that you should outsource what you do not need to do for yourself. Richard told me that, at one point, AIT had done this with catering. However, they then realised what they had lost in terms of intangible benefits. Catering had been provided in-house for several years, when the firm was smaller. Then it got to the scale where it was big enough to be outsourced. Richard related the consequences:

> 'We went from a friendly, homely, environment to this dreadful
> outside catering operation which didn't in any way catch the mood.
> Some people said it was great that they had something to complain
> about, because the catering was so terrible!'

Richard explained that the outsourcing policy had been reversed. AIT had introduced an 'artist in residence' scheme and now they had added 'a chef in residence'. The purpose of this was more than the provision of better food – it addressed the whole of the working experience in AIT.

> 'We're building a different sort of staff catering facility, which aims
> to make food an integral part of the company's experience and to

convey a sense of caring for our staff. It will give them an option to socialise in our staff restaurant both during the day and after work. It will be good in terms of staff retention. It gives us more flexible meeting spaces, and another differentiator in the eyes of our customers too.'

Richard also explained that intangible benefits from agility can come in ambassadorial terms.

'These things can also give you opportunities to create identity. Anytime you can do something for a member of staff who is about to go home, or to the pub, so that he will tell his friends or his family, 'You should have heard what we did today' Something that helps them justify to their peer group why they work here. I think AIT does really well at that – creating exceptional events that give novelty value.'

At BioFocus, the cultural freedom to innovate parallels the AIT experience. In addition, the bright scientists who joined from 'Safe Pharma' backgrounds looked forward to the opportunity to innovate. Keith Moscrop commented:

'A lot of the scientists that have joined us here have been quite innovative people. One of the reasons they joined us is to express that innovation.'

I asked Keith if this had been designed in to the organisation. He explained that BioFocus had done it right from the beginning, but it had to be 'catch as you can'. They had not raised money to invest in formal product or planned it that way round.

'It's all been a case of, while we're doing all this boring, bog-standard, service stuff for people, what can we do around the edges of it that will build us into a nice and bright future?'

Keith believed that the company had achieved a good balance between internal developments and serving the customer.

'I think that the company is outstanding in what has been achieved in proportion to the amount of external funding obtained.'

This sounds very much like a 'by the skin of our teeth' approach! Keith said that, because of the need to focus on the development of special tools, In BioFocus there is a tendency to outsource those things that can distract. So:

'There is a tendency to outsource the building blocks of what we need, and stay at the design end. We're the architects of this particular area of discovery. We tend to be leaders in the approach to it. If we want to make a special set of chemicals, if we can buy in or outsource all the bricks we need to build the wall, then we will.'

Keith said that possibilities of 'break out' could occur in customer organisations, if one took an innovative approach. He explained that some of the tools BioFocus deployed were of general use, while some were more specific. It is the mindset behind their construction that is the most important element.

> *'The basic ideas, which were worked up around one senior scientist, who was freed from constraints in his earlier life, have informed others and this has allowed further developments to take place. A senior scientist who joined us some years later was inspired to build on these ideas. He has come up with a concept that has led us into a new area. Again you see, there is break out. He'd been wanting to do this for a long while, and he has had the freedom to do it.'*

With The Generics Group, there is no shortage of talent, and no shortage of incentives for innovation, so ideas are abundant and expressed. Duncan Hine felt that, even if you couldn't totally engineer innovation or predict conception of the winning idea, you could make it more likely to happen.

> *'I think you can certainly affect it. You can influence it. And when it does happen, you can make it more likely to succeed. But I don't think actually you can affect that moment of conception. That's largely in the hands of the individuals. I could organise a brainstorm in the next hour, and you could throw a problem at us, and we will give you twenty or fifty amazing new ways of doing something. But actually that depends on the ten people in the room volunteering those twenty things.'*

However, as Duncan pointed out, merely getting bright people together to brainstorm does not necessarily bring results, whereas in Generics it has been possible to link the idea to the solution. It was not the use of techniques like brainstorming that was the secret. Duncan elaborated on this:

> *'Everybody does brainstorms these days, but in some big, bureaucratic, companies, either it doesn't lead to much of an outcome, so they think it's not really worth trying, or they do it so infrequently that they never really free fall out. They're a bit of spinning, political things, so that you don't really get a chance to be wildly creative.*
>
> *I think the other big difference here, and this is a proven thing, is that we can do something that is very unusual. We can now do the brainstorm where people say, for instance, 'You know if it was 10 per cent of the size, it would be a radically different product'. That's great, but making one that works at 10 per cent of the size is very, very difficult. But we can do that as well, because we can go into our other mode where we'll flow the output of the brainstorm on the*

*problem out to the hard end technology sphere. We have many
examples of products where we've halved the manufacturing costs,
we've put the battery life up 1,000 fold, and so on. The big difference
here is that we can have the wild idea and then produce a workable
solution to it.'*

Dianne Thompson at Camelot has already shared her views on the
issued of mixed messages because of the period of re-bidding for the
second licence, and the need now that is achieved to re-engender
creativity. As she explained:

*'Some of it is about behaviours. I think it's very much about
empowerment. As long as people feel that they are always having to
go back up the layers of bureaucracy, that stymies creativity. I think
it's about new ways of working, and new working environments. I do
believe the environment you operate in is very important in terms of
creativity and innovation. It's also about an attitude in business, and
it's about us saying that it's okay to fail. I've been saying to people,
Just take ownership of it, just go and try it. Some you'll get wrong
and some you'll get right.'*

So, I asked Dianne, how do you go about designing innovation into
the organisation? She said that Camelot had some project groups
working on innovation and change, and the people that were assigned
to those actually gained time out to brainstorm or whatever. They
have also designated a room as a 'think room'. Dianne said it always
looked a mess but at least it showed that people were being creative.
She also discussed the usual tension over balancing day-to-day
pressures on the business with innovation. She spoke of an idea she
had got from Barbara Cassani (then Chief Executive of GO, the low-
cost airline).

*'What she had was a post-it note room, where you can put post-it
notes with ideas on. The nice thing about her room is that, if
somebody writes an idea, somebody else may come along and add to
it. We haven't got to that stage yet. We're playing around with our
think room, but we're trying to do that. To be frank, the problem
we've got at the moment is that there's a lot more we'd like to do but
because, firstly, so much time has been taken up with recruitment or
induction of new people coming in and, secondly, we've got new
terminals to get out, we're all working absolutely flat out on the
current project.'*

b Not-for-profit start-up/Lymphoma Association

As in other areas, Alan Bartle felt that the Lymphoma Association was
somewhat behind other sectors. Consistent with this, he thought that
ideas and innovation were more likely to come from outside than be

generated from within. He therefore allied this with the thoughts he had on the extrovert organisation, together with giving more scope to people to act. If the Association was actually identifying trends in the charity sector in the lymphoma field that gave it the opportunity of being in the right place at the right time.

> 'If we are monitoring, if we are going out, if we are networking, if we are talking to the right people, then we will become aware of opportunities, and we'll be in a position to respond. We do know that it's a rare occurrence that somebody comes and knocks on the door with that opportunity. We have to be out there knocking on their doors and being ready for it.'

Talking about encouraging creativity and innovation, Alan said he would like to feel that each of the Association's team now was much more open to that. He thought they had had some success with it, in that there was a greater willingness now.

> 'Various members of the team actually bring ideas up at meetings. I've made it very clear that not everything has to come from my desk. If there's something on which they can act today, and I'm not in the office, just get out there and act upon it, whatever it is. If it works, that's brilliant and I'll applaud them. If it fails I'm quite happy for the responsibility it to fall on my shoulders, because tomorrow might be too late.'

c 'Phoenix' organisations

Bryan Jackson from Toyota gave an answer which accorded with my memory of Komatsu's approach. Innovation was an expectation of everybody, and therefore the approach was systematised. Employees were encouraged to join in Kaizen Action Meetings (KAMs) and particular encouragement was given by allocation KAM days, which are devoted to accelerating improvements. There is no financial reward, but great recognition of achievements. In a way that is similar to the Quality Circle movement, there is competition world wide for the KAMs, to promote the best ideas and go in for knowledge sharing.

In similar vein, to gain improvements across boundaries, the process of sharing ('yokoten', literally 'cascading') is strongly supported to promote improvements and give recognition. The classic difference with other organisations is that improvement, innovation, ideas and creativity are expected, systematised and encouraged from all sections of the workforce, not just the intelligentsia.

Some of the solutions from Unipart Automotive display similar origins to those at Toyota. Paul Forman made the connection between customer awareness and the internalising of improvements with technology that helps the spreading of knowledge.

> 'You've got to have the right mind set, being customer aware, because you can see there's a real benefit. In internalising that notion, you've got to have the tools. It's having the right databases, the right measurements. If something is merely an anecdote, and stays out in a branch in Aberystwyth, say, then that's tacit knowledge and not something that can be shared. We've created an Intranet in the organisation, which we've called the Oracle. It is a way not only of people doing their business, by accessing on-line internal job agencies, marketing programmes, and so on, but also a way of sharing best practice, and making tacit knowledge explicit.'

In terms of how to encourage creativity and innovation, Paul is on familiar ground.

> 'Create a culture of self-belief and self esteem in people, otherwise they won't think that it has any benefit for the organisation even if they are creative. It comes to mindset and tools. We have a (quality) circle programme, which we use to solve problems, and also 'pie and pint' sessions orally where we have good ideas coming up through the organisation. The branches are supportive, my directors are supportive, but it means working on middle management so that they see that upward flux of ideas up as an opportunity for them to succeed rather than a threat. You quite often need to change some mind-sets there.'

Paul was clear that the Unipart view was that you could engineer creativity, and build the resource to create the opportunity.

> 'Undoubtedly, you've got to give yourself the organisational tool-kit, to tune into the market place. By definition, if you are give people the right tools you've got to have the intranet in place already. To help them we designed the Oracle in conjunction with the business. It's a must have, an integral part not an adjunct.'

d Consultancy/Outsourcing

Tim Watts at Pertemps is on familiar ground. For him, employees or partners 'catch the moment' because they own the company.

> 'They are always keen to offer up ideas and suggestions to improve working practice. People do not hold back, they adopt the 'keep attacking' mindset.'

In similar vein, Tim commented:

> 'We encourage creativity and innovation, and allow mistakes. But I expect no one to make the same mistake twice, but rather to learn from the mistake.'

Can we engineer creativity, I asked Tim?

'It is about creating the environment to allow it to be part of the way we do things around here.'

Tim referred to the 'leaves on the tree' concept we had talked about earlier (new employees were the leaves) and how they all worked together. .

'Here, everyone is a leader and everyone should be spotting the opportunity and actively communicating.'

For Bill Penney, the requirement was about being alive to opportunities that may develop, and then committing to them. There were huge strengths in this, but also huge dangers. The approach needed to be very proactive, not reactive, in order to be selective.

'There are tracks that get you nowhere and are counterproductive and disappear. We've decided that the field of opportunities at the moment is actually so broad that we need to be proactive about it, not reactive.'

Bill and his colleagues were wary of being driven by 'more of the same' and extrapolation from where they were perceived to be. This linked with Bill's answers when we talked about the 'extrovert organisations'.

'It's trying to keep a balance between, Don't let's just extrapolate, don't let's assume it's going to be more of the same, and, Let's try and see where things are going and take advantage of that.'

Ashton Penney, in contrast with some of the other organisations we have discussed, outsourced everything they could. For instance, they were even using their own methodology of employing interim managers to find new offices and facilities!

Peter Smith, of The Strategic Partnership, believed in structural solutions to innovation. That meant having people whose job it was to think through new solutions. This was similar to how the government was structured, having an innovation unit looking at trends. This approach commenced with scenario planning, aiming to keep the 'unpredictable' in the planning process. I suspect that this would be seen as a very specialised and different approach in Toyota or Generics!

Lastly, Peter Ward of Telos summed up the situation from the viewpoint of a consultancy that thrived on innovation. He thought they were benefiting from having a group of people who had different backgrounds, which created a certain amount of stimulation about the way they did things.

> *'I can't see us twenty-five years from now doing what we do today.*
> *We'll be doing something else. I don't know what it will be, but I can*
> *tell you the themes. You'll be able to trace them, because those things*
> *are important to us as we develop and grow and change things*
> *around.'*

So, for Peter, the issue went back to making sure that you understood the point where you were on the sigmoid curve, being aware of the external world, and seizing the moment. It was doing all of those things. And Peter had recognised the key success factors that led to this way of working:

> *'What's important is trust and confidence within the business. If*
> *you've got that, people are prepared to experiment and fail. If they're*
> *prepared to experiment and fail because of their trust and*
> *confidence, you cannot help but engender new ways of doing things. I*
> *like the economic model, because that in itself stimulates you to do*
> *things. There's that edge all the time – 'I've got to make the sale, I've*
> *got to deliver the goods'. You count your money and then decide what*
> *you're going to do with it. The efficiency that you get from it, and the*
> *application of ideas to commercial situations, helps you to develop*
> *your thinking.'*

When you think about it, there are many similarities here to the Generics Group.

II   M&A/DEMERGER ORGANISATIONS

In a very similar way to other groups, the interviewees in this category overwhelmingly expressed the need and the aspiration for the whole organisation to be innovative, but at the same time described their frustrations that obstacles were in the way.

Syd Pennington of R&SA admitted that:

> *'We've not been the greatest innovators in the world. There's*
> *increasingly a realisation that we need to be more creative, and that*
> *we need to be helping create new markets. The concept of moving to*
> *a solution provider is the way we are taking it forward.'*

For R&SA the real issue has been culture change. Syd described how they had tried to encourage people to take personal responsibility and accountability for issues. The firm had a belief that the nearer to the customer decisions were made, the better they will be. But as he recognised:

> *'It's difficult to go from a blame culture five years ago to a 'can do'*
> *culture today.'*

However, Syd felt that there were hopeful signs.

> 'We have had these practice groups, networking and sharing best
> practice and trying to develop new concepts for the best way forward.
> It's beginning to happen in pockets, but we're a long way away from
> being satisfied both in terms of agility and innovation. But the
> important thing is that we recognise it.'

Mike Rake of KPMG expressed similar desires and frustrations in the
same breath, together with a typical dilemma.

> 'I think agility is fundamental to the tight/loose syndrome, to the
> way our people react, and I think we're making progress. The
> innovation factor is hugely difficult. We've tried everything. We've
> tried having innovation centres and supporting them, but they
> become too far from reality. You try to encourage a spirit of
> innovation in everything that people do, which is possibly what we're
> trying to do with Darwin. If we begin to work that, then we have
> something that encourages it. You can't have everyone innovating
> every day all the time or you'll go out of business. On the other
> hand, you have to encourage people to innovate.'

Mike related a great anecdote, which described a case where
innovation had been implemented by people close to the ground.

> 'We tried to develop a global knowledge management system. We
> spent $100m on it, based in Boston. It failed to give us what we
> wanted. They were not close enough to the market place. The guys
> here decided to develop one, and in about three months they
> developed one for about £2m. It works brilliantly and is now in use
> throughout the whole world.'

For Todd Abbott at Cisco the issue was one of encouraging people to
challenge, something that becomes even more necessary as an
organisation got larger and potentially bureaucratic.

> 'We pride ourselves on looking for outside the box, creative, risk-
> taking types of people. As you get to be an organisation of our size,
> this gets harder to do, because the bigger you become, the more people
> there are who move into jobs thinking their responsibility is to say
> 'no'. But we've continued to reward people who, as I call it,
> 'constructively disagree'. If somebody is saying 'no' or is not allowing
> you to do what makes absolute business sense, then you have to
> constructively disagree.'

We mentioned in chapter 4 Sally Vanson's analysis from MCL/The
Performance Solution of intuition being a gender issue. Essentially,
she was arguing that diversity, whether male/female, sensor/intuitive
in personality terms, and temporary or interim staff, can often give
access to agility and innovation.

III PUBLIC TO PRIVATE

In the analysis reported in chapter 4, all our leaders agree that for innovation and creativity to flourish, there must be the atmosphere within the enterprise to encourage it. Yet, together with their desire to see this happen, there is a hesitation in being confident that it is actually happening. There seem to be a number of obstacles, including:

- the historical culture – where ideas were not welcomed in a command and control ethos
- the structure – where there is too much disconnection between the ideas and the authority to commit resources
- the lack of time and space to innovate, when the 'day job' is so dominating.

Consequently, our leaders end up with a feeling of frustration despite their good intentions. This is mixed with the sure and certain knowledge that the potential for innovation is not being fully realised in their organisations. The ex-public sector organisations feel this particularly keenly, because they have come from the risk-averse, command and control ethos. Added to this is the fact that the future of their predecessors never rested on the ability to innovate.

To some, the dominant reason is the issue of size. Jeremy Long of GB Rail felt that the answer was to create new profit centres by innovation. This is somewhat similar to Generics' solution, as espoused by Duncan Hine, in spinning off businesses using the scientific intellectual capital.

Bob Mason, formerly of BT, saw it in a similar light, by advocating the creation of incubators for the ideas to flourish. He charted the difference from yesterday, which was as much a cultural shift as a deliberate change in policy on innovation in BT. The change turned upon a different view of the place of relationships in business growth. Bob explained that lots of the innovation in BT, in technological terms, had taken place at their research laboratories at Martlesham in Suffolk. Bob thought that this was a great case study. It was a top-secret research establishment, where you had to have a pass to get in, and you were held at a visitors' centre outside the wire to have all your credentials checked before you were allowed on site. Bob described how the business realised that this was crazy, because it was actually repelling ideas. It was keeping people out. So a major change took place:

> 'About two to three years ago, the fences came down – literally.'

Security was lightened. Other suppliers and innovators and partner
organisations were invited, not only to visit the site, but also to locate
on the site. So Corning, for example, who do a lot in photonics and
optical technologies, now have a facility on site. What you develop
then is not a secret research laboratory but a technology park with
ideas and where people can stimulate each other.'

The second thing BT did was with some of the bright ideas identified.
People would develop a technology; then look to see if there was a
market for it. In other words, they created an incubator to which those
researchers could then take their business idea, and with some
support, be given the time and resources to develop it into a potential
business or product. But there was still a problem of scale, as Bob
commented:

'How do you deal with all the ideas that come up? I don't know that
anyone's really cracked that.'

Again, this is a story that is very similar in concept to that of the
Generics Group.

Both Sir John Egan and Jeremy Long felt that the issue was about
giving people space to innovate. For John, it was about encouraging
employees to undertake controlled experiments as part of process
improvement. This approach owed a lot to John's manufacturing
background. And in his mind innovation was mainly about
incremental steps (continuous improvement, or Kaizen). Jeremy, on
the other hand, saw innovation competing for time with the 'day job'.

'You've got to have just a bit of slack in the organisation for people
to go and back their hunches, and also to try to get people to feel as
though it's worth their while doing that. In the short term that
nearly always means more risk or hassle for the innovator.'

Both Tony Ward of BAA and Chris Mellor of AWG focused on the
crucial area of culture as an enabler of innovation and creativity. Both
felt that, despite the massive efforts in both organisations, the culture
was not yet as helpful as it could be. Chris Mellor recognised the vital
importance of signals.

'I think fundamentally this is about trying to create the right culture
and environment. It needs a supportive environment that encourages
people to take risks and to feel that they won't get their pension
chopped off if they make a mistake. Signals are very important in
an organisation.'

He also recognised that the days of innovation coming from the top
of organisations were numbered.

'It seems to me that, in today's society which is so complex, the odds

against leaders in large organisations being sufficiently close to what's going on in the marketplace to be able to spot an opportunity are probably lengthening all the time.'

Tony Ward was frank about the issue, and acknowledged that BAA had not got this right yet. The organisation knew that there was more progress that they could make on it. He admitted:

'We're back to leadership and self-insight. One of the things we've also demonstrated is that the perspective of people at the top of the wall is quite different from the people at the bottom. We've got a cultural map which shows us that we've got a defensively aggressive type of culture; I defend myself, I don't take responsibility, I keep my head down. If that is the culture that prevails, then when I'm working towards my boss, I turn it round. I say, How do I survive in that culture? How do I manage myself, if I'm managed by someone like myself? So we've done quite a bit of work trying to build on our strengths, eg coping skills, problem solving, tolerance, etc., but our cultural weaknesses inhibit learning and innovation for example.'

In terms of whether organisations can engineer the resource to facilitate creativity or whether resourcing has to follow the idea, Tony thought in reality it was a bit of both.

'Mainly, we're in the opportunity seizing type camp, but we are trying to build the capacity to give us that (creativity) and the climate which would encourage it. We are trying to make it more constructive in its totality, and supportive of failure, hence one of our key values is learning.'

Chris Mellor felt that innovation in business development needed a focused, strategic, approach – it was not going to happen by chance.

'I think it starts with having a clear strategy. You're never going to get anywhere by just throwing darts at the board hoping they will hit something. You've got to be pretty focused, because you can't do everything, and you can't be everywhere. You have to develop teams who can make proper assessment of risk and bid for it to be visionary.'

IV PUBLIC SECTOR AND PFI

Again, drawing on our analyses in chapter 4, our interviewees were totally conscious of the key role of innovation in sustainability. Not surprisingly, the obstacles this group identified were very similar to the 'public to private' analysis, ie:

- the historical culture – ideas not traditionally welcomed
- the structure – disconnection between ideas and resources

- lack of time and space to innovate in competition with 'the day job'.

To these we can add a number of additional factors:

- If the concept of 'extrovert' is not embraced, how can innovation and agility follow?
- Innovation can be seen in technological terms and not necessarily organisationally – as in the NHS, for example.
- The macro economic view prevailing in the public sector that their role is to create stability in order that change may be free to happen in the private sector (the Treasury view) – which begs the question of how the public sector can become agile and innovate (the John Bridge view).
- To reinforce the above the view from the judgers of intellectual property, the Patent Office who encourage innovation in industry but, as we have seen, find it difficult to apply within.

To start with the Patent Office, Philip Johnson feels that more can be done to develop the resource and tap the potential of the organisation. The classic method of progression is via Civil Service vacancies, so that constituent departments within lose good people. In my experience, this is similar to the NHS. There is often too little effort to create succession plans within NHS Trusts for instance, and a reliance on the advertising of vacancies and the desire of individuals to move.

Philip Johnson concluded:

> 'At its heart is the culture of the Patent Office. The integrity of the work is sacrosanct and nothing can or should be done which might jeopardise that. However, the Patent Office has to be more than world class, and they have a role to play in all the interactions they have with potentially world-class businesses. They must question what they do and how they do it. They need a healthy turnover of people. They have somehow to break the mould, constantly challenge, and push and push. Despite the rigidity of the end product, it would be possible to change the culture. Of course their customers see their product not their culture. But how much better could it be though?'

There are few pieces of research that link internal organisation factors to customer outcomes in the NHS, and few examples of high performance working in the public sector in general (see David Ashton et al in ILO study)[1]. However Professor Michael West of Aston University[2] has produced an interesting study that links team working and appraisals within acute hospitals to mortality rates. This is in the same vein as his studies in manufacturing, which linked people- management practices with productivity and profits. (See *Beyond World Class* p134)[3]

Sir Liam Donaldson saw that major innovation has to happen in the education of professionals. He tells the entrancing story of commenting on the General Medical Council's latest draft of their *Tomorrow's Doctor* document.

> 'There are so many things that people have never asked the obvious question before. Nobody, for example has ever said, Good communication is so important to our patients. What are we doing about it? And there are big stones that have never been turned.'

Sir Liam explained how, when he got the GMC's latest draft of their document, which is basically what they send out to medical schools to tell them how to design their curricula, he took a look at it and thought that the Department of Health was not just another consultee. They were not just one of 600 people who pitched in a view. This was their service. Sir Liam acted accordingly:

> 'I wrote a couple of pages and sent it to the Chairman of the committee that was due to look it and said, We are not a normal consultee. In future, we want doctors who can work in teams, who respect other professions, who can properly communicate with their patients, who can understand how to affect the quality of their services improving, who understand how to use the information, and all the other things that we would want to see in the future. If these are the sorts of doctors we want in ten years' time, they're not just going to turn up on their own. We've got to go upstream, and going upstream is unheard of in traditional civil service work and central government work.'

The last sentence should ring in our ears. It is about fundamental challenge and moving 'up stream' to the source.

Malcolm Lowe-Lauri, speaking from the NHS Trust perspective, feels that although individuals can be agile and innovative, moving the Trust forward is more difficult.

> 'The complexity of the Trust means that, although you can harness creativity and innovation, its implementation and therefore its impact is slow. It is a super tanker rather than a speedboat. It is essential to create the right environment where highly qualified and academic individuals can be harnessed to produce results and outputs which are fully aligned to the Trust's Vision and Values. You need to have in place a change Team (such as the Transformation Project)[4] and the testimony to their skill and success is the fact that many of those team members have moved on (beyond the Trust). The skills are always developed internally – the Trust does not 'buy in' knowledge.'

This in part explains why, as good as Trust-inspired change like this is, it is very difficult to transfer such good practice to another part of the NHS.

In Regional Economic Development terms, agility and innovation doe snot necessarily equate to science and technology. John Bridge did not see necessarily the validity of duplicating, for example, the Cambridge Scientific Park in other places, or that innovation should be seen only in those terms. He argued that you could actually generate higher added value in quite a number of different areas. For example, he talked about cultural tourism. What was know was that cultural tourism was much more valuable to a region than 'tourism tourism'.

> 'By 'tourism tourism' I mean somebody who goes to Whitley Bay for a week, and spends some money in the pubs and casinos. Somebody coming into Newcastle, to go to the Theatre Royal and to a few art galleries, staying in a better quality hotel, is actually spending two or three times more per day. So cultural tourism is very important to us.'

John said that, if you looked at tourism, leisure, culture, sports, and creative industries as a whole, they probably represented well over 20 per cent of the total workforce in the North East. If you look forward about ten years then they could represent about 40 per cent of the workforce. He concluded:

> 'You have a choice. You could get there through the low value route, by providing more and more low paid jobs, more and more McDonalds, or whatever. Or you could go the high value route, by providing high quality services, very high quality facilities from which people can benefit, and which obviously will increase regional income.'

Peter Hewitt, at the Arts Council, viewed innovation and agility in much the same way as did Chris Mellor at AWG and Bob Mason at BT. For him, it was about creating the right environment in which it would flourish.

> 'The key is highly skilled, authoritative, internationally respected individuals who can see the big picture, (theatre/visual/music, etc). It comes by creating an internal environment where challenge is welcome. Internal partnership is positively encouraged. It happens where traditional demarcation lines are willingly dismantled, where space is made for the exploration of idea rather than prioritising the fulfilment of tasks.'

Talking about whether you can engineer creativity, Peter felt it was more about 'engendering'.

> *'I'm not sure you can engineer creativity. You can engender it. It's about equilibrium between building the resource and being opportunity led. If we don't have the resource, then we are unlikely to convince people that ACE has an important role to play. We need to be able to respond to opportunities with agility, but also with flexible resources to back up this agility.'*

The only interviewee to consider the issue of 'employability' in the context of agility and anticipating the future was Jenny Clarke of the Learning and Skills Council. She believed that a company must be agile and anticipate the future. Therefore:

> *'We need to prepare employees for the possibility of redundancy, by equipping them with skills which would enable them to find work elsewhere. Companies are becoming more flexible. The ability to respond to the market place and to competition through innovation is critical.'*

Lastly, Mike Walters of Bovis Lend Lease saw agility and innovation in terms of product development. He instanced the growth of PFI products in construction companies. A few years ago there were none, and now all construction companies had PFI as a business.

Bovis kept product development high on the agenda. This was integrated with the planning cycle, stimulated by the firm's research arm to highlight ideas. Mike commented:

> *'Our 'business as usual' is about always catching the moment. People are encouraged to have the ideas and bring them in. Our matrix approach encourages this. Ours is a very fast moving environment, and by being out there this encourages creativity and innovation, since things are happening all the time.'*

Mike remarked pithily about the over-application of outsourcing to concentrate on the 'core' as a route to producing agility.

> *'I am not convinced. It sounds good, but there are lots of downsides. If you outsource too far, you end up with no company. You can lose the relationship thing, and if you outsource to the extreme then you end up with just a MD talking to himself!'*

V 'BUILT-TO-LAST' ORGANISATIONS/'STEADY AS SHE GOES'

In chapter 4 we saw that Mark Hope, from Shell, viewed the issue of agility in terms both of being 'employer of choice' – 'the best people want to work here' – and more widely in terms of whoever contracts to Shell – not just directly employed staff but also contractors, consultants, and advisers. Their aspirations had to be around 'motivation, inspiration, listening and learning'. Lawrence Churchill at UNUM also felt it had to start with the atmosphere in the company.

> 'Innovation is encouraged across the organisation, and there is a lot of talk and discussion about knowledge management. What matters is getting the solution to the problem, rather than believing that an individual is the fount of all knowledge.'

He connected thinking and innovation to leadership.

> 'Strategic thinking enables you to 'catch' the moment. It is always important to have champions within the company who can drive 'new' thinking and innovation.'

When asked how you could engineer innovation, for Lawrence again this came back to leadership.

> 'Leaders should perceive the opportunity and then investigate the resource.'

This theme of the leader's role also came out strongly with David Burall, who was taking personal responsibility for new products and finding different routes to market. For him, it was the leader of the company who sparked it.

> 'I've never been leading edge but I've never wanted to be in the following pack. So in terms of designing a business... I've wanted to find new ways of attacking markets, rather than using the same ways that the competitors are doing. This means looking for innovative solutions both in terms of products and routes into the market that give you competitive advantage.'

I asked how the team viewed innovation, and about their role. Did they embrace innovation? David, not entirely confidently, said that he was sure that they did.

> 'Because I'm restless, I'm never satisfied. While I may be over-critical when I step out of the business and look at other businesses, I realise just how innovative they all are. And that's partly because they like the challenge. I've never been happy with the status quo, and I'm always looking for new ways of doing things. It does make life tough for others.'

Richard Maudslay believed, a little like David Burall, that restlessness and a dissatisfaction with the status quo, within an encouraging environment, was a stimulus.

> 'You employ the right people, and you talk to the right people, and you keep it in the forefront of everybody's mind. Yes, the quality of the people is important, but they also need to be put in an environment to stimulate them. You need to have a non-threatening, non-confrontational environment. You come up with any idea, however stupid and we'll listen to it.'

Innovation was also about the systematic integration of the varying contributions to product development, which Richard brought from Rolls-Royce, where he had been Managing Director of the Industrial Power Group. He described the method:

> 'Sales come up with the idea, a development person works out what he can do, goes back through the loop to see how much it will cost, back through the loop to see whether that makes sense regarding how much the sales guys think we can sell it for. It's this eternal loop. We get ideas about what products to make both by talking among ourselves and by talking to customers. How can we get one step ahead? It is by working out what our market is now, and what we want it to be. It is by accepting the fact, which pains many of our people, that there's going to be constant change. The models may only last forty years. If you look at our museum, a model introduced in 1890 was still selling in 1960. That isn't going to happen again.'

In such a traditional craft industry, the innovation message has to be managed carefully. Richard gave a vivid description about where the message had been misinterpreted totally. The firm had said that they were going to simplify the manufacturing process, reduce the number of standard parts, and do a lot of value engineering. Then one of the designers said he wanted to resign. When they had asked him why, he had said he had always worked in organisations dedicated to quality, and now they wanted to do away with all that. Richard described what happened next:

> 'We said, Hang on, who said anything about quality? He said, But you want to do all this cost-cutting stuff. We said, Yes, we want to reduce costs but we want to at least maintain, if not improve, the quality. And he said, Oh, is that's what you want to do. I've got lots of ideas about that. When we asked if he had ever told anyone about them, he said, No one was ever interested before. So it was very much a dictatorial environment, but in its day it was extremely successful. It's the same with all sorts of companies. M&S have to innovate in a totally different way now, to attract a new audience.'

John Cridland was taking the internal view on innovation, for CBI as an organisation, rather than for its members.

> 'We are predominantly a graduate organisation, and therefore we have a pool of people who are able to contribute very effectively. The way we try to tap into that is to run the place internally a bit like a constant brains trust. There are a lot of quality circles, and a lot of project teams where we do bring in external consultants. We insist on them working very closely with internal project teams, which usually is pushing an open door, and on strong feedback loops. So I would say we are probably a good example of an organisation which is

*non-hierarchical, and where a lot of ideas for innovation come from
the shop floor.'*

All of this sounds like an idyllic situation, until you recognise the
inevitable drawbacks. John explained that it brought risks and had
downsides.

*'The first leads to the second. First is the capacity of the organisation
to follow through. If you have a relatively small organisation with a
lot of people contributing ideas, they all expect things to happen. The
second is the nature of the people who are contributing, in that they
are very good on ideas but are less experienced. Therefore they are
occasionally a bit intolerant about things that can't happen, because
they can't understand why they can't happen.'*

John Cridland is a fan of building the resource in order to engineer
creativity, but also being prepared for 'events'.

*'Perhaps this is a bit particular to the CBI. I think in principle that
it must be right, but I come back to this concern that it's easy to get
heroic about some of this, but so much of what CBI does is dictated
by events. In a world in a state of flux, life is never what you think
it's going to be.'*

Ashridge is another organisation in the not for profit sector that
believes building in capacity for innovation. It is an intellectual capital
organisation, and we heard in chapter 4 how they have a 'creativity
week' in January of each year. One idea that came from this was to
widen roles of those at the customer interface. Leslie Hannah related
one of the consequences.

*'We've just recruited a chauffeur who turns out to be a historian.
He's started taking guided tours for visitors around the house. That's
great, because otherwise I'd have done it, being a historian myself.'*

A related Ashridge story concerned an overseas client. The client
board took an interest in sending the senior executives who were
going to make the final decision to possible contractors. The last two
schools to be evaluated were the LBS and Ashridge.

*'The Board decided they had better come over to Britain and look,
so they wrote to LBS and Ashridge. LBS said, Get the train and get
the tube and go to Baker Street, and we're just up the street.
Ashridge, in the middle of England, said, We'll meet you at
Heathrow. In the hour's drive around the M25, our chauffeur had
done the history, structure, and philosophy of Ashridge, and when
they got here the tutors had nothing to do. The chauffeur had sold it.'*

This nice anecdote also proves that a non-elitist approach can even
work in academia!

I asked Leslie if Ashridge outsourced in order to concentrate on core business. Not necessarily, he said. Some things were precious and the Board had a contrary view. Leslie explained:

> 'The thing that our Chairman of Governors is always asking us to outsource is the hotel and restaurant side. What are you doing here? What do you, Les Hannah, know about running a 195-bed hotel and a 300-km2 plot? The answer is, if you're in the middle of a forest, you've got to provide transport for your staff. You're mainly working with a very stable, and very competitive, local labour market, and we treat people very well. Every lecturer has private health insurance, and if they get ill they go to the best hospital and they know that Ashridge is looking after them. It's a very special relationship.'

However, there is a grand British compromise.

> 'We outsource our management. There are two catering and hotel managers. They're from an independent consultancy, but self-employed. They're two ex-Forte managers who set up their own consultancy some fifteen years ago. They still do a lot of work for others, so they bring in industry knowledge, but they love working at Ashridge. They work here three days a week each and do consultancy the other two days a week, and we get very good value.'

Although perhaps counter-initiative, this is an innovative, flexible arrangement.

The growing feeling in drilling deeper in this chapter is that the elements of the basic premise are strongly linked. It is becoming clear that those organisations that are 'extrovert' are also likely to be 'agile'. Further there is the issue of democratisation of ideas. The organisations that involve a wide range of their employees in being 'extrovert' ie out there engaged in their communities (from customers to consumers to local community) are also inclusive when it comes to idea generation and ability to act or 'catch the moment'.

There is contrast and learning between sectors. It is clear that SMEs find agility easier – the essence of being entrepreneurial. Large organisations conversely find agility difficult. Those that are confident put their faith in the culture that has engendered ability. Others struggle with issues of the silo mentality or inhibiting bureaucracy. The public sector struggles with issues of extroversion and agility.

The public to private experience is interesting. These organisations have had the opportunity to think hard about transition and the desire for more agility. They have struggled with the inhibiting factors of

- historical command and control structure
- hierarchical structures

- conflict over innovation versus the 'day job'.

The last factor is universally shared and represents a classic leadership dilemma. This is twinned with the dilemma of specialisation – should we cream off innovation to a research unit, a think tank, an ideas room?

In the concluding chapter we have the opportunity to pull these valuable insights together and to discover whether there is anything beyond living by your wits or by the skin of our teeth.

Notes

1   Ashton, D & Sung, J *Supporting Workplace Learning for High Performance Working* ILO 2002

2   West, M A Borrill, C Dawson, J Scully, J Carter, , Anelay, S Patterson, M Waring, J (2002) *The Link between the Management of Employees and Patient Mortality in Acute Hospitals* The International Journal of Human Resource Management 13, 8, pp1299-1310

3   Morton, C *Beyond World Class* Macmillan 1998

4   See Appendix III for results

Chapter nine

WORLD-CLASS TO SKIN OF TEETH:

CREATING SUSTAINABLE ORGANISATIONS THROUGH PEOPLE

ONCE I HAD PRODUCED A BOOK with a title of *Beyond World Class*, many colleagues and readers asked me, 'Where do you go next Clive? What is beyond *Beyond World Class?*' What convinced me that there was something more to do was the compelling evidence that the world was changing so rapidly that there was no longer a place for formulaic solutions. Our understanding of what was needed for sustainability needed to grow and mature.

The long run of the bull market for worldwide business in the 1990s produced a cushion, a level of inventory (in manufacturing terms) that hid the real problems from view. But in the last few years, corporate failure erupted as greed was exposed, and the succession of such failures has undermined confidence worldwide. As Sir Geoffrey Chandler put it, '*Financial failure undermines companies; moral failure undermines capitalism.*' We have reached a point where the formula of 'getting it right' within companies has been completely overwhelmed by distorted and discredited corporate governance worldwide. These failures are not affecting just the perpetrating companies but are a contagion that now affects capitalism as a whole.

So why is the polemic in *Becoming World Class* and *Beyond World Class* not enough? I would put forward two sets of reasons.

The first is that the world of business, economics and communities is changing at an ever-faster rate and the certainties of a decade ago have disappeared. This has made the issue of agility even more important than before. The question this study brings to the surface is that it is fine to understand the need for agility, but how do we achieve it? For the owner-operator things are not so different – entrepreneurs have always lived on their wits and have had the flexibility of direction at their fingertips. In large organisations there is always the dilemma between control and autonomy – how much freedom to give to encourage agility balanced with prudent controls. Also, what motivates the employees to engage and energise when bureaucracy and structures tend to dampen enthusiasm?

This last question links to my second reason – people have changed. This is where I depart from many other management researchers and writers who base their findings on lengthy studies of successful companies over many decades. Their painstaking studies of stock market returns linked to company strategies, valuable as they are, are dependent on the premise that managing a company requires much the same formula in 2003 as in 1953. I argue that this cannot be so, since not only has the pace of change accelerated so much but also people have different expectations and priorities. The company of the 1950s to 1970s, almost without exception, was run as a top-down hierarchy. The issue of agility was relatively simple – it depended on the ability of those at the top to understand the trends (to be what I am now calling the extrovert organisation) and to act upon them (agility, seizing the moment). In my terms, this brought the autocratic organisation nearer to the one-man-band entrepreneur – there was little challenge to the authority at the top.

For these large organisations the issue then was how to run numbers of largely compliant people. The prevalent culture related to stability, status quo, length of service, job protection and resistance to change. An obvious product was the entitlement culture for those in organisations. The challenge, if there was one, came from organised labour and then only as to how the cake of corporate earnings was divided up. Thirty years ago, the prevalent role was administration of an organisation that was akin to sailing an ocean-going liner – maybe not unsinkable but certainly almost unstoppable. Today, management of these organisations presents a very different challenge and the leadership role has changed significantly.

In 1973, Henry Mintzberg published his seminal work *The Nature of Managerial Work*. In 2002, researchers from Gothenburg University in Sweden, Professor Stefan Tengblad and Professor Sten Jonsson produced a fascinating study for the 6th IFSAM World Congress in Brisbane, Australia, entitled: *Is the nature of managerial work a stable one? – a replication of Henry Mintzberg's classic study thirty years later*. Broadly, the researchers found significant differences, indicating that the nature of the managerial role has changed from that of administrative manager to institutional leader. Largely this was because *'a top leader should command the organisation through communicating ideas rather than giving instructions and setting rules'* and as one of those studied expressed, *'You can't build a culture or create commitment for company goals and visions by sending written instructions from the head office. You have to meet and talk with the people where they work.'* An interesting incidental finding was that the average working week for managers had climbed from forty-six hours in the Mintzberg study to seventy-six hours today!

Today, none of our organisational equivalents of ocean-going

liners can be regarded as either unsinkable or unstoppable, and little
of institutional leadership is plain sailing. Equally, the people engaged
are not compliant crew trained to carry out commands without
question. As I described in *Beyond World Class*, from Amin Rajan's
work we now have the concept of the 'self-employment mindset'
within our organisations, where employees regard their employers as
'customers for their labour', where the culture of jobs for life has
ended, and where employees assume responsibility for their own
development.

World-class – necessary and sufficient?

Hence my basic premise, tested throughout the interviews reported
here, 'world-class in all we do' has been a product of the 1970s and
1980s as has, typically, the quest for consistent quality and
repeatability in organisations. It has been a necessary discipline to
ensure that companies can support their reputation of producing
quality products, from automobiles to wine, from healthcare to clean
water, effectively and efficiently.

This was fine on its own for the 1980s and some of the 1990s,
when being world-class could differentiate organisations from their
competitors. But by the middle 1990s, companies could at least aspire
by their rhetoric to being world-class in quality terms. Since
everybody was doing this, the differential was gone. Yet, as we will see,
the reality is that there is a great gap between rhetoric and reality in
terms of world-class performance.

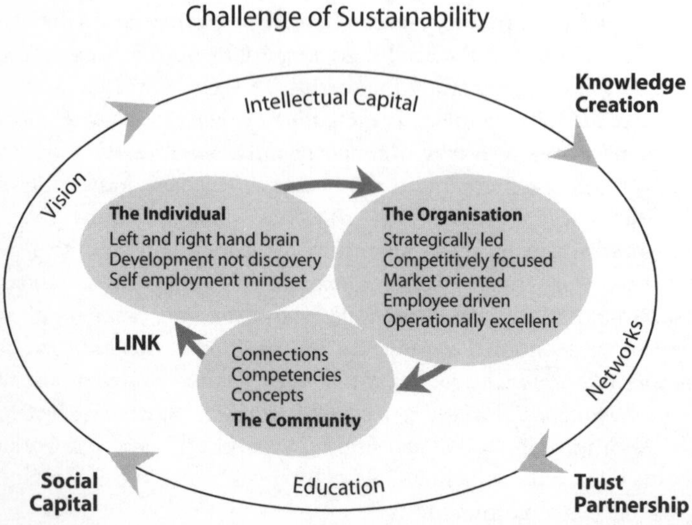

Challenge of Sustainability

Figure 9A

The *Beyond World Class* model demonstrated that organisations were not islands. For sustainability they needed continually to recognise their inter-dependence with individuals and communities. This gives rise to the emergence of the 'extrovert organisation' concept – a proactive version of the stakeholders idea in which organisations are active in their communities, however these are defined. This activity does not just provide a listening post but, typically, is one where a range of employees get involved outside the organisation, sometimes as ambassadors, but all the time increasing the organisation's intelligence and profile.

Last is the agile, proactive, seizing-the-moment factor. *Beyond World Class* recognised this as well, in the discovery that the bottom-up change stimulated by the quality movement was not enough for sustained results. We had to achieve top-down led change (including changed behaviour by top management) and re-invigoration of middle management as the 'knowledge engineers'[1] of vibrant organisations. Recognition of all this came from my hard-fought experience of achieving change post Komatsu UK in leadership roles within Northern Electric, Rolls-Royce, Anglian Water and the NHS, and latterly as a consultant working in other organisations.

Progression from world-class to skin of teeth

Book title	Systems	Drivers
Becoming World Class	World-class attributes Total quality Process Re-engineering	Bottom-up change
Beyond World Class	World-class attributes Board development Learning organisations Inclusive/stakeholder methodology	Top-led change Middle energised and facilitated Gestalt of individual/ organisation/community
By the Skin of Our Teeth	World-class in all we do Extrovert organisation Agile, innovative, seize the moment	Survival in the market Trends are the oxygen Entrepreneurial leadership A hierarchy of needs?

By the Skin of Our Teeth broadens this experience by testing the premise in thirty-three different organisations and, as the research shows, their leaders do:

- focus on world-class attributes – they have got the message on quality and listening to customers, and they focus on and communicate constant values in a world which, for a variety of reasons, is in a state of flux

- value and use emotional intelligence and right hand side of the brain approaches in developing leaders

- consciously or unconsciously develop the extrovert organisation (with broadly the exception of the public sector) so that antennae are tuned and messages are received. They often recognise the business case for an inclusive approach to stakeholders.

However, almost universally our leaders struggle with issues over agility, innovation and creativity in their organisations. All of them wish their organisations to embrace these. All recognise that for survival, re-invention and renewal, it is vital that the whole organisation becomes more innovative. Also, all recognise that the ability to be agile is a function of culture, and that it is still a great challenge to get all levels to take responsibility for this and to feel free to contribute. They are frankly unsure about this. They are unconvinced that in their organisations the culture is right to promote an atmosphere of agility.

This presents the first *By the Skin of Our Teeth* challenge. In a changing world order, how can we make our organisations as swift of foot as the one-man-band entrepreneurs? We can all agree it takes collective effort but in an age of extreme individualism with increasing independence via the self-employment mindset, the now familiar adage that management is like herding cats or squirrels comes to mind.

The second major challenge (as outlined in Chapter 1, who do we trust to tell the truth?), in terms of the biggest threats to corporate existence, is that trust and the reputations of the most stable of organisations are now at stake from, for instance, the extremes of creative accounting and the use of distorted auditing practices hence the sagas of Enron and WorldCom. Many cry for increased rules and regulations, but I argue these are merely safety nets around or through which determined fraudsters can always navigate. A better route in my view is that of process, using the principles of openness and transparency with a wide range of stakeholders, including employees, who not only provide the check and balance on management decisions but who can also influence direction and the ability to innovate, as well as providing the energy for sustainability. We will turn to the roles of directors and the board and their development later in this chapter as the route forward.

Element 1: World-class in all we do?

In summary, our leaders do focus on world-class attributes – they have got the message on quality and listening to customers. However, realism has set in from the heady days of TQM. Then, total quality was intended to pervade every nook and cranny of the organisation. You had to be world-class in every function – not just production, where it all started. To be fair, even Japanese companies, which have been the most enthusiastic about TQ, have struggled to apply its principles to all functions. However, they were the most thorough and persistent in the quest, as the interview with Bryan Jackson of Toyota shows. The productivity results also shine through, as the ILO study on 'high performance working' demonstrates.

What we need to clarify is whether organisations are taking a realistic view that being world-class in all we do is just unachievable, or is it seen as too difficult so that selection of what it should apply to is used in an expedient way? Or, is it not clear what is world-class?

Being world-class is clearly wider than quality, and some would say that it has to be modified in relation to response to customers. Sally Vanson of MCL/The Performance Solution:

> 'I actually don't believe in the total quality route any longer. I actually think people will give up part of the quality in order to get the fast response, so it's very much the 80/20 rule now. If people get 80 per cent of it right, that's okay. The days of zero defects have gone.'

Another pragmatic view comes from Richard Maudslay of House of Hardy:

> 'You've only got to be better than the other chap. It's a bit like being chased by the bear. It doesn't matter how fast you can run, as long as you can run faster than your pals. That's it in its crudest way.'

Dichotomies seem to operate here. More and more organisations seem to want to compare themselves with others in world-class terms, even though the definition of world-class is open to doubt, and even though these organisations may not compete on an international basis. To add to this, benchmarking is seen with some scepticism by those who see it as a levelling down rather than up – comparing with the average rather than the best. Malcolm Lowe-Lauri of the NHS:

> 'The challenge is how you use that benchmarking to push the standards towards leading-edge. As a generalisation in many parts of the NHS the attitude would be to accept mediocrity.'

Why should organisations compare internationally when they don't compete internationally? For Camelot it was about being the best lottery operator and improving performance internally. For the NHS it's also about internal performance, especially with regard to technology.

Comparisons between sectors are important. For John Bridge, the issue of bringing the public sector up to world-class standards is key to progress for the private sector. However, for Peter Hewitt at the Arts Council, the international perspective works against the government agenda. Nevertheless the focus is value for money, which means we must compare to raise standards.

To a lot of our leaders it depends what you mean by world-class. Bryan Jackson of Toyota felt that each organisation needed to ask what world-class meant to them. For him, it was all about what was needed in the marketplace and, further, what would provide for this need and sustain delivery.

Todd Abbott was of the view that being world-class was defining what really added value to the business model. But John Cridland of the CBI feared that the term world-class was aspirational and lacked benchmarks.

Sir John Egan gave a universal three-part model:

- *satisfying customers*
- *engaging employees*
- *involving stakeholders*

which is the only definition that appears both inclusive and dynamic.

The factor cited by the greatest number of these leaders was that of listening to customers. They ranged from Alan Bartle at Lymphoma Association, '*We want to meet the needs of every one that approaches us*' to Marion Weatherhead at Gardiner and Theobald for whom it was about being '*customer-focused*' to Richard Maudslay at House of Hardy who took great deliberation to ensure his Japanese customers were encouraged to articulate their needs (in contrast to their previous experience).

> '*I said, 'I've dealt with the Japanese before and I know that you always want something that's different. We're going to sit here and you tell us what you want.' There was a deathly silence, a lot of muttering in Japanese and then huge smiles spread across their faces. They said, 'This is very good – we've been coming here for six years and this is the first time anyone has asked us what we want.' They said, 'What we want is very simple. We are little people fishing for little fish on little rivers and we want little fishing tackle, please.'*

Several organisations defined world-class as knowledge sharing, capturing what was out there, keeping up-to-date and applying it. Mike Walters of Bovis Lend Lease:

> '*We make extensive use of circles of quality to look at lessons learnt. We use our Intranet to open up channels about who to contact to get information, rather than putting everything on the system and then*

trying to keep it all up-to-date. We also encourage team and peer reviews as another way of transferring knowledge, that is getting people to speak to others on the other side of the world. When we were looking at how to create effective knowledge transfer we used BP Bovis Alliance as a benchmark and listened to many of the lessons they had learnt.'

The process appeared for some as:

- define your core competence
- make it world-class, and
- outsource the rest to people who can perform at that level.

Paul Forman of Unipart saw the need for an opportunity for *'access to world-class capability'*.

Chris Mellor of AWG was in tune with both John Cridland and Paul Forman:

'First of all, world-class in all we do – yes, that's an aspiration but is that an unrealistic aspiration? Isn't that really why many companies have gone down the outsourcing route, recognising that you can't be world-class at everything?'

Mark Hope of Shell was direct:

'If you're not world-class, you don't do it. You get someone who is to do that bit.'

As was Jeremy Long of GB Rail:

'I actually think that, in all truth, there are very few organisations that will try to do that. I think what you find is that successful organisations are clearer about what it is they're trying to be world-class in.'

The immediacy of the issue was shared by many. Bob Mason saw it as an entry ticket for business:

'Being world-class gets you into the game. It's a bit like getting to the Olympics because you've met the Olympic qualifying standard. Because of globalisation, companies (who don't understand) will get a very rude awakening.'

Philip Johnson of the Patent Office, observing British business, was convinced that businesses must increasingly be of world-class standard to survive. Mark Hope of Shell conceded that in the short run, due to poor communications, you might be able to get away with being less than world-class for a time, but the standard of world-class was being ratcheted up continuously:

'If you're world-class today and you're just doing the same thing next week, you're in danger of not being world-class next year.'

LSC work showed that the 'best' are never satisfied:

> *'The 'best' companies always look outside the box, never stand still and are never satisfied with the status quo.'*

This resonates with David Burall's comments on the subject. His preoccupation is with his restlessness:

> *'It's never being satisfied with the status quo, being curious and innovative, not wanting to tread the conventional route.'*

This is about willpower, which is a necessary starting point for Peter Ward of Telos Partners:

> *'You can be world-class in a process, you can be world-class in thinking, and that buys you the right to start off. Then, if you're world-class, you're probably thinking about regeneration. It's a will to continue, to be self-determining.'*

The last and most important area of consensus is over this dynamic, how to produce a world- class result on a continuous basis. The key is world-class people.

'*World-class assets equal world-class business*' is the Generics theme. Generics is a classic example of the 21st-century company in that at least 70 per cent of its assets are the brains of employees. The release of potential comes from linking bright people with bright ideas to the commercial opportunity. The other high-tech companies sing to the same tune. Richard Hicks of AIT says that to be world-class is to be the supplier of choice – where people want to work. What do they gain? Exceptional skills, which are a passport for mobility.

This is echoed by Todd Abbott of Cisco Systems. Now stock options are unattractive, what motivates and retains the best people? The answer is the development of the individual. Keith Moscrop at BioFocus believes it is all about people and motivation, giving them space for development of world-class technology – an opportunity which many were denied in the 'big pharmas'.

Mark Hope of Shell takes the 'employer of choice' view another stage, by embracing all those supplying to or contracting with Shell:

> *'The best people must want to work here. I don't think it matters whether people are staff, consultants, advisers, whatever. If you are running a business of any sort or size you want there to be a hum around the place.'*

To some extent this brings us full circle. The TQ philosophy espoused by Deming and Juran, and most thoroughly implemented by Japanese manufacturers at home and abroad, was all about gaining quality in all elements of the process, including suppliers.

We will examine the other aspects of the basic premise, the

'extrovert organisation' and 'agility', later in the chapter. However, I can't escape the conclusion that western organisations (with the exception of many in this study) generally do not take the issue of world-class standards seriously enough. It's a bit like the response many have to issues of corporate governance – let's tick the box and move on. The evidence from the ILO study on high performance working (which includes issues of quality) shows that too few businesses are world-class in this sense, and the DTI has shown that many go in for self-delusion and believe their own rhetoric.

It is a pity that change is not always internally generated to produce a better outcome. But the good news is there are two unconnected movements that are putting organisations under pressure to produce the right result.

The first pressure is an odd benefit of globalisation from 'the bottom up'. Francis Fukuyama[2] sees governance from the bottom-up via universal standards that progressively apply globally. Examples are air traffic control, product standards and safety standards, all of which are agreed industry by industry for the benefit of worldwide trade, commerce and communications.

The second pressure is through 'corporate governance'. This is a top-down process, and is gaining momentum in the wake of recent spectacular business failures such as Enron, WorldCom, Marconi and others. Here the rules and penalties imposed on businesses are multiplying as a reaction to these events.

I see this movement as parallel to what happened in the birth of the environmental movement. Peter Marshall, editor of Whole Earth magazine, sees the disaster at Chernobyl as eventually leading to the collapse of communism.

> '…in 1986, Chernobyl exploded. And with that, faith in the communist regime of the Soviet Union fell apart, leading to the eventual downfall of communism.'

In other words, unless the corporate disasters such as Enron are checked and corporate governance improves, confidence in capitalism can continue to be undermined in the same way as communism was destroyed by its own internal disasters. There is a severe danger that capitalism could similarly implode if governance is not faithful to moral and ethical values.

The key issue is do we treat symptoms or causes? Rules and penalties are likely to treat only the former.

Vision and values proposition

In the last decade, there has been a trend towards the adoption of vision and values in organisations. Where did this come from? Why do companies do it? Does it achieve anything? Or is it another example in the hall of fame exhibition of management fads?

Like all of these examples, it is a product of pendulum swings from previous experience. TQM was seen by many to be too mechanical and production-oriented, often related to systems, and aligned to the '*mechanistic*' perspective on organisations to take the term from Burns and Stalker's seminal work *The Management of Innovation*[3]. Business process re-engineering followed this inexorable logic and concentrated on a '*zero-base*' approach to what was needed to produce at minimum cost. Then siren voices chimed that all this was logical and left-brained but took no notice of issues of the organic side of organisations – the need to engage hearts and minds, the need to motivate and capture human imagination inside and outside the organisation. The vision and values movement was greatly stimulated by the findings of Collins & Porras in *Built to Last*[4] where stock returns were correlated to constancy of purpose and values.

In parallel, as we've seen, the debate started in the 1990s about the purpose of a company, with the famous '*pebble dropped in the pool*' by Charles Handy, at his RSA lecture '*What's a company for?*' in 1990. Then, universally, the answer would have been that the company existed for its shareholders, and the returns they receive or hope to receive. After all, without their capital, the enterprise would not exist. A decade later the philosophy of the stakeholder enterprise has taken hold. Many of the organisations that provided the information for this book would subscribe to that. However, Charles Handy in his more recent writings argues that a much more fundamentalist approach needs to be taken in today's circumstances towards the constitution in law of the company. In the *Harvard Business Review* for December 2002, in a challenging article entitled *What's business for?* he writes:

> '*We cannot escape the fundamental question, who and what is a business for? The answer once seemed clear, but no longer. The terms of business have changed. Ownership has been replaced by investment, and a company's assets are increasingly found in its people, not in its buildings and machinery. In light of this transformation, we need to rethink our assumptions about the purpose of business.*'[5]

And on shareholders' needs and purpose:

> '*…to turn shareholders' needs into a purpose is to be guilty of a logical confusion… The purpose of a business, in other words, is not to make a profit, full stop.*'

Handy points out that the origins of company law saw those who provide the finance as the company's rightful owners, that the company is a piece of property and employees are treated as property and recorded as costs not assets. But as he points out:

> '*A good business is a community with a purpose and a community is not something to be owned.*'

And of more sharp contrast:

> '*In the world of talent businesses, employees will be increasingly unwilling to sell the fruits of their intellectual assets for an annual salary.*'

The mismatch between outdated laws and executives' perceptions is repeatedly shown in surveys carried out by the company which colleagues and I have established, Board Performance Limited. Less than 5 per cent of directors surveyed recognise that their primary duty, under even this outdated law, is to the company and its livelihood, not shareholders or even shareholder value.

Nature and purpose of vision and values – balancing corporate and stakeholders' views

With this background, it is hardly surprising that there is confusion. What is remarkable is that so many organisations* are now subscribing to the concept of vision and values where it encapsulates the purpose of the organisation. As many said, it is about having something constant in the midst of change. But there are other motives.

Richard Hicks of AIT saw this as a means of alignment (which included some of the owners of the business):

> '*It's the way you keep everybody within the organisation thinking alike and pursuing the goal in a co-operative way. For me that's one of the things that vision and values are about.*'

Keith Moscrop of BioFocus saw it as more a collection of personal ambitions (some of which were those of founder/owners of the business).

Duncan Hine, formerly of the Generics Group, saw different routes to it. For the company, it had to explain itself to potential investors and therefore was able to articulate this down the organisation. However, in essence, it clearly means different things to different people and, Generics being an intellectual property company, it is about the peer group relationship. This is not dissimilar to the NHS as Professor Sir Liam Donaldson describes it in chapter 5. Also similar is BioFocus, where the technology and the ability to make money from it come together (in both Generics and BioFocus

---

* In a 2003 survey of 1000 CEOs in 43 countries PriceWaterhouseCoopers found that 87per cent had implemented policies on values, ethics and codes of conduct

there are no dividends for shareholders only the hope of shareholder value, not being fulfilled in the current bear market!).

Dianne Thompson demonstrated what many in this study have said, that the vision may change with the external environment. It was to be 'the best lottery operator', all about efficiency and achieving recognition. However this wasn't effective, because it was process-led, and was not about creativity and innovation. Now the vision is about 'serving the nation's dreams'. The values are unchanged but they are not seen as delivery behaviours necessary for creativity and innovation. Hence the organisation re-working on alignment.

In the Lymphoma Association the vision and values are all about 'commitment to the purpose' – commitment to patients on information and support in order to empower them. Here there is no potential divide in vision and values or agenda for the Association or its employees. Charles Handy says something about this situation with which I wholeheartedly agree. There is something the private and public sectors can learn from such charities as Lymphoma Association.

> *'We should, as charitable organisations do, measure success in terms of outcomes for others as well as for ourselves.'* [6]

In one of our two examples of employee-owned companies, Tim Watts of Pertemps partly puts the issue of vision and values back to the employees, as part owners of the enterprise.

When we look at the small start-ups, discussion of vision and values gets close to what the personal ambitions of the founders are. Bill Penney shows how he balances being both a clergyman and an entrepreneur:

> *'What I think our life is about is*
> *(a) fulfilling one's own life and, equally importantly,*
> *(b) helping individuals or organisations realise more of their potential.'*

and:

> *'What I'm aiming for is an integrated, meaningful, rewarding existence. Some of it will earn cash and some of it won't.'*

Echoing Charles Handy, Peter Smith of The Strategic Partnership says:

> *'Vision must encompass the values and relationships with stakeholders. Boards cannot do this on their own. At the end of the day, employees want to work for someone whose values link to their own.'*

It is clearly possible to exploit opportunities on a transactional basis –

but that is short term. Peter Ward of Telos sees relationship-based businesses as being more durable and flexible than pure transactional businesses.

For large organisations that have history and form, vision and values can have a different underlying purpose. In Royal and Sun Alliance it was clearly a way of aligning fifty-two different organisations around the world, with the aim of rationalising delivery and gaining shared knowledge.

For KPMG, the agenda was to loosen up the organisation, make it more agile and aligned, bust the silos, and reduce bureaucracy and rules; an ambitious programme for such an intangible instrument.

In Cisco it was a policy of containment and continuity. The previous incentives that gave such spectacular results in the boom growth times were irrelevant in consolidation and downturn. Vision and values were aimed at consistency and maintaining the stance of training and development. Even the vision was not to be modified too frequently.

Sally Vanson saw the issue from the employees' point of view. Change was the constant, the traditional rewards were transitory, the meaning of it all was the issue. This resulted in the growth of interest in spirituality and the follow on, gaining skills for employability. The spiritual dimension was echoed by both Chris Mellor of AWG and Tony Ward of BAA. Again, there were common issues of continuity, aspiration and intellectual and emotional engagement.

The leaders in the public-to-private category all saw the link of vision and values to stakeholders, in particular the community.

For the public sector, any statement of vision and values had to align with government policy, which of course can change with the electoral cycle. However, it had to be about stability and continuity. 'When does something become a value?' asked Liam Donaldson. Also, where members of the professions are involved, does their value set align with that of their employer?

In local delivery terms within the NHS, vision and values have been used in Peterborough to make sense of these dichotomies by helping break down the barriers between professions and employers and aiming for alignment. The results have been startling*. There have been gains in efficiency, reduced waiting times, recognition as a three-star hospital and now a prospective Foundation Trust.

'Built to last' organisations share many of the problems of size with the mergers and acquisitions category. Shell, having learnt some hard lessons, sees philosophy as seamless with vision and values, and could relate closely to the concept of the spiritual expressed by AWG and BAA.

* See Appendix III for details on the results

The philosophy of vision and values is a touchstone for Lawrence Churchill of UNUM with his virtuous circle:

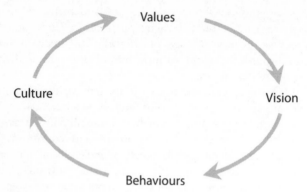

Figure 9B

The Burall philosophy, which is discussed in Appendix II, is a great story of consistency leading to employee ownership.

Lastly, Ashridge Trust encapsulates the purpose of vision and values:

> 'First, it is a people business. Values are very related to human resource type values – respect for people. Second, it's about what gets you out of bed on Monday morning – that's not in essence about creating shareholder value – the latter is a by-product of vision and values which are broader and were purposeful.'

And this takes us full circle back to Charles Handy's remarks quoted on page 206 in this chapter.

Work/life balance

As an extension of the discussion on vision and values, I encouraged the interviewees to talk about the work ethic and the work/life balance. One thing was clear – the work ethic doesn't mean the same today as it did two or three decades ago. This was not a case of a lot of grey-haired males complaining about restless and fickle youth. It was a recognition that, probably, previous generations had got it wrong and there did need to be a balance, a better balance, which honoured families and dependents in a way that didn't happen before.

The other trend all will agree upon is that later generations have moved up Maslow's hierarchy of needs, possibly to the need for self actualisation, hence the search for meaning and purposeful work. Sally Vanson would argue that this has accelerated in the wake of 9/11, when so many perished in New York when just about their daily work.

Oddly, the issue of decreased job security and its impact on work/life balance came from the charity sector (the Lymphoma Association). Maybe their experience means that other sectors have it as de rigueur. Peter Ward saw the biggest impact on work/leisure was happiness and satisfaction in the job.

Several of our leaders saw the issue not as one of separation but of integration:

> 'I don't think there is a work/life balance, and as soon as you start thinking in terms of work/life balance you've probably missed the point. It's work/life integration. You shouldn't need to make choices if you're working with an organisation that believes in your beliefs.'

Chris Mellor, Tony Ward and Mark Hope were of the same view, but all felt the pressures were several times those of yesterday, and that a lot of these were emotional and psychological. However, if lived out, the vision and values philosophy helped, together with greater understanding and flexibility. Many organisations felt that this was having a positive effect, although not necessarily at senior level.

Vision and values and major disruption?

Several of our organisations have had the experience of major disruption following their establishment of vision and values. With Camelot, it was the roller-coaster ride of first losing and then regaining the franchise; with AIT, it was the fall from grace on the Stock Exchange. For Royal and Sun Alliance it has been the last, post-merger, tumultuous years and for Cisco the change from bull to bear in short order.

There are other examples of changes and challenges. They include:

- MCL to Performance Solutions in Sally Vanson's case
- AWG acquiring Morrison Construction and asking 'Shall we extend the vision and values?'
- BT and AWG – what happens to these subsidiaries in new markets?
- BAA moving away from the core business
- Bovis plus Lend Lease with two sets of vision and values wondering whether they will match
- Shell with shocks on environmental and ethical fronts.

All these changes present big dilemmas to the boards of the companies concerned, and we will be looking at the leadership dimension next. What is common is that none of these organisations abandoned their vision and values in the face of these major disruptions. Rather, they often used them to get through the challenge and to the other side, perhaps modifying the vision but holding to the values. This reflects a search for constancy in a world in a state of flux.

Leadership and dilemmas

Our thirty-four interviewees showed a high sensitivity to the issues involved in developing leaders. The vast majority agreed with the approach put forward in the first three bullet points:

- knowing yourself and others
- the role of emotions and emotional intelligence
- the individual and the team
- if leadership is about effectively dealing with and resolving dilemmas, what experience rings true?

Again, nearly all were happy with the fourth as a definition of leadership and gave a variety of examples that illustrated the point.

Technology-based companies are very well aware of the need to balance technology with leadership skills and are equally aware that their bright employees often have little interest in management and leadership. Typical examples are AIT, BioFocus, Generics, Cisco, the NHS, Gardiner and Theobald and – in a different, non-technological but specialist way – the Arts Council and the CBI.

Richard Hicks of AIT saw how important leadership was in terms of engaging hearts and minds, the emotional engagement of people. In the knowledge-based organisation you depended on commitment, agility and imagination.

For Keith Moscrop at BioFocus the issue was the growth from small beginnings – when scientists could collaborate without structure, to the plc status – when formality, hierarchy and distance intervene.

Duncan Hine at Generics was sensitive to the need to recruit 'polymaths' – those who had good 'right hand brain' skills as well as the scientific intellect. Leadership potential would be there. Development came through having a minimum hierarchical structure, peer group reviews and project management with clients.

Todd Abbott at Cisco talked about the effort to identify the top 15-20 per cent in leadership development. He found with the bright technologists that continual emphasis was needed on teamwork, and with directors the emphasis was that 80 per cent of their jobs were about people. As he says, ears have twice the capability of the mouth! On emotional intelligence, along with many others interviewed, he felt that education about this was in its infancy. In common with

Chris Mellor of AWG, he believed in constructively confronting issues so that everybody 'owned their own part'.

The NHS, despite its gargantuan size, shared some things with tiny BioFocus. Clinicians, according to Professor Sir Liam Donaldson, had received little management training and leadership development. The activity was growing, but mainly from the managerial, non-clinical areas of the NHS. At local level in the NHS, Malcolm Lowe-Lauri saw an increase in empowerment, great dedication and the breaking down of traditional barriers.

Gardiner and Theobald employ specialist quantity surveyors who can ply their trade for any similar professional practices. They become attached more to the industry they work in than the structure of the firm. Hence leadership needs are low, and interest in vertical progression is similarly low.

Peter Hewitt of the Arts Council has to bridge between artists, who typically have no interest in management, and the governance of the ACE who have to take a hard-nosed view with restricted finances and a need to consolidate from the previous Regional Arts bodies. The CBI, as John Cridland admits, takes an amateur approach to leadership. It sees it as being about organising and motivating specialists at one end, and satisfying corporate members at the other. Quite understandably, although not in the technical specialist camp, the Lymphoma Association acknowledged that it was stronger on caring than leadership – which some would say was no bad thing!

The next grouping that has synergy is the large organisations that are going through major change, where their workforces need leadership of a differing sort. Some think this is about the particular point in the life of the organisation and 'situational leadership'. Winston Churchill was the leader in wartime, but the electorate decided in 1945 that different leadership was required in peacetime. Two of our interviewees mentioned this trend. Sir John Egan was one:

> *'Firstly, you actually have to know yourself, and know what you're good at and, particularly, what you're bad at because it could be that some people for example are brilliant in a crisis and tend to emerge with solutions which are fundamentally better.'*

Paul Forman at Unipart linked this with emotional intelligence. For him, you had to:

> *'...have the emotional intelligence to understand there is a multiplicity of styles you have to adopt with people.'*

Camelot, for example, changed leaders in natural succession from the avuncular Tim Holley, who was always relating to individuals within the rather smaller organisation, to Dianne Thompson, feisty 'Camelot Queen', who was ready to don the breastplate (or was it steel balls!) to do battle with the knight of the round table, Sir Richard Branson and the regulator. Mass meetings of over six hundred were managed effectively, with general approval at the end. As with other organisations, cross-functional working was encouraged. What is clear is that without Dianne's leadership and high profile, jobs would have been lost, not saved.

Similar change was afoot at KPMG, with the dramatic shift to vision and values and the change programme, Project Darwin, merging the 'silos'. It was led by Mike Rake, who is convinced you can teach management but not leadership, which requires such a mix of skills.

> *'I think it's very difficult to train good leaders to be leaders. I think you can bring out the leadership qualities with people, and give them the opportunities to see whether they have those leadership qualities, but I think real leadership is about an extraordinary balance between sensitivities, self-confidence, emotional intelligence, and communication skills...'*

Mike, like others, sees the need for differing personalities on the team to provide balance. This issue of balance was taken up by Syd Pennington at R&SA, who could see the gain, in leadership terms, from diversity and cross-functional working.

One of the most innovative leaders has been Chris Mellor of AWG who embraced wholeheartedly the premise on leadership as fundamental to development. In his view, in AWG the introduction of emotional intelligence re-invented the business and changed it from one that was risk-averse to one that was entrepreneurial. As he says:

> *'We're human beings and we've got two parts to our brain. I've seen so many examples that demonstrate that you don't get very far until the whole brain is engaged. At the very best you only get half the result you were looking for.'*

Although not associated with revolutionary change, very different approaches come from Toyota. There, leadership is not seen in the Western, macho, sense of crisis management or interventions. It is about systems, competencies, very careful recruitment, and a blame-free culture with attitudes seen as crucial. The atmosphere is one of mutual respect.

Other contributors embraced facets of the emotional intelligence issue. Peter Ward at Telos made the clear link with the constancy of purpose and values:

> *'We are greatly influenced by Level Five leadership (Jim Collins* [7] *).*

It involves quiet influencers, pushing people, encouraging people, working through people. I think leadership is about consistency and constancy. It is about allowing the purpose and values to determine what you will do in certain situations. That's why your purpose has to be unchanging.'

And others made the link to the extrovert organisation, by talking of shared leadership with stakeholders. They include Tony Ward of BAA, Sir John Egan with the Heathrow Express story, and Mark Hope at Shell with the development of the portfolio experience.

The last frontier, many agree, appears to be the board. Those of this opinion range from Bill Penney, who has struggled to promote emotional intelligence amongst colleagues; to Peter Smith on the revolution that's needed in board composition and management; to Sally Vanson who confesses failure at being able to align the board with necessary change in the organisation (which, in her words, delayed the change programme); and to Bob Mason who sees it as necessary that institutional investors and the City value, and buy into, these definitions of leadership.

That such development can be instrumental is without doubt. AWG's Board development gave the signal for leadership development elsewhere in the organisation. At One NorthEast, John Bridge was able to revolutionise strategy by the same means.

In passing, one important manifestation of the rate of change facing organisations is 'Executive Churn', the rapid turnover of people in top management positions. This study demonstrates this short 'self-life' very clearly. It is interesting to note that, in the time between interviews and final script (eighteen months), over one third of our CEO interviewees have left their job or changed employers!

The extrovert organisation

What is the incentive for organisations to spend their time being extrovert – in other words committing resources to the external world?

Customer focus

For some it is as simple as keeping in touch with customers and consumers. Keith Moscrop of BioFocus saw it that way. Duncan Hine at Generics related this issue to engagement in the selling process, and it was as much about encouraging specialist technologists to engage with the commercial aspects of business. For Dianne Thompson at Camelot it was about being 'out there' to protect market share and to anticipate what change will be needed:

'I'm not sure it helps us anticipate external change but it helps us anticipate where we will have to change in the future.'

Sensing trends was the agenda for Jeremy Long at GB Rail, this time looking at what competitors provide for consumers.

'The confident management team is the one that is out there'.

Syd Pennington of the R&SA also saw the extrovert aspect as re-aligning with customers and producing change within. An apparently more strategic, growth approach is taken by Cisco, 'to look for markets and economic disruption'. When EEC markets collapsed, Cisco bought into those markets to reap the benefits later.

Chris Mellor saw economic growth as being part of two other irreconcilable aims – protecting the environment and becoming a good citizen.

Mike Walters is very clear that the way to meet clients is by being involved in so many organisations. This is rather similar to David Burall, with his non-executive connections on behalf of the group.

Richard Maudslay thought the extrovert term was embroidery – *'Work out what your customers want by asking them. Nothing fancier than that!'* This goes together with his delightful story about listening to Japanese customers.

Lastly, Ashridge Trust deliberately makes the agenda for their academic staff to consult for one day a week, thus keeping in touch with customers and bringing ideas inside.

Company reputation

There was a strong view that company reputation was the reason that being 'extrovert' was important. Bob Mason, formerly of BT, was very clear that being 'out there' helped with company reputation, and that this formed part of the sales proposition. He believed that reputation on ethics and attractiveness of product were key determinants in consumer choice. Bob instanced Tesco ('A grocer for God's sake!') facilitating the provision of computers in schools, and the degree of brand enhancement that was achieved as a result.

Syd Pennington of R&SA pointed out the clear interest link between R&SA as insurer against calamities and the Red Cross and Red Crescent as 'pickers up of the pieces' after natural disasters. Their involvement even extended to the more tenuous links of helping clear up the Antarctic of debris and concern for the ozone hole over the South Pole.

Partly playing the long game, and also helping the organisation's reputation, Cisco has been investing in the developing world as a responsible enterprise, including in war-torn Afghanistan.

These views are supported by the results of the PWC survey of 1,000 CEOs, referred to earlier. Seventy-nine per cent of the CEOs said that reputation and brand have a great impact on sustainability.

Sometimes the external effort is directed towards damage limitation, as in the case of GB Rail, which sees one dimension of relationship building as an insurance policy. Similar defensive approaches are taken by House of Hardy, which works to demonstrate, to those who want to hear, that rivers that are fished are better conserved.

Belief and trust in stakeholder relations

The most fundamental belief in the extrovert organisation probably comes from Richard Hicks. It is an act of faith with him which drives his commitment as Chairman of the think-tank, Tomorrow's Company. His reading supports his instinctive view. In *Bowling Alone*, Robert Putnam talks of 'bonding capital' and 'bridging capital' in order to build trust. Trust relationships, as Francis Fukuyama points out, reduce transaction costs. What is one of their characteristics? In Richard's view, it is one of openness: honesty and clarity in relationships with customers, employees and the community.

Several others of those interviewed paralleled the depth of Richard's beliefs. Chris Mellor, of AWG, sees the opportunity to reconcile the irreconcilable and produce sustainable development. He talks of three levels of impact:

The first level involves:

- economic growth
- protecting the environment
- being a good citizen.

The second level concerns:

- balancing the objectives by involving staff; gaining their contribution, and achieving pride; and having products which are consistent with the values and giving the benefit of working in teams.

The third level consists of:

- gaining competitive advantage by knowing how to succeed at the earlier levels. It is about maturity and gaining optimal whole-life costs.

So, in the terms Richard borrowed terms from Putnam, it involves working through bridging capital to bonding capital.

Tony Ward of BAA, whose views are reinforced by Sir John Egan, the former CEO, is convinced that stakeholder relations give the business longevity. This belief has been tested in the severest of circumstances. These include relationships with customers (that is, the airlines) and government when BAA expressed its belief, during the T5 enquiry, that a third runway should not be built at Heathrow, but of course it would be the government's decision. Also, supplier relationships, where BAA adopted partnership in the face of the tunnel disaster on the Heathrow Express rather than fighting through the courts.

Dr Bryan Jackson of Toyota and Paul Forman at Unipart both treat trust in stakeholder relationships unquestioningly as the only way of conducting business. Bryan says business cannot afford to operate in a vacuum. For him, the argument is one of integration:

- employees come from the community
- the community provides customers
- the company needs to know community views and to improve communication.

Paul Forman sees the goal as supplier and client teams being indistinguishable.

Mike Rake at KPMG sees a great range of internal benefits from KPMG staff getting involved, including recruitment, fostering internal change, and breaking down the 'silo mentality'. The extrovert organisation is consistent with the values, and has longevity stronger than the will or desire of any incumbent CEO. Mark Hope of Shell found his work outside Shell gave insights, and a perspective, he knows would not otherwise be there.

Lawrence Churchill, formerly at UNUM, made a strong link between bottom line performance and the extrovert organisation.

'We cannot sustain shareholder value without the stakeholder view.'

This view is reinforced by Leslie Hannah, as we discussed in chapter 5. The ultimate step of faith in terms of trust was taken by the Burall family, when they passed control of the business to the employees as majority shareholders.

Before leaving the topic of belief, I have been struck by the number of interviewees who have pursued the extrovert path as a matter of personal conviction. Many have even made their external activity a pre-condition of their employment in particular organisations. As a result they have created 'portable community involvement' (or in some cases this could be the foundation of a future portfolio career).

What is clear is that boards face dilemmas over sustainability with which they must deal. What time and emphasis should be invested? The PWC 2003 CEO survey cited previously showed that 79 per cent of CEOs believe that sustainability is vital to profitability and that 71 per cent are prepared to sacrifice short-term profitability for long-term shareholder value through sustainability programmes. But one question that arises is whether those shareholders who are only investing for the short term value this.

Linkage with agility

It seems to me that the evidence is mounting that there is a clear linkage between the extrovert organisation and agility. Those organisations that have effective antennae are more able to be agile. At face value this is stating the obvious. Unless you have antennae and can read the trends, you don't know where to act.

However, I believe there is another dimension. The more of an organisation's staff that are involved in the reconciliation of customer and consumer views and those of the company stakeholders, the more prepared those staff are to be agile. You should not be able to hear people saying 'We've always done it this way, and why should we change?' in extrovert organisations.

Our sample contains several examples of this link between extrovert and agile. Paul Forman at Unipart said that the antennae had to be keener now, due to the pace of change. Syd Pennington wanted to substitute 'innovative' for 'extrovert' – integrating 'extrovert' with 'agile'. Jeremy Long saw the team that was 'out there' as one that was creative. Mike Walters of Bovis saw the extrovert organisation as being all about 'anticipating the future'. Dianne Thompson at Camelot saw it as anticipating changes that would be necessary. John Bridge took an economist's view and advocated the decoupling of people and products so that people were the key to sustainability. Lastly Leslie Hannah, supporting John Bridge, saw that business leaders needed to understand that the 'built to last' formula worked for organisations that developed and nurtured the human resource – but not necessarily for their products where agility took over and where the order of the day needed to be 'creative destruction':

> The most effective strategies, he states, are built on values established in the past.

Agility

This is clearly an attribute for which all our interviewees wish.* Certain preconditions become clear from the interviews:

- small organisations find agility easier than large ones. The more entrepreneurial they are, the quicker they are to react to or seize opportunities
- as such companies increase in size or become quoted companies, the formalities increase and perceived agility dissipates (eg BioFocus)

---

*This is in line with the PWC 2003 survey of 1,000 CEOs who felt the most effective business lever in today's uncertain environment was innovation.

- large companies regard the quest for 'catching the moment' a continual challenge. Those that believe they are most successful at being agile feel it is 'in the blood' (Camelot) or essentially a cultural thing. Some feel that it can be inhibited by silo mentality (KPMG) or the dominance of 'how we've always operated' (R&SA)
- the public sector finds this even more difficult than the rest.

The group of organisations which most consistently come to remarkably similar conclusions are in the 'public-to-private' category. They see the obstacles to agility as:

- the historical culture – which essentially was one of command and control
- the hierarchical structure
- the battle to give people time and space to innovate.

This last obstacle, the pressure on time, is one recognised by a number of interviewees. It is fine for the CEOs to encourage giving people time and space but the middle managers often receive mixed messages. Mike Rake of KPMG puts this dilemma succinctly. He says that you can't have people spending all their time on innovation, otherwise you'll go out of business, but nevertheless you have to encourage it.

Another common dilemma related to innovation is whether it should be left in the hands of specialists, or whether it is best given to a wider audience. Those that like the innovation 'think tank' idea include Camelot (with their 'think' room), The Strategic Partnership, KPMG (having, in one sense, tried innovation centres), and incubator theory and practice with Generics, BT, GB Rail, the NHS and the CBI. The other school of thought argues that, provided you can balance the time and resource effectively between day job and innovation, as many as possible in the organisation should be encouraged to innovate.

Many organisations have aspirations in this area but those with the most comprehensive 'systems' approach have their roots in the quality movement. Toyota, Unipart and Sir John Egan's experience from Jaguar give unstinting allegiance to the continuous improvement philosophy. In these cases, despite all we have seen about the ever-increasing pace of change, Bryan Jackson of Toyota points out that it takes five years to design a car and to speed the cycle up would build in too much obsolescence. Here there is a difference in what is meant by agility. Often the western concept is the 'eureka moment', leaping out of the bath with a formula to end all formulae. The total quality movement favours the iterative, continuous improvement, approach which has the capability of involving everyone.

Both Bryan Jackson at Toyota and Paul Forman at Unipart put the priority on people motivation. They see the need as one of taking people with you, and Paul sees 'catching the moment' as the second tier of development, beyond motivated and galvanised employees.

Sir John sees the issue as having an alert workforce and to engage their brains with a licence to experiment and space to innovate, not just the top of the organisation leading the change. Chris Mellor at AWG sees it as the aim of the whole organisation to spot opportunities, with people being motivated and empowered to do something about it. Mike Rake of KPMG, having tried dedicated innovation centres. is convinced that they can get too far from reality and that innovation needs to be close to the ground. In similar fashion, Syd Pennington of R&SA believes that the nearer to the customer they are taken, the better-informed decisions will be.

This sentiment is echoed by both Chris Mellor of AWG, who believes that leaders are not close enough to the market place, and Tony Ward at BAA who states that the perspective of people at the top is quite different to those at the bottom. Mark Hope of Shell is also in tune – he takes the 'employer of choice' route, which applies to all who contract to Shell, and brings the total organisation together to innovate.

There is a good degree of consensus over the right culture with which to overcome some of the obstacles. Richard Hicks equates diversity with creativity and tolerating mistakes. Duncan Hine talks of engendering innovation, creating the expectation, by being prepared to experiment and fail. Paul Forman at Unipart invoked Abraham Maslow (to whom we shall return later) by making agility a function of self-belief and self-esteem. Both Pertemps and Telos advocate encouraging creativity by diversity and allowing for mistakes.

Similar themes are picked up by Chris Mellor, who describes culture as being the enabler and stresses the crucial importance of signals to employees when moving from a risk-averse organisation, and Tony Ward, who desires an ethos of opportunity seizing but recognises that this needs a climate supportive of failure where the key value is learning.

The public sector is not immune to this debate. There seem to be two opposing views. One is that the public sector led policies are there to create stability (often macro-economic) so that the private sector can innovate and take risks. Alternatively, John Bridge advocates that 'we need an entrepreneurial public sector that continually innovates and becomes more agile' (for the benefit of the economy).

We have discussed, in turn, the different elements of the basic premise but we also need to explore whether, as might be predicted, there are linkages between them. In fact the interviews did reveal such linkages. The most striking area of consensus over linkages between the separate elements is about the links between the extrovert organisation and agility, which we recognised above while analysing interviewees' comments. Looked at from the other end of the loop, several of our interviewees made the connection.

Duncan Hine at Generics saw the client relationship being 'out there' as meaning that the organisation was continually agile, due to the extrovert nature of that relationship.

Similarly, the intense watching of the markets by Cisco and swift action in acting in a counter-intuitive way was a classic example of the extrovert-agility link. Dianne Thompson's view of what was happening with lottery opportunities and trends gave her the chance for agility.

Richard Hicks saw the extrovert link as ambassadorial, not just advertising AIT but giving knowledge for action. In a similar but non-commercial way Alan Bartle, through maintaining and networking, saw the extrovert-agile link as giving opportunities to improve the situation for Lymphoma sufferers and carers.

Peter Ward related the opportunity to Charles Handy's famous sigmoid curve describing the life cycle of an organisation. What the extrovert process did was to inform the business when to go for re-invention and to choose, as Charles Handy recommended, to reinvent at the top of the curve and not when sliding uncontrollably towards 'Paddy's Bar'.

This strategic approach was endorsed by Chris Mellor, who saw that companies needed to be selective in innovation and business development, selectivity which is informed by the extrovert nature of the organisation.

Learning between sectors

The connections between aspiration to world-class, engagement as an extrovert organisation, and ability to be agile, transcend the sectors in which the organisations within the book fit. As we have seen, the more experience of being extrovert the organisation has, the more able it is to judge the trends, understand customers, anticipate demands and markets and therefore to seize opportunities when they arrive. Further, it is clear that the wider the franchise is the better. The more employees that are involved in contributing to the antennae of the extrovert organisation, the greater the awareness, the easier the change process, and the more agile the organisation is collectively.

However, the public sector struggles with the concept. As we saw in chapter 7, the public sector has little incentive to attract more custom for its services. With stretched resources and politically limited budgets, it is obsessed with producing value-for-money solutions and justifying existing spends. Nothing happens without an invention of a target to measure outcomes, all perfectly logical and defensible in town halls and parliament. However it often amounts to a blinkered concentration on outcomes preventing time and opportunity being spent on policy and strategy. This is frequently because stakeholder views are not rated as important as satisfying centrally devised targets. Hence the benefit of the extrovert organisation is lost. Arguably without the practice of the extrovert organisation a wider view is not available, staff do not see the value of stakeholder views and the organisation is less agile. Professor Bob Garratt has helpfully demonstrated the tension here in his 'Learning Board' model, which we will dip into later in the chapter.

The public-to-private sector has realised this and, in the transition from public authorities to privatised companies, have consciously developed the extrovert organisation, thus becoming stakeholder organisations, sensitive to their communities and thus able to sense opportunities.

John Bridge of One NorthEast bemoans the lack of agility of the public sector. Perhaps here is a potential learning point between sectors. If public sector reform could see its focus not just as efficiency (a world-class aspiration) but effectiveness (to include being extrovert and agile) and practise being stakeholder organisations, then perhaps some of the competitive practices could become transferable, creating a more agile public sector. Similarly, other sectors can learn from 'not-for-profit' experience, as Charles Handy points out, the inherent ability of charities to measure their results by their effect on a range of stakeholders.

Individuals and organisations – the search for meaning

I believe there is a model formed by the linkages and dependencies between the attributes, from world-class to vision and values, to leadership, to extrovert and agile. What we have studied, across a wide-ranging number of organisations, demonstrates what I see as a hierarchy of needs for the organisation. I think this will have its parallels in Abraham Maslow's now famous and broadly accepted hierarchy of needs for the individual:

Hierarchy of needs for the individual

Maslow developed the hierarchy of needs to demonstrate that given the right environment, individuals could transcend subsistence or survival modes.

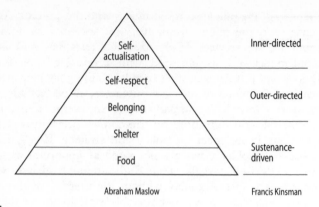

Figure 9C

Subsequent commentators have not received Maslow's hierarchy totally uncritically. In *The Empty Raincoat*[8] Charles Handy wrote that, as it stood, the hierarchy was rather self-serving, and he proposed that it should have a further stage of 'idealisation' in the search for meaning and purpose:

There could be a stage beyond self-realisation, a stage which we might call idealisation, the pursuit of an ideal or cause which is more than oneself. It is this extra stage which would redeem the self-centred tone of Maslow's thesis which, for all that it rings true of much of our experience, has a rather bitter aftertaste.

Francis Kinsman in *Millennium, Toward Tomorrow's Society* borrowed three psychological types developed by the Stanford Research Institute to describe the world as he saw it:

- sustenance driven
- outer-directed
- inner-directed

In Figure 9C I have related Kinsman's definitions to Maslow's hierarchy.

The search for meaning has been a recurrent theme in this research. There is little doubt that 9/11 has provoked this difficult issue to resurface. The parallel of Maslow and Kinsman with progression through a hierarchy of needs, spiritual and physical, is striking. Following Maslow, it would be tempting to take the earlier fundamental needs for granted, that is that individuals progress up the hierarchy not needing to attend to the earlier rungs of the ladder. In reality we all know that, despite the aspirations to self-actualisation and beyond, the experience is that the lower rungs of the hierarchy need to be maintained and not neglected.

Evidence in the research of the need for a spiritual dimension ranges from the Etzioni quotation in chapter 1 to the comments of Chris Mellor and Tony Ward in chapter 4. Scott Peck, the noted author and psychiatrist in *A Different Drum*[9] defines different stages of spiritual development for the individual.

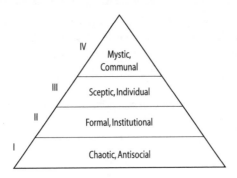

Figure 9D

The Stage I characteristics that Scott Peck describes are typical of teenage years, self-centred and disregarding of others' needs. Stage II is characterised by formal membership of religious bodies of whatever persuasion; in extremis this can feature fundamentalist or exclusive approaches. At Stage III is found the sceptic, agnostic, atheist, rejecting stages I and II, but often still very individualistic. Stage IV is about community, understanding, maturity of behaviour with others, wholeness and connectedness. These are typified by the Kinsman concept of inner-directedness or Charles Handy's idealisation as a stage beyond Maslow's self-actualisation.

Scott Peck makes a similar point about travel between the stages. Individuals oscillate between the stages, sometimes skipping a level. Just as with Maslow, there is a need to retain the experience of lessons from earlier stages ensuring good foundations are there.

Hierarchy for sustainable organisations?

I find an uncanny link between the progression for the individual as put forward by Maslow, Kinsman and Scott Peck and that applicable for the organisation. Arie de Geus, in *The Living Company*[10] published by Nicholas Brealey in 1997, produced some parallel evidence from Shell studies to the famous Collins & Porras work in *Built to Last*. Shell found that long-lived companies were:

- sensitive to their environment
- cohesive, with a strong sense of identity
- tolerant
- conservative in financing.

Arie de Geus puts these conclusions into context in *The Living Company*.

> *'Defining the living company:*
>
> *Over time, the same four factors that we developed in our study of long-lived companies at Shell have continued to resonate in my mind. Gradually they began to change my thinking about the real nature of companies and about what this means for the way that we, managers at all levels, run those companies. I now see these four components in this way:*
>
> *– sensitivity to the environment represents a company's ability to learn and adapt*
>
> *– cohesion and identity, it is now clear, are aspects of a company's innate ability to build a community and a persona for itself*
>
> *– tolerance and its corollary, decentralization, are both symptoms of a company's awareness of ecology; its ability to build constructive relationships with other entities, within and outside itself*
>
> *– and I now think of conservative financing as one element in a very critical corporate attribute: the ability to govern its own growth and evolution effectively.'*

Moreover, the question remains: why would these same characteristics occur again and again in companies that had managed to outlive others? I am convinced that the four characteristics of a long-lived company are not answers. They represent the start of a fundamental enquiry into the nature and success of commercial organizations and their role in the human community.'

I believe we can take the evidence from the interviews in this book and the basic premise and construct a 'Maslow's Hierarchy' for organisations.

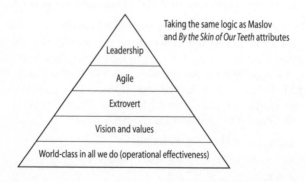

Taking the same logic as Maslov
and *By the Skin of Our Teeth* attributes

Leadership

Agile

Extrovert

Vision and values

World-class in all we do (operational effectiveness)

Figure 9E

From our studies in this book the linkages, dependencies and co-dependencies can be seen in this hierarchy. The parallels with Arie de Geus, Maslow, Kinsman and Scott Peck become clear. To take this in sequence:

	Organisation	Individual
1st Step	World-class (operational effectiveness) survival mode	Food (sustenance)
2nd Step	Vision and Values (frameworks, expression of persona)	Shelter (sustenance)
3rd Step	Extrovert (learning and ecology)	Belonging (outer-directed)
4th Step	Agile (only with confidence)	Self respect (outer-directed)
5th Step	Leadership (learning and evolution)	Self actualisation inner-directed)

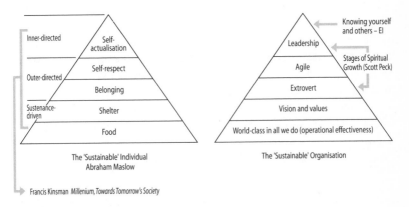

Figure 9F

So far so good. We have put forward an equivalent hierarchy of needs for the organisation to that for the individual. But what happens when we try to integrate them? Does it work? Who should act as the bridge? Or should we accept that the individual's needs at work are different and irreconcilable with the needs of the organisation?

My view is that bridging this gap is the most important challenge we face. Second that it is very clearly the Board's role to oversee this. If so, how?

Here I propose that an 'upside-down' pyramid can dovetail between the individual and the organisation and provide 'the bridge'.

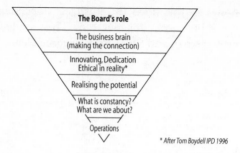

Figure 9G

The board's role

Putting it all together, what should the board do to create the dynamic and give the best chance of sustainability?

The board's role is deliberately dovetailed in this model as a bridge between hierarchy for the individual (Maslow) and the hierarchy for the organisation (for sustainability). While most of the prescription for the board is obvious by inspection, it is worth expanding a little on the model.

Working upwards, it is significant that the lower tip of the triangle covers the smallest area. Boards should not spend a great deal of their time on operations, which are matters for the executive. However, too many boards do get dragged into detail and micro-management.

'What is constancy?' What are we about? addresses the focus on vision and values, with which we dealt in some detail in chapter 5.

Combination of models

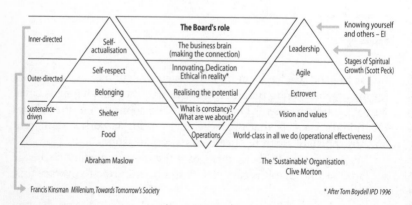

Figure 9H

'Realising the potential' is the board fulfilling its role in creating the atmosphere in which individuals and teams develop for their own and the organisation's benefit, giving a sense of belonging as well as learning and an outward focus.

'Innovating, dedication, ethical in reality' is about living the values and behaviours, about commitment to stakeholders, giving agility and self-respect. Significantly, each higher layer demonstrates a greater need for investment of the board's time.

What is the Business Brain?

The 'business brain' is the cerebral cortex of the organisation. This is where self-actualisation and leadership come together to deal with the tricky dilemmas between today's operations and the future strategy. What is the business brain and how can it be engaged? My colleague in Board Performance Ltd, Professor Bob Garratt has developed a powerful model of the Learning Board:

The Learning Board

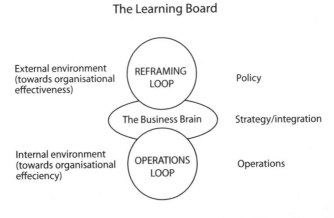

Figure 91 Professor Bob Garratt in *The Fish Rots from the Head* Harper Collins 1996

Bob Garratt's point is that the Business Brain needs to be fed in a balanced way from both the data rich element of current and past operations together with visions from the external environment allowing the 'reframing' of strategy. Few Boards properly achieve this.

This research has, I believe, helped us to further understand the necessary left hand (logic, reason) and right hand (emotion, spirit) brain activity of that 'business brain'. Modified it looks thus:

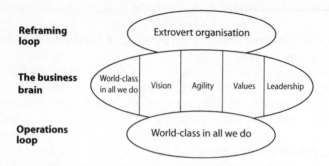

Figure 9J The Three Learning Loops – after Bob Garratt Defining the cerebral cortex

This is where we come full circle, from the individual needs for development through the organisation's needs, to the 'business brain' of the board that will need to set the policy and strategy for the sustainable organisation in the 21st century.

The board, let's face it, is made up of individuals, and they are the people who will determine success or disaster. My colleagues at Board Performance share with me the necessity and urgency of getting this right. Bob Garratt, in his latest book, *Thin on Top* published by Nicholas Brealey 2003, argues that, in the face of increasing corporate governance rules and expectations, board directors need to 'professionalise or face incarceration'. Also, we argue that the performance of directors and boards needs to shift upwards a gear – to raise their game in today's terms to fact the complexities, chaos and uncertainties we have acknowledged in this book. In the context of a loss of confidence in UK Boardrooms the Higgs Review of the role of non-executive directors commissioned by the UK Government in 2003 has put forward a powerful principle – the need to evaluate and develop the board.

Evidence, from the successful leaders who granted me interviews and the other experience I have contributed, is that boards have a key role in ensuring sustainability. Indeed, as Bob Garratt shows, this is their legal duty to the company and its prosperity and not, as is often assumed, focusing on short-term shareholder value.

The key role of the board is to balance prudent control with entrepreneurial activity for the future – a classic dilemma. We have seen that leadership is all about managing dilemmas, and that it is about knowing yourself and others. I have also the temerity to suggest that leaders need to aspire to the higher stage of spiritual growth as defined by Scott Peck. This is not necessarily spiritual growth in religious terms, although it might be. An up-to-date, classic example in terms of world leadership would be Nelson Mandela who appears, despite (or because of?) the deprivations of twenty-seven years on Robben Island, to have reached Stage IV of spiritual growth and is full of emotional intelligence.

We can't all be Nelson Mandelas, neither can one leader encapsulate all that a board needs in order to grapple with the dilemmas it faces. We know that the obverse operates – dysfunctional leaders mean dysfunctional boards which mean organisational demise. However if boards evaluate, review and develop against the criteria for a sustainable organisation developed here, I believe it gives the best chance of survival and growth.

As we have seen, this is not a formula. It is more a sustainable process acknowledging the cycle of organic development envisaged by Arie de Geus in *The Living Company*. Bob Garratt acknowledges this in the Learning Board model. The business brain must be fed by both the operations loop and the reframing loop.

This research shows that the business brain is capable of development. Naturally that brain is the sum total of the individual contributions around the board table and other contributions – often from outside. I argue that the often-neglected element in this is the right hand side of the individual and collective brains, hence the emphasis in the diagram above of the contribution of leadership, values and agility, all of which are predominantly right hand brain activity. My conclusion is that, to ensure sustainability, it is on the development of these attributes that organisations, their leaders and their boards need to focus.

A way forward

At the beginning of this chapter I put forward the proposition that the world we live in today is too complex, too fast-moving for formulaic solutions to give the simple answer to organisations in their quest for sustainability. My view is no different and having pursued the research summarised in this book I am not about to produce a manufactured toolkit that is 'one size fits all'.

However there is a wealth of difference in the effectiveness and performance of our organisations whether in the private, public or not-for-profit sectors. Many literally survive on their wits, 'by the skin of their teeth', with little prospect of longevity whereas others exhibit resilience, coping with all the unpredictability thrown at them, surviving and prospering.

This research has shown that long-lived, resilient organisations do share similar characteristics, which go beyond efficiency, operational effectiveness and transactional system based solutions. These characteristics include

- clear and meaningful vision and values
- ability to inculcate meaning and purpose for employees, customers and other stakeholders
- being connected with communities, outside the organisation – 'extrovert' in the definition within this book, listening, understanding trends
- agility in every sense of the term as a cultural ethos – embraced by the widest constituency
- transformational leadership that responds to the needs of those in and 'outside the organisation – not focusing on task- based transactional priorities.

These distinctions could lead the reader to conclude that there are two opposing methodologies for organisations – the first that is about short-term results, profits, targets, costs, mechanistic, logic, facts and figures (transactional based) and the second about long-term, intuition, big picture, meaning and purpose, organic growth, empowerment culture and change (transformational).

In one sense this is true. In another the trick, the solution, is to see them as complementary. Both methodologies have their place and the truth is that either one (Ying or Yang) cannot last long without the other. Hence the challenge in leadership terms is to balance the seemingly conflicting philosophies.

Finis Coronat Opus
(Motto of Isleworth Grammar School – my attendance 1954–1961)

Notes

1   Nonaka, I & Takeuchi, H *The Knowledge-creating Company: How Japanese Companies Create the Dynamics of Innovation* Oxford University Press 1995
2   Fukuyama, F quoted in *What's Next* Global Business Network Wiley 2002
3   Burns, T and Stalker, G *The Management of Innovation* Tavistock 1961
4   Collins, J and Porras, J *Built to Last* Century 1994
5   Handy, C *What's business for?* Harvard Business Review Dec 2002 p51
6   Harvard Business Review Dec 2002
7   Collins, J *Good to Great* Random House 2001
8   Handy, C *The Empty Raincoat* Random House 1994
9   Peck, S A *Different Drum* Simon & Schuster 1987
10 de Geus, A *The Living Company* N Brealey 1997

Appendix I

BACKGROUND ON PARTICIPATING ORGANISATIONS

I   START-UPS/ENTREPRENEURSHIP/PHOENIX

A   NEW START-UPS IN THE FIELDS OF TECHNOLOGY

AIT plc

Interviewee: *Richard Hicks, Non-Executive Chairman*

AIT is a software solutions company producing innovative IP programmes for the financial services industry. AIT was voted number 5 in *The Sunday Times 100 Best Companies to work for* in 2002. *The Sunday Times* said:

'*The entrepreneurial brothers Richard and Clive Hicks, along with Dave Woodhead, an IT expert, say they set out to redefine the experience of work in 1986. They chose a business – helping banks and building societies manage customer accounts through multi-media – that has since exploded. While other companies suffered, AIT's sales went up by more than half last year (2001). Despite the growth, staff at the Henley offices, surrounded by the green fields and the calming waters of the Thames, say the firm has done much to preserve its small-company feel.*'

See chapter 4 for subsequent events.

BioFocus plc

Interviewee: *Keith Moscrop, former Business Development Director and co-founder*

The company started in 1997 when a number of senior chemists who worked for Wellcome decided to leave after the Glaxo takeover and, with Keith Moscrop, to set up their own company in combinatorial chemistry to subcontract to the big 'Pharmas'.

'*We were fortunate that we were able to pick up the very cheap labs at Sittingbourne Research Centre, where everything worked when we walked in and turned on. We paid about £8 per sq ft for this fully serviced chemistry suite, which was amazing. Five thousand sq ft to start with and we had a couple of lorry loads of equipment that we inherited from Wellcome when they closed the labs down. We filled up the labs with all this equipment, recruited one or two people to start with and away we went.*

So it was complete start from scratch with a bunch of people who were all chemists and had no commercial background.'

In three years, BioFocus went from zero turnover to £5.7m turnover and £1.4m profit. In 2001, BioFocus took over a biology company in Cambridge expanding to three sites.

Scientific Generics

Interviewee: *Dr Duncan Hine, former Chief Executive*

'Generics Group is a Swiss registered, publicly listed group. It has around 275 people working for it. It's a collection of things rather than a highly integrated company. So the fundamental part of it is a large consultancy business based in the UK and America. There's another division which exploits intellectual property based in the UK, although registered in Switzerland for Treasury reasons and a third division that invests in third party businesses which are actually very small but quite significant in the overall activity. In terms of size, turnover and so on it's quite difficult to state in a meaningful sense because the turnover is a combination of organic trading and realisations of transactions and one transaction could be half or more of a year's organic trading so depending on whether there is one (transaction) or there isn't one, the results can be up and down 50 per cent. Organically we do about £20m a year roughly. In terms of profile, it's quite high profile for a business. I think it punches above its weight in terms of it is a little SME in European terms but actually is quite notable in other ways. Market niche is very much high technology but all technology so we go right across from optics, advanced materials, life sciences, chemistry, engineering, product development, communications and business strategy.'

Camelot Group plc

Interviewee: *Dianne Thompson, Chief Executive*

'We're an organisation founded in 1994. We're a single-purpose private company originally owned by five shareholders, then went down to four when GTECH left as a shareholder and back to five when the Post Office joined, when we actually won the latest bid. So the five shareholders are Cadbury-Schweppes, ICL or Fujitsu as it's now called, Racal as it was, which is now owned by Thales, the French electronics company, the Post Office or Consignia and Delarue, and that's the way it will probably stay. We have the two largest brands in the UK with the National Lottery Game, which is the six from forty-nine game that gets played on Wednesdays and Saturdays. Despite falling sales, we've still got about thirty-million people playing on a very regular basis – 65 per cent of the

adult population. On an average week our sales are now around £86m per week in total across all games.'

B   NOT-FOR-PROFIT

Lymphoma Association

Interviewee: *Alan Bartle, former Chief Executive*

Lymphoma Association is a relatively new charity that started in the 1980s in Tim and Felicity Hilder's dining room. Tim had non-Hodgkin's Lymphoma and survived for over twenty years after the initial diagnosis - which was quite exceptional. Tim and Felicity realised from experience that there was little co-ordinated non-medical help for sufferers, relatives and carers; hence the Lymphoma Association was born out of voluntary help to meet the need.

'The organisation aims to provide information and emotional support to people who are affected by lymphomas, ie cancer of the lymphatic system. That provision is made primarily through a telephone help-line service augmented with printed and video information, a network of support groups around the country, an annual national conference and a quarterly publication and also we have increasingly made use of the website. We are the only organisation that works exclusively in the lymphoma field.'

C   PHOENIX

Toyota   Manufacturing UK Ltd

Interviewee: *Dr Bryan Jackson OBE, Deputy Managing Director*

Toyota MUK is a wholly owned subsidiary of Toyota Japan established in 1992, with an investment of £1.7bn, on a green field site at Burnaston, near Derby. It employs 3,800 people in the UK and produces 22,000 vehicles pa on the basis of two-shift production. Turnover of Toyota MUK is £2bn pa. Vehicles are manufactured from rolled steel to finished vehicles and engines built in a separate plant at Deeside. Toyota is seen as the most successful large volume producer in an extremely competitive market.

Unipart Automotive plc

Interviewee: *Paul Forman, former Managing Director*

Unipart was originally the parts side of British Leyland (BL), which was government-owned in the 1980s and it started as a buy-out when Rover was sold to BAe. It is in the business of provision and distribution of parts to original equipment manufacturers (OEMs) and replacement parts to distributors. It has grown organically at 5 per cent year on year to £650m turnover employing 6,000 people by 2001. Hence, a start-up but with people, equipment and other inheritance from BL. The other link of interest between them is that Unipart quickly saw itself as a learning organisation and, under its first Managing Director, John Neill, adopted many Japanese manufacturing techniques and disseminated these amongst its suppliers and employees through Unipart U, its corporate university.

D   Consultancy/Outsourcing

Pertemps Ltd

Interviewee: *Tim Watts, Chairman*

Pertemps provide temporary or permanent staff in various sectors including commercial, technical, industrial and executive. Its philosophy is that it can recruit anyone for any type of job. Pertemps has an annual turnover £600m, it employs 2,000 staff and places more than 30,000 flexible workers per week.

Ashton Penney Ltd

Interviewee: *Bill Penney, co-founder*

'Ashton Penney is a company I started seven years ago which started as just me with a database promoting the concept of interim management and it's grown in the first two or three years simply on the back of more business than I could handle and some of my friends and people I'd worked with in my past life walked past the door and I put out my hand and grabbed them. So we've evolved a fairly unusual structure, I think. We are, to all intents and purposes, a virtual company. Our fear is that, we are now thirteen or fourteen, all relate to the company through their own personal services company and we work on a margin split on the business that's generated. We've grown now to be, probably one of the biggest players in the interim management market. Our turnover last year was about £6.5m, which is the first year when we haven't more than doubled in growth.'

The Strategic Partnership

Interviewee: *Peter Smith, Chief Executive*

A Management Consultancy with scope to create growth on valuable assets, eg relationships, culture, values, knowledge and leadership. There is a virtual team of four at centre and sixty-five consultants dotted around. It measures success through client satisfaction, successful acquisition of business, professional development and its ability to innovate.

Telos Partners

Interviewee: *Peter Ward, Principal*

> *'It's a business that's built on beliefs. There's a fundamental belief that organisations are more important than just economic vehicles. I have a belief that too many people see companies as nothing more than the sum of their transactions whereas I see them as products of their relationships.'*

II M&A/DEMERGER ORGANISATIONS

Royal and Sun Alliance plc

Interviewee: *Syd Pennington, Director of Customers and People (now Group Director Executive Office and Change Management)*

R&SA is one of the world's largest and oldest insurance groups that has been through enormous upheaval in recent years in terms of products, position in the marketplace and financial viability. An incredible range of insurance 'from pet insurance to nuclear power stations', diverse origins pre-merger and 520,000 employees. The big issue has been to grapple with size and diversity and increasing challenges from shareholders.

KPMG

Interviewee: *Mike Rake, Chairman KPMG International*

> *'KPMG is an accounting firm, split between four major divisions, assurance, tax and legal, consulting and financial advisory services. The total of all of that is about $14billion revenue, although we are in the process of separating consulting which we've partially separated and floated off, which would reduce our ongoing revenue, without consulting, to about $10billion. In the UK we have about £1.5bn of revenue, about 11,000 people. Again in reality about 25 per cent of our revenue is in each of those businesses and we are in the process of integrating our practices in Europe, where we have about 50,000 people and about 5 billion Euros of revenue. In the last three to four years, we've more or less doubled our profitability and had compound growth of about 20 per cent. So we've done OK in the last few years against a good economy and we think gained market share in most key areas in recent years.'*

Cisco Systems EMEA

Interviewee: *Todd Abbott, former Group Vice President, EMEA*

The *Sunday Times 100 Best Companies to Work For* said this in 2002 about Cisco:

'Last year's number one (number seven in 2002), has endured a difficult year with 5,000 redundancies worldwide. The Internet specialist has not been immune to the pressures in this sector but employees still trust the firm's vision and flexible, egalitarian approach to work. Cisco was launched in 1984 by scientists from Stanford University and grew phenomenally. Tough times in the market triggered job cuts. Employees say the redundancies were handled well. Teamwork is encouraged and 88 per cent of staff said that management genuinely seeks suggestions. One said: 'From the day I joined, I felt part of a winning team. Everybody in the business has time for you and will help in any way they can. The company's whole ethos is based around working as a team and supporting others.'

Cisco has acquired to build capability over the last decade. Todd Abbott expressed it:

'As the largest manufacturer of networking solutions we're very much focused on three segments in the market and the enterprise, the small and medium enterprise or business so we look at it amongst those three. Historically we've come up from being an enterprise-focused company and expanded it to commercial and service provider, which was always really a vertical-within enterprise historically from our early days. About six to seven years ago we started to evolve into infrastructure types of equipment for service providers as what's happening is the network of the enterprise and the small and medium business and the service provider and all really starting to converge.'

MCL – The Performance Solution

Interviewee: *Sally Vanson*

'MCL…started life as Mazda Cars UK, importing Mazdas into the UK twenty-seven years ago. Major shareholder was Itoshu which is a Japanese trading house and about five years ago decided to diversify out of the motor industry, either by organic growth or acquisition and ended up unbundling all the internal services like logistics, event management and so on and setting up separate companies. They ended up with thirteen companies, £800m turnover, UK based and we now have companies, e-commerce, fulfilment, logistics, financial services which are limited companies in their own right with external clients.'

'The Performance Solution…as a result of [the demerger] I set up a company called The Performance Solution with three external partners.

So it's more of a strategic alliance than a wholly-owned business and it focuses on personal and organisational development, particularly the areas of leadership, team development and coaching.'

III PUBLIC TO PRIVATE

AWG plc

Interviewee: *Chris Mellor, former Chief Executive* described the business then:

'I would describe AWG as a business in transition. It's become two fundamental businesses in one – a water utility and a business that we aspire to of what we call our whole line managing the infrastructure operating across the utilities, the government sector and so on, and on an international basis. We have been pursuing two growth strategies, one to expand internationally in water and one to expand into other areas in the UK and we hope eventually to square that circle by using the international platform to establish water as the bridgehead to move into other areas, just as we've done in the UK.

We set out to be the leading company in water and we got there two years early in terms of overall performance but the other key measure for us is growth and ultimately it's shareholder value. So I adopt a balanced scorecard approach to setting of targets in four main areas: what our shareholders want which is really totally shareholding returns, what our customers want and that depends on the customer, what processes need to be excellent and what do we need to learn and grow.'

G B Rail plc

Interviewee: *Jeremy Long, Chief Executive*

'GB Rail is the owning group behind three trading operations. Anglia Railways passenger franchise, operating from London Liverpool Street up to East Anglia, which is a seven-year franchise. The second passenger business is a business we started. It is not a franchise. It's therefore ours to develop Whole Trains, which is an open access business, which we hope to be able to go on and expand and develop. The third is our rail freight business, also started within the last year, which again is not a franchise, it does not have any limited timescale to it, it's a case of how quickly we develop and grow that business.'

In achieving the franchise as a rail operator from the privatisation of British Rail in 1996 GB Rail is both public-private and a start-up. Jeremy Long believes their rail experience at the start made a difference.

'There are very real barriers to entry into railways generally. One has to

have a licence, one has to have a safety case. Achieving those from a standing start is non-trivial. It would be very difficult for a would-be railway company to set themselves up from scratch. But if you already have a railway operation, to then put in place a new management team with some common aspects is still difficult but not nearly as difficult as doing it from nothing. So we set up GB Railways in the same way as Whole Trains with two completely separate management teams and got consents.'

BT plc

Interviewee: *Bob Mason, former HR Director, BT Wireless*

'BT is today a global, multi-national business which operates in the communications market place which is a little different to its origins in the post office and then in the telecommunications market. It is a business of approaching 130,000 people worldwide with a turnover of £15bn with a profit of around £2bn which is substantially down on where it was just a few short years ago. And a business that is under a good deal of pressure in terms of the amount of debt it has taken on to fund its international expansion. That's forcing the business now to review its international reach and indeed some of the businesses have retrenched into a western European area, particularly the mobile business, by selling off some of the international operations in Asia, the US and places like that. It is however one of the highest revenue earning communications businesses in the world. So then it was a business that was starting to question, does it remain a single business or does it break itself into four or perhaps five different businesses, able to compete more aggressively in each of the relevant areas of its market. Subsequently they demerged the mobile business so that a mobile company could compete against very specific competitors in mobile communications.'

BAA plc

Interviewees: *Sir John Egan, former Chief Executive (now Chairman at Inchcape)* and *Tony Ward, Group Services Director*

Tony Ward described the situation in the UK and abroad:

'BAA is the world's leading airport management company. We operate airports predominantly in the UK but also in the US, Australia and mainland Europe. We have about 13,000 employees, the majority of which are in the UK and they are engaged in front line services to passengers and to airlines but also in facilities development as well as retail space management. The privatisation of airports all round the world following the UK lead is a bit erratic and we've taken some of those so our biggest representation now is in Australia where we have Melbourne, Perth, Northern Territories and we operate one airport in the US and we own Naples in Italy.'

IV PUBLIC SECTOR AND PFI

NHS/DoH

Interviewee: *Professor Sir Liam Donaldson, Chief Medical Officer, Department of Health*

The National Health Service and Department of Health are separate but linked. The NHS was established in 1947 by the post war Labour administration for the provision of healthcare nationally 'free at point of delivery'. It employs well over one million staff and has the largest departmental budget at over £70bn pa. As such, it is always a subject of controversy.

Sir Liam described the DoH and his role:

'My role is as one of the two most senior executive posts within a central government department, which is responsible for health policy and resource allocation mainly to the NHS and responsibility for regulating social care and responsibility for performance management of the NHS.'

Peterborough Hospitals NHS Trust

Interviewee: *Malcolm Lowe-Lauri, former Chief Executive*

Medium/large acute hospital provider with some particular specialisms (eg inhalation unit for those affected by smoke/burns etc). Turnover currently £100m which increased by approx £10m with the merger with Stamford Hospital. 2,700 employees. Second largest employer in Peterborough. High national profile and under the government's 'star' rating system the Trust has received highest 'three star' assessment for two years running. Also the Prime Minister's personal award for clinical excellence in Ophthalmology.

One NorthEast (Regional Development Agency)

Interviewee: *Dr John Bridge, Chairman*

'One NorthEast is one of the nine regional development agencies in the English regions which includes London. Its size in terms of its actual spend is coming up to the £250m level this financial year. That relates to about 220 people employed. Its scope is to lead economic, social and environmental improvement in the north east. That's a very, very wide agenda. Obviously the economic is relatively straightforward. It's about business improvement, improving the quality of the infrastructure, innovation, technology transfer, providing finance for business, all those sorts of things. In terms of social improvement it's about making people

ready for the marketplace, bringing people out of social exclusion, working with communities. Looking at the environmental side it's ensuring that whatever you do, now and over the next five to ten years you do it in an environmentally friendly way. So interestingly enough that's created a whole series of new relationships and partnerships that we have in the region.

£250m sounds like a lot of money to a lot of people, but it probably represents 2-3 per cent of public expenditure in the region, so it's not a big number. What we can do is influence through strategic approaches, in much bigger areas of public expenditure. An obvious example would be education skills.'

Arts Council England

Interviewee: *Peter Hewitt, Chief Executive*

The Arts Council England is the national agency charged with the responsibility for developing opportunities for artists and the arts in England. Its budget is £500m; it employs 600 people and has experienced recent financial growth. It occupies a 'monopoly' position but is open to audit and accountable to parliament.

Success is measured formally through financial, quantitative and qualitative measures and informally through:

- the scale of financial opportunity that is generated for new initiatives in the arts
- level of regard the arts are held in
- financial health of the arts community
- public perception of art
- level of partnerships, numbers of engaged people and the quality of that engagement, public coverage.

Learning & Skills Council West of England

Interviewee: *Jenny Clarke, Head of Workforce Development*

Jenny has responsibility for pulling together the strategic initiatives for workforce development in the geographical area covered by this Skills Council. Effectively it covers the 'old' Avon district plus Bath to the East. Jenny's particular remit aims to co-ordinate, share and spread best practice, learning from those employers who apply leading-edge principles of employment. The nature of the Council's work is one of persuasion in a part of the country that has low unemployment and where the challenges are to maximise performance and strengthen leadership. The modus operandi is to establish networks of recognised leading and successful companies. These 'pathfinder' networks comprise approximately ten companies, sharing issues and sustaining the networks to learn from each other.

The Patent Office

Interviewee: *Philip Johnson, Head of Marketing*

Philip Johnson is Head of Marketing at the Patent Office, an Executive Agency of the DTI based in Newport South Wales. The Patent Office moved to Newport ten years ago from Central London. They employ 950 with a further twenty in the London Office. It is an executive agency of the DTI. Turnover £55m derived principally from patent renewals. The Office grant trade marks/design registrations/copyrights as well as developing policies in the whole arena of intellectual property.

Bovis Lend Lease

Interviewee: *Mike Walters, Executive, Lend Lease Europe*

'*Bovis Lend Lease is part of Bovis Lending Europe, with 2,000 employees. Bovis Group is scattered across twenty-two countries. Bovis Global is a major international player in the construction field. We measure success through financials, but also sales and other areas such as knowledge transfer. The number of hits on the system measures the latter. Then there are safety measures and performance agreements. We looked at balanced scorecard but this had too many measures. We make extensive use of circles of quality to look at lessons learnt. We use our Intranet to open up channels of who to contact to get info rather than putting everything on the system and then trying to keep it all up to date. We also encourage team and peer reviews as another way of transferring knowledge i.e. getting people to speak to others on the other side of the world. When we were looking at how to create effective knowledge transfer we used BP as a benchmark and listened to many of the lessons they had learnt.*'

V   'BUILT-TO-LAST' ORGANISATIONS/'STEADY AS SHE GOES'

A   PRIVATE SECTOR

Shell UK Exploration & Production

Interviewee: *Mark Hope, Director of External Affairs*

'*The operating company I work for is the exploration and production company for the UK so that means we explore for and produce and process oil and gas from the North Sea and that involves something over thirty platforms offshore and it involves gas processing plants onshore in Scotland in Fife and in East Anglia at Bacton where the southern North Sea Gas comes in and Shell in the UK operates on behalf of itself and Esso or now Exon Mobil and a number of other smaller partners because most of the North Sea licence blocks are licensed to a number of companies, not just to one. So there are a lot of joint ventures. The scope of the business, we produce a bit less than 20 per cent of the oil and gas for the UK so we're one of the bigger players alongside BP and Exon Mobil. We produce something like 500,000 barrels a day of oil and gas equivalent. Turnover is, well it goes up and down with the oil price like a yo-yo but is of the order of billions of pounds a year. Growth, well the business, again is hugely dependent on the oil price. Over the last ten years we've about doubled our production of oil and gas and the profitability of the business varies massively. Three and a half years ago when the oil price was around ten to twelve dollars, the business was slowly making money. In current, the last year with oil prices in the mid-20s, it's a hugely profitable business so it oscillates massively with price being largely outside the oil companies' control. Size – in terms of employees, we directly employ something like 2,500 people and via various, depending on how you count it, there's probably about the same number of contractors directly working on our business and then through the supply chain obviously a lot more people involved in the business. The market niche is oil and gas upstream, so exploration and production in the oil and gas sector.'*

UNUM

Interviewee: *Lawrence Churchill, former Chairman and Chief Executive*

'*UNUM is a niche player in disability insurance with a turnover of £250m, average growth of 23 per cent pa (over the last four years) and 650/700 employees.*

It was established in the UK in 1970 but was originally established in the US in the nineteenth century. We have branches in the UK and small operations in France and the Netherlands.

We are part of UNUMPROVIDENT Corp USA, which has a turnover of $7bn and is world leader in this specialised insurance. We provide Group and Individual income protection in the event of accident/sickness. We sell via brokers but also supply the product under other labels, for example HSBC.

We have seven UK competitors. For Group business (which tends to focus on companies with 50-500 employees) UNUM has a 30 per cent market share, Royal & Sun Alliance has 14 per cent and Legal & General 7 per cent. For Individual business UNUM has 18 per cent.'

Burall Ltd

Interviewee: *David Burall, Non-Executive Chairman*

'The business was started by my grandfather in 1890. Grandfather died rather suddenly in 1924 when my father was twelve years old and my aunt took the business over. She was grandfather's secretary. It was quite a big business in the mid 20s employing 120 -140 people in label printing, general printing and stationery.

It was a national business with a fairly wide distribution network through sales people. Father joined up in the Second World War and was killed in a jeep accident in India in 1946, just after the end of the Japanese war. So Aunt Kathleen kept the business going and I joined it in 1963. The Board of Directors were Aunt Kathleen, who ran it, my mother, my grandmother and my step-aunt. A matriarchal society! Aunt Kathleen and the business were both a bit tired. It was under-capitalised and not making money - £100,000 turnover, which doesn't sound very much now. This was in 1963 when I came into the company at the age of twenty-two or twenty-three and it took me quite a while to get to grips with the challenges of an under-capitalised business. We began to have some small wins in terms of expanding the business and beginning to invest in new plant and equipment and to get the sales and marketing structures to be more effective. And the business grew slowly but surely – nothing dramatic. I remember I wanted to keep the business small and decided that we shouldn't employ more than 100 people. We employed ninety-five. I then embarked on the policy of having more than one small company so we started our first venture with a new business starting a small creative design company and through the 70s and 80s things went pretty well for us. By 1990 I think we had three or four operating companies and by the mid-1990s we were rolling up to a £15-20m turnover.'

House of Hardy

Interviewee: *Richard Maudslay, Managing Director*

'House of Hardy was formed in 1872 as gun makers by the two brothers Hardy. They then changed a year later and concentrated more on fishing tackle although they did make the guns for many years. Then were incredibly innovative and made an awful lot of new inventions both in rods and reels and the company then changed ownership to another family in the 1960s and brought in the first outside manager in the 1980s. Scope of the business - we make fishing rods and reels. We also have a spin-off business, which has been going for about thirty years, which makes composite tubes. Because we're good at making carbon fibre fishing rods we are making any kind of carbon fibre tubes so we make tiny ones for the defence industry, radio aerials, military aerials, for aerospace, canoe paddle shafts, golf club handles from time to time, formula one car struts, *you name it. Size of the business in turnover terms roughly £4m but 20 per cent being industrial business and the rest fishing tackle. We have another brand – Grade. There was Mr Grade who used to work for Hardy who made fishing rods then he left and set up his own business that went through a lot of different ups and downs then finally it went into receivership. It was subsequently bought by House of Hardy.'*

Gardiner & Theobald

Interviewee: *Marion Weatherhead, Salaried Partner*

'Gardiner and Theobald are an international practice of project managers and construction cost managers with a global alliance based in Levitt and Bailey who work from Hong Kong, China and the East Pacific Coast and then Ryder Hunt who are based in Sydney who have got offices in Australia, New Zealand and on the west coast of the USA. We've got offices on the east coast of the United States and we've got offices in Europe particularly Eastern Europe, like Hungary, Czechoslovakia, Poland, Romania. We've done work up in Russia and Latvia and the Baltic States and all over the place actually and then in the Middle East we've got offices and we've done projects in India and projects in China even when that overlaps with Levitt and Bailey and we go out there with them so there is a cross-fertilisation. We've also got an association with a practice in South Africa and I don't think we have an office there at the moment but we have operated in South America so it's global. But as with many of these large practices we all have developed other aspects to our services. Construction becomes much more sophisticated, you're much more likely to be able to serve your clients well if you can get in early on when they're thinking about the initial ideas so we have a number of exclusive services that help the consultancy and that's the area in which I work. I tend to be involved particularly with businesses related to property. I work quite a lot on soft management issues, developing tool kits, working with the construction industry folk in developing learning sets, with corporate clients in helping them to develop their ideas of what they want, etc, understanding the law and property and their business.'

B   NOT-FOR-PROFIT

CBI

Interviewee: *John Cridland, Deputy Director General*

'The CBI is a membership organisation representing the interests of British business. It has an annual income of about £17m and employs 210 executives. We judge success by how far we are able to persuade governments here and internationally to adopt policies at the request of the business community and ultimately corporate members will judge whether

we've added sufficient value to their operations to justify their subscription.'

Ashridge Trust

Interviewee: *Professor Leslie Hannah, formerly Chief Executive*

'Basically it's a largish British Business School. The only one that's larger is the London Business School. We're bigger than them in executive education but of course we have much fewer students on qualification programmes. The MBA side is only 5 per cent of our turnover. So we've a turnover of £26m, a faculty of eighty, total staff 400. We're at the upper end of the British Business School scale but smaller than Instead or LBS. We're much more focused than most on executive education and I would say the FT ratings are about right. They rate us top in the UK in tailored executive education, third in open executive programmes and seventh in the MBA. We're probably not as good at research as the top universities but we're excellent in many areas. Someone like Gould and Campbell, say, would be top ranking in research on strategy and organisation and the Ashridge Centre for Business and Society is a leader in corporate social responsibility. How do we measure success? Partly prestige. Growth? Yes, we like growth. We've been growing at 8-10 per cent a year for the last ten years, like most people, and this year we've grown minimally. That's probably something to do with recession or economic slowdown. The decline has come in airlines, banks and telecoms: most other business is healthy and growing.

So we're not experiencing a recession. We're slightly up overall on last year - slightly worse in some areas and slightly better in others and steaming ahead in some areas like on line learning. We're massively over budget revenue on our virtual learning resource centre, which is basically becoming a major European e-learning for business product. We got £1m subscriptions this year against a budget of £0.5m. It's selling like hot cakes.'

Appendix II

EXAMPLES OF VISION AND VALUES STATEMENTS

1 KPMG

Our Values Charter

To achieve our overall vision and apply our values, we will conduct ourselves in line with this charter.

- We will put KPMG's interests above our personal business agendas
- We will remain courteous and good humoured in all of our dealings, thus creating an environment where cynicism, oppression and rudeness are not acceptable
- We will be proactive and innovative with our clients, and will respond to their needs quickly, effectively and objectively
- We will listen to and aim to understand alternative perspectives and put our own points of view across openly, honestly and constructively
- We will support our leaders, encourage our peers and develop our people
- We will openly and proactively share knowledge
- We will respect all of our people and the contribution they make to the firm
- We will obtain the facts before making judgements on people or issues
- We will respect our own and our people's need to balance personal and business lives
- We will learn from our experiences and will take the time to enjoy our successes in the company of those we work with

Partners, as the leaders of the firm, are seen as role models for our people and the wider business community. They recognise their particular responsibility to live our values and to help embed this charter in our business.

'Success through shared values'

2   **AWG plc**

Our Vision and Values

Purpose: (the business we are in)

To deliver consistently superior returns to our stakeholders through the sustainable and profitable management of essential infrastructure.

We own, create and manage infrastructure (in the utility, government, property and transport sectors) in the UK.

Vision and goals:

To lead in infrastructure management

To achieve this we will:

- exceed client and customer expectations
- embrace the concept of sustainability

Strategy: (how we will achieve our goals)

Exceed client and customer expectations

- understand and anticipate customer needs and expectations
- operate in a safe and sustainable way
- make every employee an ambassador for AWG

Develop and promote our business

- utilise our heritage and capabilities in the water sector as a demonstration of our expertise
- develop AWG brand awareness and understanding to attract new business
- develop value-adding partnerships
- focus on ways to improve profitability

Embrace sustainability

- recognise our responsibilities to the communities in which we work
- ensure responsible use of resources
- develop a Learning organisation

Values:

- our success will be built on our common values

Safety:

- always our first priority

Integrity:
- delivering a quality service
- dealing openly and honestly with customers, clients, staff and partners
- operating in a sustainable way
- enhancing the well-being of communities

Intelligence:
- providing tailored, flexible solutions
- innovative and differentiated
- embracing change
- expert

3. Burall Limited

Burall Limited
Company Philosophy

- **is on course to be, and will remain, an employee-owned company**
- **recognises responsibilities** to customers, staff, shareholders, trading partners and the community
- **looks for an above average return** on capital in the long term without exposing shareholders to high risks and will retain sufficient profit to fund growth
- **nurtures and supports entrepreneurship** creating the best environment for successful operating companies which should be focused, flexible, dynamic and innovative, practising an open and participative management style
- **agrees marketing policies** which aim to satisfy customers with useful products and services within the information industry, particularly specialist print and publishing
- **encourages operating companies** to trade with each other on competitive terms
- **is committed to Burall Total Quality (BTQ)** – striving for total customer satisfaction through teamwork and continual improvement
- **seeks to create the circumstances for all staff to take a pride** in their company and to enjoy coming to work
- **offers equal employment opportunities** and seeks to ensure employment security avoiding job losses through the introduction of new technologies

- **offers training facilities** for a wide range of skills, opportunities for advancement and job enrichment within and between operating companies
- **sees all staff as individuals** and respects individuality and aims for honesty and fairness in its dealings

Strategic Intent

Burall Limited will develop a portfolio of dynamic businesses in the print, packaging and information sectors by providing:

- the best possible environment in which Burall companies can deliver long-term shareholder value
- a stimulating and supportive organisation structure which will recognise how exploiting synergies can create business opportunities

Burall companies should:

- aspire to the company philosophy of Burall Limited
- develop robust business plans
- demonstrate continual improvement to ensure cost competitiveness in chosen markets
- focus on markets with significant potential
- exploit market opportunities through synergy
- develop strategic partnerships to build competitive advantage
- plan to exploit emerging technologies

Appendix III

CASE STUDY 2: WHOLE SYSTEMS APPROACH – PETERBOROUGH TRANSFORMATION TEAM

STAGE IN THE CHANGE MANAGEMENT MODEL	*'To change the process of patient care – to improve it and make it more efficient. Whole systems approach involving both primary and acute sector.'* **Key challenges** • Introducing something new • Trying to introduce a change across the different departments • Convincing people of new ways of working • Success could be dependent on the type of project, the aims of the project, and the characteristics of people involved **Key learning** • Need to pick the right people and support them; people need to have the right personal characteristics; they need to be resilient, have stamina and a sense of humour – they can come from any professional background • Message needs to be that the change process is not forced or dictated • Need someone who is well known in the organisation and experienced enough to lead the whole project • Needs top level commitment • Changes take time • Need to have dedicated team to take forward the issues as clinicians and other staff are too busy • Need to keep working at it and keep going back and doing regular reviews to ensure that the things that are meant to be done have been done properly **Key methodology** • Whole systems approach **Key tools** • Process mapping • Facilitated workshops • Best practice research • Coaching and support

1 **Recognition of the need for change**	Peterborough Transformation Team was established seven and a half years ago and pre-dates the publication of the NHS Plan or establishment of the Modernisation Agency. It operates as a mini agency for the Peterborough health and social services community and is a development of the initial reengineering projects at King's Healthcare in London and Leicester Royal Infirmary. The imperative for the project was the need to change healthcare processes and reduce workloads in the face of a continual increase in demand for treatment within the then financial constraints.
	Key success factors: Buy in from the Trust's staff, particularly clinicians and local general practitioners
	Key hindering factors: The time required in the early stages to enlist participation of key personnel and develop examples which encourage further involvement.
2 **Start of the change process**	A project plan was agreed by the Trust Board and presented to the regional and local health authorities for support. Running parallel with this were a series of visits to every GP practice in the catchment area explaining the purpose behind it, the realities faced by everyone in the NHS and a request for active participation and support. A similar serious of presentations was given to all departments, specialties and professions within the Trust. A key element of the plan was the recognition that for patients their care started and finished with the GP and that any review of the processes involved must be total and not simply the acute element. Details of the project were advertised locally, and volunteers invited on secondment basis from any of the local health and public service organisations. 70 applicants were interviewed and 22 were accepted to the training, from a range of professional backgrounds. Three GPs were also recruited as active participants and advisors. Formal training in the tools and techniques of change projects was provided by an external consultancy but that was the limit of any management consultant involvement, a deliberate decision as it was felt that locally owned and managed project would have a better chance of success. All the other aspects of the project have been managed and directed by Bill.
	Key success factors: Commitment from all organisations involved and active participation of primary and secondary clinicians.

	Key hindering factors: No major hindering factors. Mostly to do with the fact that the project was something new, different and difficult, as it aimed to change the way services had been provided for many years. It took some time to convince people that this was something they should aim for.
3 Diagnosis	Out of the 22 trained, 12 were then selected to form the first Transformation Team for a 6-12 months period of time to start the work in reviewing how health services were organised. A broad remit for the group was set. The high level review of health care provision in Peterborough included: referral system, emergency admissions, elective admissions and public consultation. Out of the four initial pieces of work, areas of work were prioritised for developing better services to the patients.
	Key success factors: Key factor was to ask people their opinions instead of telling them the priority issues. Broad involvement of different staff groups.
	Key hindering factors: Sheer scale of the task and the need to determine priority areas for review.
4 Planning and preparing for implementation	The principle behind the Transformation Team is to provide an example to others. In practice this means that individual teams have a maximum amount of delegated responsibility and freedom without very hands on management input. For example the team does not have a secretary or admin support – individuals are responsible of their own work. 'We ask you to do things differently and we show example'. Also, there is no manager between the team members and the director.
	Out of the four initial workstreams, topics ('building blocks') were identified to take work forward. The aim was that when each of these 'building blocks' where put together and in place, it would result in a better service. Each of the 'building blocks' formed an individual project. For example, in emergency admissions, they broke the types of admissions down into individual components. All different 'building blocks' contribute to a different and better emergency care system for patients and staff.
5 Implement change	The 12 members of the Transformation team were split into three groups (emergency admissions, outpatients and GPs, and elective admissions). The three teams were responsible for facilitating discussions between all participants and doing the research to find out about best practice in health

	care, in the particular area. The small team would then be responsible for making it work.
	For example the early work in emergency admissions (1996), introduced the principle of 'assessment rather than admission' was quite a radical change. It was recommended that an assessment area in which patients could be diagnosed by a consultant be established, and that the decision to admit or discharge back to the care of a GP made. Admission pathways were followed through in other 'building blocks' as well. Examples of other changes include:
	• Allowing GPs to refer individuals with DVT directly for tests, and deciding whether to admit the individual or refer them back to the GP based on the test result;
	• changing the working patterns of physicians (physician of the week – one physician responsible for all the emergency admissions during the period); and
	• agreements between consultants and GPs regarding who should be admitted (for example consultants to always have mobile phones so they could speak to GPs and provide required support and advice).
	These resulted in an approach where only those who needed to be admitted were admitted.
	Key success factors: The whole process took time. Involving staff in the process, to give directorates examples and opportunities for change. This is an ongoing process. Staff have realised that the Transformation Team was serious and credible and involved people rather than telling them what to do.
	Key hindering factors: People, professional roles, number of discussions required and the need to continually audit outcomes prior to wider rollout
6 Review	Two levels of review:
	• the initial review following the change, which leads to further adjustment; and
	• ongoing monitoring and review.
	There is no set approach to the issue - it varies according to the topic and speciality. For example in ophthalmology the Transformation Team supports the audit of patients' experience and they look at the audit results to ensure that any changes made have led to an improvement. Weekly meetings are penned in to ensure regular feedback and dissemination. In addition, monthly and quarterly reports are produced. Generally the Team supports the departments undertaking the work to review results.

	Key success factors: The need for comprehensive and accurate data, regular monitoring and analysis **Key hindering factors:** Information not always available and systems need to be designed to collect it.
Mainstreaming	There is a need to have examples that work and a need to spend time with staff talking and explaining what has been done. There is no magic answer. People need support, including financial support. However, most of the time it is about changing the culture and persuading people to do things differently without feeling that it is wrong or feeling isolated. Bill is now in his fourth team of Transformers. The project is essentially a high level training programme in change management. People who have joined rarely wish to go back to their previous roles and instead have taken up many of the opportunities, which now exist in the NHS at a more senior level. For the ophthalmology Transformation Team, for instance, there is a commitment to continuity and sustainability. In addition, there are intentions of working more closely with other partners in health such as the PCTs, social services, and the council. **Key success factors:** The need to maintain credibility and be seen as a source of help and support. **Key hindering factors:** The time it takes particularly when there is primary care involvement. We have 50 referring practices and 250 GPs. Any change needs to be implemented across all to achieve a new improved and standard system. In addition there is a need to achieve and demonstrate progress in implementing the NHS Plan.

For more information please contact Sarah Butler, the project lead for the Peterborough Transformation Team **sarah.butler@pbh-tr.nhs.uk**

Useful Contacts

Board Performance Limited
www.boardperformance.com or info@boardperformance.com

The Morton Partnership
www.themortonpartnership.com or info@themortonpartnership.com

Tomorrow's Company
www.tomorrowscompany.com

Royal Society of Arts and Manufactures
www.thersa.org.uk

Association of Management Development
The Director Development Network
www.management.org.uk

Campaign for Leadership
The Director Leadership Programme
www.theworkfoundation.com/solutions/leader/dlp1.jsp

The Success Group (Director Coaching)
www.thesuccessgroup.co.uk

Index

259